BRISTOL
for young people

1st Edition

Editors
Rachel Miller
Lindsey Potter

The Freedom Guide, Bristol for young people

1st Edition

Published by

Freedom Guides Limited
PO Box 296, Bristol BS99 7LR

Published

June 2006

ISBN

0-9534648-5-7
978-0-9534648-5-2

Cover design

karen painter design
karenpainter@blueyonder.co.uk
www.karenpainterdesigns.co.uk

Printed by

AST Print Group Ltd
www.astprint.com

Cover photographs courtesy of

QEH (basketball)
Tim Potter (harbourside)
Sea Cadets (canoeist)
Bristol Old Vic (drama production)
Cherry Hersey (partying)

Special thanks to

- Destination Bristol for their support and loan of maps
- Sport Services, Bristol City Council
- Our advertisers
- QEH and Nick Hand for their generous supply of photographs
- See also the acknowledgements at the back of the book, pg 261

Book orders

Email: books@freedomguide.co.uk
www.freedomguide.co.uk

CONTENTS

BRISTOL
for young people

Welcome to the first edition of the Freedom Guide, Bristol for Young People.

Written and researched by Bristol parents and teenagers, this book is unique. It's aimed at 10-18 year olds, encompassing the years that begin with secondary school and leading up to the point at which young people venture out into the world, whether it's for work, university or travel.

When we started our research, we didn't anticipate just how much there is for teenagers to do right here on our doorstep. Bristol and the West Country are teeming with activities, courses and clubs. Now, for the first time, all the details are collected together in one place, The Freedom Guide.

So if you are looking for some serious fun and excitement, look no further than this book. It will show you where you can awaken your talents and sense of adventure. There are some amazing opportunities and challenges out there. Grasp them and you will find out more about yourself and what's important in your life.

The editorial in this book does not just talk to young people but their parents too. The years before leaving home can often be challenging. Indeed, we chose the name Freedom in recognition of the fact that parents often worry about giving their children freedom when freedom is all they want! We hope this book gives confidence all round.

Bristol is a fantastic city to grow up in, a place where young people can spread their wings and have fun with their families at the same time.

Best wishes

Lindsey Rachel

Lindsey and Rachel

PS This is your book, let us know
your views via the website:
www.freedomguide.co.uk

SPORTS & OUTDOOR PURSUITS

Rachel Miller

CONTENTS

INTRODUCTION

Bristol is an incredibly sporty city. Everywhere you turn, there are people skateboarding, running or cycling up a hill. As well as having great sporting facilities, we're also incredibly lucky to live in a city with so much green space and surrounded by fabulous countryside, with everything from hills and forests to rivers and beaches.

This chapter gives you all the contact details for sports clubs of all types, including basketball, fencing, football, cricket, rugby and hockey. There are also martial arts classes galore along with competitive swimming and diving.

For those that love a new challenge, there is an array of activities from surfing and sailing to orienteering and even flying. You can enjoy peaceful fishing, an invigorating climb, a stomach churning parachute jump or an adrenalin pumping paintball session.

SPORT

Useful sports websites

www.bristol-city.gov.uk

The Bristol City Council website has details on leisure passes, sports clubs, facilities and activities. Click on Sports, Clubs and Leisure.

www.sportslinks.info

A comprehensive sports database, everything from clubs and leagues to help getting funding.

www.southglos.gov.uk/southglos/leisureandsport

Clubs, events and activities in South Gloucestershire.

Bristol Ability Sports Club

St Brandon's House, 29 Great George St, Bristol, BS1 5QT
0117 902 0090
bookings@abilitysports.org.uk
Fortnightly, on Saturdays, 10am-12pm

Fun sports sessions for disabled children and their siblings, aged 8-16yrs. Held at St Pauls's Community Sports Academy, Newfoundland Road, Bristol. Door to door transport can be provided.

Sports centres

Bristol has good sports facilities and they are improving all the time. For the full list of sports centres and details of what they offer, see the tables at the end of the central colour reference section.

We also provide details of the private health and sports clubs on page 17 in this chapter. Membership is not cheap but most of them offer discounts to children and young people.

ATHLETICS & RUNNING

Bitton Road Runners

www.bittonrr.co.uk

Training for fun and for competition. Junior runners from 5-15yrs as well as older.

Bristol and West Athletic Club

Whitchurch Stadium, BS14 0XA
01275 833911
www.bristolandwestac.org.uk

All athletics events including track and field, road and cross country running.

Kingswood Triathalon Club

0117 909 1435
www.kingswoodtri.co.uk

Triathalon

www.sped-web.pwp.blueyonder.co.uk

This website lists many Triathalon events in the West as well as offering advice and links to local clubs.

UK: Athletics

0870 9986800
www.ukathletics.net

For information on athletics facilities near you.

Westbury Harrier and Cross Country Running Club

University of Bristol Sports Complex, Coombe Dingle
0117 973 5124
www.westburyharriers.co.uk
Mon/Thur 7pm-8.30pm, Coombe Dingle
Other sessions at Yate ACT, call for details
50p per session

The club offers qualified coaching for all levels, from beginners to elite runners. Juniors from 10-18yrs.

Yate Tristars

www.yatetristars.org.uk

Junior Triathalon Club 8-18yrs.

BADMINTON

Beaufort Badminton Club

Kingsdown Sports Centre, Portland St, BS2 8HL
0117 957 4706
shears.home@blueyonder.co.uk
Junior coaching, Mon and Wed, 7pm-8pm

Junior badminton coaching and play for ages 13yrs+. Beaufort takes players that are already at a good standard and there is a waiting list. There are also four after-school coaching sessions at Kingsdown Sports Centre and two at Horfield Sports Centre, see Bristol Leisure Centre tables for contact details.

BASKETBALL

Bristol Academy Basketball

WISE Campus, Filton College, New Rd,
Stoke Gifford, BS34 8LP
07747 487914
www.bristolbasketball.com/bristolacademy/
danny.james@filton.ac.uk
Tue & Thur pm: U16s & U18s; Sat am: U12s & U14s

Thriving basketball club with opportunities for all ages from 8yrs.

Bristol Pirates

Paul Mundy: 07788 666 405
www.bristolpirates.co.uk

A thriving basketball club which meets at St Bernadette RC school in Whitchurch, with junior teams playing in the local league (West of England Basketball Association). The club promotes "basketball for all", so everyone is welcome to come along and train. The season starts at the end of August.

BOXING

The National Smelting Co Amateur Boxing Club

Barracks Lane, Avonmouth, BS11
01454 898549

If you fancy getting in a boxing ring, this is the place to be. It promotes fitness, discipline and fair play for all ages from 10yrs.

CRICKET

Bristol West Indies Cricket Club

0117 951 5569

Four youth teams for ages 10-18yrs, based at the Rose Green Centre, Gordon Road, BS5.

Bristol Youth Cricket League

0117 330 6502
www.bristolycl.play-cricket.com
bycl@blueyonder.co.uk
Season runs from April to August
Facilities for indoor nets from February to April

There are around 40 youth cricket teams in and around Bristol, with players ranging in age from 6-18yrs. Teams are organised by age, from the U9s through to U17s, playing in leagues and knockout cups. Whether you live in Bristol or outside, call to find your nearest team. Register before November to ensure you get a place.

Damian Forder Cricket Academy

07771 560338
www.dfca.co.uk

Cricket coaching for all ages and abilities, including groups and one to one. Focusing on batting, bowling and fielding, designed to improve basic skills. Classes are held at different venues and take place after school and at weekends. Check the website for more information. Parties also available.

Gloucestershire County Cricket Club

The County Ground, Nevil Rd, Bristol, BS7 9EJ
0117 910 8015
www.gloscricket.co.uk

Aimed at boys and girls aged 8-16yrs, GCCC offers professional coaching for all abilities in the school holidays. Courses take place over two or three days from 10am-4pm. There are also courses at Cheltenham Cricket Centre. Young cricket fans can become Junior Gladiators at a cost of £29, providing entrance to domestic matches, 10% off cricket equipment in the shop and discounts on courses. Family membership is also available.

The Bristol YMCA CC

Golden Hill, Henleaze
www.ymcacricket.com

This is one of Bristol's oldest cricket clubs, founded in 1878. It has an excellent youth set-up with teams for U11s through to U17s with natural progression on to the adult teams. From February it provides indoor net sessions and competes in the Bristol Indoor Cricket League. It hosts social events, with a cricket theme, for all the family.

Thornbury Cricket Club

www.thornbury.play-cricket.com

Youth teams from U9s to U17s, playing at Alveston.

Twyford House Cricket & Social Club

Penpole Lane, Shirehampton, BS11
www.twyfordhouse.org
Tue: U11s and U13s; Thu: U15s and U17s;
Sun: youth league
Subs £10 a year

Friendly cricket club offering coaching and the chance to play in the local youth league.

FENCING

Bath Sword Club

01225 761788
www.bathswordclub.co.uk
Mon 7.30pm-9.30pm, Thu 7pm-10pm

The club meets twice a week at Bath University Founders Sports Hall, with juniors (U15s) meeting on Thursdays at 7pm-8pm. All new members take a six-week beginners course. These run throughout the year.

Bristol Fencing Club

Redland High School for Girls, Redland Rd, BS6
01934 843984
www.bristolfencingclub.com
Saturday 10am-12am

Juniors from 8-14yrs, seniors 14yrs+.

FOOTBALL

Amateur Football Alliance

www.amateurfa.com

There are loads of football teams and leagues all over Bristol and this is the place to find them. Click on Find a Club and enter your age group and postcode to find a boys or girls' football club close to home.

Avon Sports Academy

0117 904 6686
www.avonsportsacademy
info@avonsportsacademy.co.uk

A wide variety of opportunities for football fanatics, from holiday soccer schools to after school clubs. There are opportunities for advanced players to attend the Football Development Centre, the only FA-sanctioned academy in the south west. All enquiries are dealt with by email, full details on the website.

Avon Sports Soccer Camps

0117 904 6686
www.avonsportsacademy.co.uk

Sessions offer a balance between coaching skills and small side team games, taking place at Stoke Lodge Playing Fields and Combe Dingle Sports complex in Stoke Bishop.

Bristol 5 Football Club

Moorlands Rd, Fishponds, Bristol, BS16 3LF
0117 965 6948
www.youth-club.co.uk

The Harry Crook Activities Centre is home to the Bristol 5 Football Club, with teams for U10s, U12s and U14s.

Bristol City Football Club

Ashton Gate Stadium, Bristol, BS3 2EJ
0117 963 0619
www.bcfc.co.uk

The club visits local schools to host football coaching and extra-curricular sessions. There are also coaching courses during the Easter and summer holidays. Call 0117 963 0636.

Bristol Rovers

0117 952 2581
www.bristolrovers.co.uk
brfccommunity@btconnect.com

Holiday soccer schools for girls and boys aged 7-13yrs are held at Gordano Sports Centre, The Grange School, Warmley and at the Filton WISE campus in Stoke Gifford. Bristol Rovers also offers after-school clubs and football training in schools, by arrangement with head teachers. Talented players can attend the Rovers' School of Excellence and may even end up playing for Bristol Rovers! Any junior football team can arrange to visit the Bristol Rovers ground on a match day to have lunch, watch the game, meet the players and have their picture taken on the pitch.

Down's Football League

0117 973 7861
www.bbc.co.uk/bristol/sport/down_league

Every Saturday afternoon, more than 700 players representing 56 teams play on 28 pitches on the Downs. If you turned 15 in the July before the start of the football season, you could be there too! You can ring secretary Owen Dow in advance, or just turn up, with your boots, and ask around. You will need written permission from your headteacher.

Gloucestershire Football Association

www.gloucestershirefa.com

Gloucestershire FA oversees all the youth football leagues in the Bristol area, of which there are many. The GFA website is a great place to find all the necessary contact details.

The Avon Youth League

www.avonyl.co.uk

With its four divisions, from U12s to U16s, there are some 4,500 young people playing football every Sunday as part of the Avon Youth League. It is also connected to the local Under 18 competition, the Bristol Combination league.

GOLF

Ashton Court Golf Course

Top end, Ashton Court, Bristol, BS41 9JN
0117 973 8508
18 Holes: juniors (U16s) £4.00, adults £5.35,
Club hire £5 deposit

Henbury Golf Club

Westbury-on-Trym, Bristol, BS10 7QB
0117 950 2121
www.henburygolfclub.co.uk

The club has a large junior membership.
There are also lessons for non-members.

Knowle Golf Club

Fairway, West Town Lane, Brislington, BS4 5DF
0117 977 9193
www.knowlegolfclub.co.uk
£4 per hour

Coaching sessions take place every Saturday
and Sunday mornings for ages 5-17yrs. All
equipment is provided. Book in advance.

GYMNASTICS

Baskerville's Gym

Englishcombe Court, Englishcombe Lane, Bath, BA2
01225 339991

Classes every day for all ages. Courses are
made up of ten sessions per term, four terms
a year. BGA grades followed.

Bristol Hawks Gymnastic Club

Gymnastics World, Roman Rd, Lower Easton, BS5
0117 935 5363/973 7481

Structured classes for advanced gymnastics in
the evenings. BGA grades followed.

Bristol School of Gymnastics

Old Bishopston Methodist Church, 245 Gloucester
Rd, Bristol, BS7 8NY
0117 942 9620

General gymnastics with apparatus, for all
ages up to 18yrs. Opportunities to progress
towards competitive gymnastics.

Fromeside Gymnastics Club

Watleys End Rd, Winterbourne, Bristol, BS36 1QG
01454 776 873/777749

All classes taken by qualified coaches.
Children participate in the BAGA Scheme and
they can progress to competition level.

HOCKEY

Firebrands Hockey Club

Longwood, Failand, Bristol, BS8 3TL
01275 393392
www.firebrandshockeyclub.co.uk
Youth training, Tue 6pm-7.30pm

Opportunities for boys and girls to play hockey
in friendly fixtures and tournaments, for ages
9-15yrs. Holiday coaching academies are
also available.

Redland Ladies Hockey Club

01454 898384
Sun 10am-12pm & Tue 6.30pm-8pm
From £30 per year

Juniors (9-14yrs) train at Redmaids School on
Sunday mornings, while Seniors (15+yrs) train
at Golden Hill on Kellaway Avenue on Tuesday
evenings. All matches take place at Redmaids
School as part of a league organised by
Sports West. Annual subs increase from £60
for juniors playing competitively to £90 for
seniors playing competitively.

ICE SKATING

Bristol Ice Rink

Frogmore St, Bristol, BS1 5NA
0117 929 2148
www.jnll.co.uk
Session times vary, call for details
From £5.50 including skate hire

General skating and disco sessions for all
abilities. Long sleeves, trousers and gloves are
recommended. Tuition available for all ages
and abilities and courses run to the NISA fun
skate programme. Junior Ice Hockey (U19yrs)
on Tuesdays. Skating sessions for disabled
people. Also ice karting for over 18s. Also see
Parties on pg 165.

Christmas Ice Rinks

There are usually ice rinks at Castle Park in
the City Centre, the Mall at Cribbs Causeway
and Queen Square, Bath. They run from
late November to mid January — great for a
Christmassy skating session.

ICE HOCKEY

Bristol Ice Hockey Club

Frogmore St, Bristol, BS1 5NA
0117 929 2148
www.jnll.co.uk

Junior Ice Hockey (under 19yrs) on Tuesdays.
Competitive league team training. New
players must start in the beginners group
which plays from 5pm-6pm.
U12s: 6pm-7pm
U14s: 7pm-8pm
U16s: 8.15pm-9.15pm
U19s: 9.30pm-10.30pm.

LIFESAVING

Junior Lifesaving

Winterbourne Swimming Pool
0800 953 0059
Friday evenings
£25 for ten week course

Children aged 8-14yrs can become a
Rookie Lifesaver. The programme has four
components: water safety, rescue, self rescue
and emergency response.

National Pool Lifeguard Qualification

01454 319373

This 37-hour training programme is available
to competent swimmers aged 16yrs+. The
course is available at several pools in Bristol,
call for further details.

MARTIAL ARTS

Bedminster Judokwai

Ashton Park Sports Centre, Ashton Park School,
Bower Ashton, BS3
07834 619437
www.bedminsterjudokwai.co.uk
Tue 6.15pm-7pm (U16s, beginners)
Tue 7pm-8pm (graded juniors)
Tue 8pm-9pm (over 16s)
Fri 7.15pm-8.45pm (all ages)

Judo for all ages from 5yrs to adults.

Bristol Karate Club

Holy Nativity Church Hall, School Rd,
Totterdown, BS4
0117 977 9029
www.bristolkarateclub.org.uk
enquiries@bristolkarateclub.org.uk
Junior classes: Thur 6.30pm
£3 per session

New members are welcome at anytime and
there are no age limits.

Bristol Martial Arts

Louise: 07866 723631
www.bristolmartialarts.com

Taekwon-Do classes for all ages held in Clifton
and Henleaze. Bristol Martial Arts also offers
a FAST self-defence course that covers anti-
bullying and anti-abduction strategies.

Bristol School of Tai Chi

0117 949 3955
taichi@bristoltaichi.com

Tai chi for children 7yrs+ at the following
venues: Gloucester, Glastonbury, Yate,
Thornbury, Bishopston, Nailsea,
Weston-super-Mare and Clifton.

Karate

Tim: 07980 863061
Tue 6.30pm-8pm, Bradley Stoke Community Centre

Karate for all ages and abilities. You can pay
£5 to drop in but there's membership for
those that want to come regularly.

KEBBA

07989 773950
www.kebba.co.uk
mail@kebba.co.uk
Tue & Wed, Staple Hill
Thur, Keynesham
Sun, Warmley

Martial arts classes for ages 7+yrs. One
month free trial available.

Levan Taekwondo

Dung Levan: 07966 763407
Tue 6.30pm-7.15pm, Bishopston School of
Gymnastics
Fri 6.30pm-7.30pm, Henleaze United Reform Church
£20 per month

Aimed at all ages from 5-16yrs, this
Taekwondo class also offers anti-bullyng
strategies, anti-drugs courses, first aid courses
and self defence for children as well building
respect and confidence.

Matt Fiddes Academy

0800 0354660
www.mattfiddes.com

National martial arts chain offering a mix of
kick boxing, TaeKwonDo and Kung Fu. Call for
further details of clubs in Bristol.

ShotoRyu Karate

814 Filton Ave, Filton, Bristol, BS34 7HA
0117 969 5697
www.shotoryukarate.co.uk
Nick Moller: 0117 969 5697
www.shotoryukarate.co.uk

Sessions are held throughout the week at
Horfield, Easton & Henbury Sports Centres,
see Leisure Tables at the end of the Central
Reference section; also at Greenway Centre
and Kingswood 17th Bristol Scouts Hall.

Taekwon-Do

0845 6001967
www.puma-uk.com

Taekwon-Do is the Korean martial art of
punching and kicking, offering improvements
in strength, endurance, flexibility, stamina,
self-control, confidence and relaxation.
Sessions held at many venues across Bristol.
Phone for more information.

NETBALL

Crossbow Netball Club

01454 327566
www.crossbow.0catch.com

Juniors are very welcome at this well-established and friendly netball club. There are teams for U12s, U14s and U16s. Over 16s join the seniors. The club trains in Bradley Stoke on Monday evenings.

ROWING

Avon Rowing Club

0870 163 4091
www.avoncountyrowingclub.org.uk
juniors@avoncountyrowingclub.org.uk
Junior squads meet Sat and Sun am

Junior rowing at Saltford for all ages from 11yrs. The club has lots of beginner boats as well as racing boats. Beginners meet on Sunday mornings. There is a waiting list.

City of Bristol Rowing Club

Albion Dockside Estate, Hanover Place, BS1 6TR
0117 954 4621
www.bristolrowing.co.uk
cbrc@bristol.rowing.org.uk
Juniors: Tue, Thu & Sun

The club welcomes everyone from beginners up to national level rowers. It runs learn to row courses in the harbour for ages 10yrs+.

RUGBY

Bath RF Club

01225 325 200
www.bathrugby.com

There's loads on offer for children and young people at Bath RF Club. There are holiday rugby coaching camps at Easter and during the summer. There are birthday packages including a tour of the grounds, the chance to meet players and to have a coaching session. There's also a Question Couch at every match where U16s can come and speak to the

players after the game. The club has a girl's development team for 12-16yrs and there's a children's Christmas party every year. Bath RF Club also has a special Community Foundation which aims to improve the lives of young people through sport.

Bristol Saracens Rugby Club

Bakewell Memorial Ground, Station Rd, Cribbs Causeway, Bristol, BS34
0117 950 0037
webmaster@bristolsaracensrfc.co.uk
Training for U12s, Sun 10.30am;
U14s to U17s, Wed 6.30pm

Young Saracens offers qualified coaches for teams starting from the U7/8s up to U17s.

Bristol RF Club

0117 952 6114
www.bristolrugby.co.uk

Bristol Rugby Club has an active community programme in local schools and sports clubs, as well as holiday rugby camps.

Clifton Rugby Club

Cribbs Causeway
0117 950 0445
www.cliftonrugby.co.uk
Sun 10am-12pm

Mini and junior rugby for all ages up to 18yrs.

SWIMMING & DIVING

Amateur Swimming Association

www.britishswimming.org

Clubs, news, information and links.

Backwell Swimming Club

Backwell Leisure Centre, Farleigh , Backwell, BS48 3PB
01275 463726
www.backwellswimmingclub.me.uk

Training and competitive swimming for ages 5-19yrs. Friendly galas and tournaments.

Badminton Pool

0117 962 7972

Term-time swimming courses, including a beginners course for teenagers who can't swim on Thursdays at 8.15pm. Also, four-day intensive courses in diving, snorkelling and octopush (like underwater hockey!) run three times a year in April, July and December.

Bradford-on-Avon Swimming Pool

St. Margaret St, Bradford on Avon, Wilts, BA15 1DF
01225 862 970
www.bradfordswimmingpool.co.uk
enquiries@bradfordswimmingpool.co.uk
Daily, call for more details

Special activities in school holidays, including lifeguard courses, diving, canoeing and distance swims.

Bristol Central Swimming Club

0117 968 1650
www.swimbristol.btinternet.co.uk
swimbristol@btinternet.com

Bristol Central Swimming Club runs sessions for swimmers at all skill levels, from learners to international level swimmers. The club offers the chance to take part in swimming, synchronised swimming and water polo.

Bristol Henleaze Swimming Club

www.bristolhenleazesc.org.uk
info@bristolhenleazesc.org.uk

This friendly and competitive swimming club offers swim schools as well as competition squads for all ages. Based at Clifton High School and Horfield Pool.
Swim School: Liz Richardson, 0117 969 8276
Development and competition squads:
Judith Bush, 0117 935 5636.

Clifton Swim School

0117 973 7245

Long established Easter and summer swim school. Beginners to ASA challenge awards, snorkelling and diving. Blocks of ten lessons every morning over two weeks. Friendly tuition in small groups, held in pool in Clifton. Call for reservations and further information.

Greenbank Outdoor Pool

Wilfrid Rd, Street, Somerset, BA16 0EU
01458 442468
www.greenbankpool.co.uk
May-mid Sept: Mon-Fri 12am-6.45pm term time,
Sat-Sun 10am-6.45pm, summer hols 10am-6pm.
£4 adult, £3 child.
Ring or see website for details of season tickets

This pleasant heated outdoor pool surrounded
by grass is less than five minutes' walk
from Clark's Village. There are two pools, a
separate children's area, a new Wet Play Area
and refreshments. Picnics welcomed. Small
car park.

Henleaze Swimming Club

Henleaze Lake, Lake Rd, Westbury on Trym, BS10
0117 962 0696

For those that prefer swimming in natural
surroundings (with the fish!), this former
quarry with its rolling lawns, leafy outlook and
diving boards is hard to beat. It's a members-
only club and you must be a strong swimmer.

Newport Centre

Kingsway, Newport, South Wales
01633 662 662
Daily

Public sessions seven days a week including
most bank hols. Warm leisure pool with wave
machine and slide. Spacious changing rooms.
Other activities include canoeing, archery,
trampolining and water polo. Holiday activities
for all age groups.

Portishead Open Air Pool

Esplanade Rd, Portishead, BS20 7HD
01275 843454
May-Sep

Heated open air swimming pool with
sunbathing terraces.

Sedgemoor Splash

Mount St, Bridgwater, Somerset, TA6 3ER
01278 425 636
Open daily, please call for details.
adult, £3.85; child, £2.75; family tickets £10.50.

Fun pool with two water flumes, river run,
bubbles, water jets & wave machine.

Soundwell Swimming & Diving Club

0117 957 4042
www.soundwellswim.org.uk

This club offers the chance to learn to
swim for all ages from 6-18yrs, as well as
competitive swimming and diving. It meets at
Kingswood Leisure Centre.

Splash Happy Swim School

0117 979 8266
splash_happy@hotmail.com

Swimming lessons with qualified teachers
at Badminton Girls' School and Clifton High
School for children up to 16yrs, of all abilities,
including special needs. Classes held at
weekends and some weekday evenings.

Thornbury Swimming Club

01454 772249

Competitive swimming squads for 7-17yrs.

TENNIS

Bristol Box League

0117 923 8896

This league operates all year in 6-8 week periods, during which players organise their own matches against others in their box. It is not club based and is for players of all abilities up to 16yrs who want to play friendly competitive tennis.

Bristol Central Tennis Club

Derby Rd, St Andrew's Park, Bristol, BS7
07887633095
www.bctc.org.uk

There are regular coaching sessions on Saturday mornings and during school holidays. The junior squads train on week nights after school in term time.

Bristol Lawn Tennis & Squash Club

Redland Green, Redland, Bristol, BS6
0117 973 1139
www.bltsc.co.uk

After-school and holiday classes for all ages.

City tennis courts

0117 922 2789 hireline
£4.90 per court for adults
£2.55 per court for children

There are municipal tennis courts at Canford Park, Horfield Common, St George's Park, Redcatch Park and Eastville Park. You can pay on the spot or book on the council hireline.

What's your sport?

Let us know if we have missed anything. Tell us about the sports clubs and courses that you rate and send us your pictures — you could be in the next issue of the Freedom Guide:

editor@freedomguide.co.uk

City Tennis Programme

0117 962 6723
www.bristolcitytc.totaltennis.net
St George's Park (Sat)
Eastville Park Tennis Club (Sat)
St Paul's Tennis Club (Wed, Thu & Sat)
Horfield Park (Sat)
Canford Park (Sat & Sun)
Ashton Park (Sun)

Bristol has an LTA-accredited City Tennis Programme. Some 21 schools benefit from coaching initiatives. There are also city clubs, to make tennis more affordable for all ages. Sessions take place mainly at weekends and there are also school holiday courses.

Clifton Tennis Club

Beaufort Rd, Clifton, Bristol, BS8
0117 968 2653

This is a private club but non-members can take advantage of the coaching.

Coombe Dingle Tennis Centre

Coombe Dingle Sports Complex, Coombe Lane, Stoke Bishop, Bristol, BS9
0117 962 6718
www.peterbendall.org.uk
Peter Bendall: 07973 641132

Ten-week courses run after school for all ages and abilities. Youngsters showing promise will be invited to join Junior Select, a competitive squad that meets three times a week. Holiday courses are also available.

Cotham Park Tennis Club

71 Redland Rd, Bristol, BS6
0117 974 1044
www.cothamtennis.net

Regular coaching in the holidays and during term time as well as junior squads.

Henleaze Tennis Club

Tennessee Grove, Henleaze, BS9
01275 543449

Coaching starts with mini tennis and goes on to a more structured programme. There are courses after school, at weekends and during school holidays. During the winter months, coaching is offered at the indoor tennis centre at Coombe Dingle.

Kings Tennis Club

Maplemeade, Kings Drive, Bishopston, Bristol, BS7
0117 942 7667
www.tennisleisure.co.uk
tennisleisure@hotmail.com

Drop-in sessions

Sat 10.30am-11.30am for 9-12yrs, £2

Teaching the FUNdamentals of tennis in a non-competitive environment.

Mini Tennis

For more aspiring youngsters, classes are held after school throughout the week, teaching not only the technical skills but also scoring and playing in team competitions.

RAW Tennis

Teenage tennis is very popular at Kings. The fun element is kept and competitions are team-based. There are tricks and skills sessions and leagues, many of which are doubles-based, playing in both county and national divisions.

Holidays

Week-long courses are available in all the school holidays.

Knowle Tennis Club

Wells Rd, Knowle, Bristol, BS4
0117 977 3996
www.knowletennis.pwp.blueyonder.co.uk

Thriving junior coaching programme with sessions on Saturday mornings for all abilities, as well as ten-week courses during term time.

Westbury Park Tennis Club

Off Springfield Grove, Henleaze, BS9
0117 962 2663
www.westburyparktennisclub.co.uk

Saturday morning coaching for all ages.

VOLLEYBALL

Hornets Volleyball Club

07941 027446
www.horfieldhornets.co.uk
Mon 8pm-10pm Henbury Leisure Centre

Friendly volleyball club, for all ages.

SPORTS CENTRES & PRIVATE HEALTH CLUBS

Full details of Bristol's many sports centres can be found at the end of the Colour Reference Section. There are several private health clubs in Bristol. Joining fees and monthly membership (often with minimum terms) can be very motivating! Most have classes, gym and spas, some have pools. A few are open to non-members off peak but unless stated, assume the clubs are members only.

Better Bodies

94 High St, Portishead, BS20 6AJ
01275 845353

David Lloyd Club

Ashton Rd, Ashton, BS3 2HB
0117 953 1010
www.davidlloydleisure.co.uk

En Forma Health Club

Bath Hill, Keynsham, BS31 1EB
0117 987 3262
www.enforma.co.uk

Esporta Health and Fitness Club

Hunts Ground Rd, Stoke Gifford, BS34 8HN
0117 974 9740
www.esporta.com

Fitness Factory

17 Broad Rd, Kingswood, BS15 1HZ
0117 935 2060
www.fitnessfactoryltd.co.uk

Livingwell Health & Leisure Club

Cotham Gardens, 80 Redland Rd, BS6 6AG
0117 942 5805
www.livingwell.com

Next Generation Club

Greystoke Ave, Westbury-on-Trym, BS10 6AZ
0117 959 7140
www.ngclubs.co.uk

Redwood Lodge

Beggar Bush Lane, Failand, BS8 3TG
01275 395888

Riverside Leisure Club

Station Rd, Little Stoke, BS34 6HW
01454 888 666

OUTDOOR PURSUITS

There are many excellent outdoor pursuit companies in and around Bristol that offer adventure days with a whole range of activities. And, from the Mendips to the Wye Valley, we've got some great countryside on our doorstep to tempt us. These centres are listed first, followed by the specialist organisations. All outdoor activity centres should be licensed by the AALA, see below.

AALA

02920 755715
www.aala.org

The Adventure Activities Licensing Authority inspects and licenses outdoor activity centres. All good centres should be AALA licensed.

Aardvark Endeavours

Broadway House, Axbridge Rd, Cheddar, BS27
01934 744878
www.aardvarkendeavours.com
burt@bc1.net

Aardvark is a non-residential outdoor pursuits company but it's based at a caravan park if you do need somewhere to stay. It offers abseiling, gorge walking, rock climbing, archery, rifle shooting, caving, pot holing and kayaking. Most activities are suitable for anyone aged 7yrs and over.

Black Mountain Activities

Three Cocks, Brecon, Powys, LD3 0SD
01497 847897
www.blackmountain.co.uk

Rock climbing, abseiling, caving, mountain biking, canoeing, raft building, white water rafting and more. Minimum ages apply for some activities. Please call for details.

Black Rock Outdoor Education

16 St Andrews Rd, Cheddar, BS27 3NE
01934 744389
www.blackrockoutdoors.co.uk

Black Rock offers the full gamet of outdoor activities including: caving, abseiling and climbing, kayaking, archery, ropes, off-road biking and mountain weekends away. Most activities are suitable for everyone from 8yrs and Black Rock caters for all types of groups from schools and clubs to families.

Bristol Activities Centre

Avonquay, Cumberland Basin, Bristol, BS1 6XL
0117 353 2299
www.bristolactivities.org.uk
bac@bristol-city.gov.uk

Activities include: caving, climbing, kayaking, team building, hillcraft, abseiling, canoeing, orienteering and mountain biking. Sessions take place on weekdays as well as weekends and last 2½ hours. BAC caters for established groups such as schools and youth clubs, but you can put your own group together and they also do activity parties.

Chepstow Outdoor Activity Centre

01291 629901/0870 609 4439
www.chepstowoutdooractivities.co.uk

Activities include paintball, quad biking, archery, clay pigeon shooting and off-road driving. There's also Spheremania, in which two people are strapped inside a 12ft inflatable ball and rolled down steep hills. By all accounts, it's great fun!

Go Ape

www.goape.co.uk
0870 444 5562
Mar-Oct, and weekends in Nov
Closed Mon in term time
£20 per adult, (gorillas) £15 per child (baboons)
Mallards Pike Lake, Forest of Dean, Gloucs
On the Nibley (nr Blakeney) to Parkend Road, entrance is 1½ miles east of Parkend.

An adventure course made up of a network of rope bridges, trapezes and zip slides set some 30ft high in the treetops. This new location in the Forest of Dean is bound to prove popular. Perfect for school outings, family days out and parties, Go Ape is open to anyone over 10yrs and taller than 1.4m. You must weigh less than 20 stone.

Mendip Outdoor Pursuits

Laurel Farmhouse, Summer Lane, Banwell, Weston-super-Mare, BS24
01934 820518
www.mendipoutdoorpursuits.co.uk

Caving, kayaking, abseiling, orienteering, archery, raft and bridge building, assault courses and hill walking, all in the beautiful Mendips. For ages 8+yrs.

Motiva

Christchurch, The Forest of Dean, Near Symonds Yat
01594 861762
www.motiva.co.uk
info@motiva.co.uk

Rope courses and adventures for 10+yrs.

Rock Sport

Cheddar Caves & Gorge, Cheddar, Somerset, BS27
01934 742343
www.cheddarcaves.co.uk
rocksports@visitcheddar.co.uk
All year caving, Mar-Oct climbing & abseiling
£16 adult, £12.50 11-16 yrs for 1½ hour
30 mins SW of Bristol on A371, between A38 & A37

Supervised beginners sessions in caving (beyond the Black Cat in Gough's Cave) and climbing & abseiling on a 50-foot abseil pitch in Cheddar Gorge. Sessions every day, lasting up to 1½ hours. Booking recommended, age and height restrictions apply.

Symonds Yat Canoe Hire

Symonds Yat West, Herefordshire, HR9 6BY
01600 891069
www.canoehire.com
Mar-Oct 9am-6pm

Located on the opposite bank of the River Wye from Symonds Yat Rock. Canoes and kayaks can be rented from one hour to a week. They can also transport boats up river so you can just paddle down.
Camping available.

The Action Centre

Lyncombe Drive, Churchill, N Somerset, BS25 5PQ
01934 852335
www.highaction.co.uk
info@highaction.co.uk
9.30am-10pm
Costs vary according to activity
(Start at £4.50 for toboganning)

Floodlit dry ski slope open all year. Any age permitted providing they can snowplough, stop, turn & use button drag lift, booking not necessary. Lessons available for all abilities. Also toboganing, snow blading for established skiers and snowboarding from 7yrs (dependent on height). Activity days run by a qualified instructor, teaching skiing, archery and rifle shooting. Also quad biking, power kiting and mountain boarding. Booking essential for all activities except recreational ski-ing. Also see parties on pg 166.

The Adventurous Activity Company

0117 925 3196
www.adventurousactivitycompany.co.uk

The Adventurous Activity Company works with schools, clubs or any group to provide challenges and activity days, featuring everything from canoeing to rock climbing and abseiling. Available to children aged 8yrs+.

Wye Pursuits

Riverside House, Kerne Bridge, Nr Ross, HR9 5QX
01600 891199
www.wye-pursuits.co.uk

Large range of outdoor activities on offer as well as canoe and kayak hire. Activities for groups of eight, families welcome. On offer: climbing, abseiling, caving and white water rafting. For all water activities you must be able to swim 25 metres.

Wyedean Canoe & Adventure Centre

Holly Barn, Symonds Yat Rock, Coleford, GL16 7NZ
01594 833238
www.wyedean.co.uk
Easter-Oct: daily 8.30am-5pm, winter by appt.

As well as canoe and kayak hire, this centre has a vast range of activities for all ages over 8yrs. Canoeing, kayaking, raft building, abseiling, climbing, high and low rope courses, team-building, caving and archery. It caters for individuals and groups. It is essential to book in advance.

Young Bristol Outdoor Activities

0117 953 7921/07812 151131
www.youngbristol.com
rw@youngbristol.com

Half-day outdoor pursuits events in and around Bristol for groups of eight, including canoeing, kayaking, sailing, raft-building, abseiling, caving, climbing and rock sports, mountain biking and archery.

ARCHERY

Bristol Bowmen

Keynesham Rugby Club
0117 933 2934

Archery tuition and competition. A weekly session is held indoors on a Friday evening. Club afternoons every Sunday at 2pm on Keynsham Rugby Field between April and October. Beginners courses take place during the summer months. Book in advance.

Cleve Archers

01454 852181
www.clevearchers.co.uk
clevearchers@uk2.net

This archery club has a thriving Junior Club and meets every Saturday morning between April 1st and October 31st at Moorend, near Hambrook, Bristol. There are beginners courses during May/June for 7-18yrs. Junior membership costs £20 a year. There is an additional fee to shoot indoors during the winter months.

BALLOONING

Bailey Balloons

01275 375300
www.baileyballoons.co.uk

Bailey Balloons offers balloon flights from Bristol, Bath and South Wales. Prices vary, with special offers from £125 per person. U18s must be accompanied.

Bristol Balloons

0117 963 7858
www.bristolballoons@balnet.co.uk

Children can fly as long as they are aged over 9yrs and over 4ft 6 inches tall. Standard flights cost £130 but some specials from £95.

CAVING

Cheddar Caves and Gorge

01934 742343
www.cheddarcaves.co.uk
rocksport@cheddarcaves.co.uk
11-17yrs (height restrictions apply)

Rock Sport offers caving for beginners as well as adventure caving, taking you into caves and passages the tourists don't get to explore! Sessions last 1½ hours and are available every day. All equipment is provided. There's also climbing and abseiling on the 50ft abseil pitch in the gorge.

CLIMBING

Bristol Climbing Centre

St Werburgh's Church, Mina Rd, St Werburgh's, BS2 9YH
0117 941 3489
www.undercover-rock.com

This dedicated indoor climbing centre features over 150 climbs up to ten metres high, catering for all abilities from complete beginners to national champions. Taster sessions for beginners, Fridays 5pm-6pm for children aged up to 15yrs, cost £10, pre-booking necessary. Beginners courses, taking place over two consecutive weekends, cost £29. Climbers that complete this course can then attend supervised sessions three times a week and also get the chance to climb outdoors, including Avon Gorge.

The British Mountaineering Council

0870 0104878
www.thebmc.co.uk

The BMC website tells you where to climb walls, hills and mountains in your area.

The Warehouse

Parliament St, Gloucester, GL1 1HY
01452 302351
www.the-warehouse.co.uk
Mon-Fri 12pm-10pm; weekends 10am-10pm

Impressive climbing venue with up to 180 routes. The main room has walls up to 13 metres. Rock Rats club for 8-16yrs. Taster sessions available. Also caters for children's parties.

CYCLING

Black Mountain Activities

Three Cocks, Brecon, Powys, LD3 0SD
01497 847897
www.blackmountain.co.uk
Bike hire: £30 for full day, £20 for half a day

Offers mountain biking along with many other outdoor adventures.

Bristol BMX Club

The Tumps, Waterside Drive, off Coniston Rd, Patchway, BS34
07875 146489
harry.price@hotmail.com
Wed, 5pm onwards, Mar to Sep, weather permitting
Membership £15 a year.
Members £3; non-members £5 on the night.

The BMX Club is open to all ages. Bring your own BMX bike with padding, wear long sleeve tops and long trousers and gloves as well as a helmet. Stump pegs on bikes must be unscrewed. Races start at 6.30pm and you'll be entered according to age. The top two go up into the next group. You can take part in regional and national events.

Cycle Paths

See cycle routes on pg 174. The Forest of Avon have details of cycle paths on their website, check out the following (www.forestofavon.org.uk):

The Avon Timberland Trail, Ashton Court: built by mountain bikers for mountain bikers.

Bristol and Bath Railway Path: 16 miles of flat cycling through beautiful countryside.

Leigh Woods: Special marked cycle paths.

River Avon Trail: Pill to Bath (23 miles).

Cycling in Bristol

www.bristol-city.gov.uk
Bristol City Council offers a range of services to cyclists:

Free cycle route maps

To obain maps covering the Greater Bristol and Avon Cycleway, call 0117 903 6701.

Bristol's Biggest Bike Ride

Annual event attracting thousands of cyclists.

Car Free Day
Held every September.

The Bristol Bike Shed
The Grove, Queen Sq, BS1 4RB
www.mud-dock.co.uk
Provides secure bike parking, showers, lockers
and maintainence facilities as well as cheap
coffee at Mud Dock, by the harbour.

Life Cycle UK

86 Colston St, Bristol, BS1 5BB
0117 929 0440
www.lifecycleuk.org.uk

Group cycling courses for 8-11yrs at venues
in Bristol. Also courses for 11-18yrs with one
instructor to two teenagers, cycling on and off
road, teaching road safety.

Mountain Bikers

www.mtbr.com

A useful website reviewing trails and giving
information on length, level and type as well
as directions.

Mountain Biking UK

www.mbuk.com

Details on mountain biking routes in the
Forest of Dean, the Mendips and South Wales.

Sustrans

0845 113 0065
Safe cycling to school: 0117 915 0100 Mon-Thu
www.sustrans.org.uk

Sustrans is the UK's leading sustainable
transport charity. It provides information on
the National Cycle Network and other routes.
Sustrans' vision is a world where people
choose to travel in ways that benefit their
health and the environment.

The Burnham Tigers

www.burnhambmx.co.uk
Tue/Thur 6pm-9pm

The track at Apex Leisure and Wildlife Park is
considered by the British Cycling Federation to
be one of the best in the UK.

DRIVING

Bristol Off Road Driver Training Centre

0117 986 1097
www.bristoloffroad.co.uk

Wide selection of off-road tracks and experienced instructors for ages 13yrs+.

Castle Combe Skid Pan & Kart Track

Castle Combe Circuit, Wiltshire, Chippenham, SN14
01249 783010
www.castlecombecircuit.co.uk

Junior kart racing for 10-15yrs (with a min. height of 4'8") on first & third Sunday of every month. Pre-booking essential. Phone for possible summer school sessions. Party bookings taken. See advertisement pg 177.

Jumicar Bristol

Dormers, Mead Rd, Stoke Gifford, BS34 8PS
01454 250219
www.jumicarbristol.co.uk

Road safety instructions for children, aged up to 12 in real junior-sized cars. Currently run at ASDA WallMart car park, Cribbs Causeway.

Supakart

Units 10-11, Leeway Industrial Est, Newport, NP19
01633 280808
www.supakart.co.uk
Sun 10am: Junor club (must be over 4ft10in)

Indoor kart centre with hairpin bends, a tunnel and a bridge for a real Grand Prix experience (ages 14yrs+).

The Raceway

Avonmouth Way, Avonmouth, Bristol, BS11
0800 376 6111
www.theraceway.co.uk

Huge indoor racing track offering the chance to get behind the wheel for all ages. There's a youth club for ages 8-15yrs on a Sunday morning. Then there are opportunities for driving practice for anyone over 12yrs. To take part in the full-on Grand Prix Experience, you need to be 16yrs+.

The Under 17 Driving Club

www.under17-carclub.co.uk
Venues vary, weekends Mar-Nov, ages 12-17yrs
£160 per person, £240 for 2 or more,
£50 joining fee per family

An opportunity for U17s to practice and improve their driving skills legally and safely in a variety of different vehicles. Supervisors encourage an active interest in cars and motor sports. Members are taught to drive by their parents in their parents' cars, with the help of club instructors. Members must have an associate member (preferably, but not necessarily, a parent) responsible for him/her. You must join before you turn 15 years of age. Additional one-off events are held, giving members the chance to go off road in 4x4 vehicles and drive trucks and single seater racing cars. The club is a non-profit making organisation. One of the key venues is Castle Combe.

West Country Karting

The Lake, Trench Lane, Winterbourne, BS36 1RY
01454 202666
www.westcountrykarting.com

A 350 metre outdoor karting circuit. You must be at least 5ft1in for karting, if you're shorter then you will not reach the pedals! Quad biking is available for children up to 12yrs. It's open all year but closes on very quiet days, so call for opening times and prices. Party bookings taken.

FISHING

There are plenty of places to fish in Bristol, without having to go far. If you're a member, you can fish at Henleaze Lake. You can buy day tickets on the banks of Bitterwell Lake, Henfield and Duchess Lake, Stoke Park. You can also fish in Bristol Docks for free, where we are reliably informed there's very good freshwater fishing. You'll need a rod license from the Post Office (£10) wherever you fish.

Big Well Fly Fishing

Tinmans Green, Redbrook, Monmouth, NP25 3LX
01600 772904 or 07748227347
Open daily, dawn to dusk

This trout fishery in the Wye Valley has three lakes and a novice pond, which provides anglers with the opportunity to practice and improve technique. There's free tuition, with a range of refreshments and rod hire. Inexperienced anglers are initially encouraged to attend with an adult.

Bristol, Bath & Wiltshire Amalgamation

0117 967 2977
The fishing season runs from 16 June to 15 March.
Adults: £35 Juniors (U17s): £12
Special adult and junior card: £37.
Discounts if you buy before March

This organisation is an amalgamation of 11 fishing clubs and as a result, it offers fishing along nearly 100 miles of banks, including rivers, lakes and reservoirs. Membership cards can be bought at most tackle shops within 50 miles of Bristol.

Chew Valley Lake

Woodford Lodge, Chew Stoke, Bristol, BS40 8XH
01275 482948
Prices vary, around £7.50 for children
£15 for adults

Fly fishing for trout is available on Chew Valley lake for children aged 12yrs+. There are also guided walks, a restaurant and a shop.

Go-Fish

www.go-fish.co.uk/avon.htm

Great website that has information about lots of fishing spots in in the UK, including plenty of Bristol locations, such as the harbour as well as local ponds and lakes.

Henleaze Lake

Lake Rd, Westbury on Trym, Bristol, BS10 6YD

Popular place to fish with carp, bream, tench, perch, pike and eels. Day and season tickets from Henleaze Lake Angling Club.

The Royal Forest of Dean Angling Club

01594 543796
webmaster@fodac.freeserve.co.uk

For great fishing in lakes in the Cinderford area, either buy day tickets from Wye Angling tackle shop in Ross-On-Wye or start fishing on the bank and you'll be able to buy a ticket there. There are golden tench on Marion's pool, big carp and bream on Steam Mills and a mixed bag at Meadowcliffe, Waterloo and Lightmoor. Plump Hill is also a lovely spot.

FLYING

Aeros

Filton Airport
0117 936 4495
www.aeros.co.uk

If you want to learn to fly, the good news is that you can start from the age of 12. The not so good news is that it's not cheap. You could spend about £6,500 getting to the point where you have a license. You can start logging flight time at the age of 14 and you need 45 hours to get a license. You can go solo on your 16th birthday and once you've done the time, you can get a license when you are 17yrs old. Then it's chocks away and the sky's the limit!

For more flying experience also see 2442 Squadron ATC on pg 47.

Airtopia

Unit 9, Button Mill, Lower Mills, Bridgend,
Stonehouse, GL10 2BB
01453 827202
www.airtopia.com

If you are over 16, you can try paragliding.
You don't need to be big and strong but you
do need to be fit and have a head for heights!
Taster sessions, tandem flights and training
are all on offer at Airtopia.

Bristol & Gloucestershire Gliding Club

01453 860342
www.bggc.co.uk

See the world from a whole new perspective!
You can fly in tandem with an instructor using
dual controls. There are no age restrictions
but you need to weigh at least 6-7 stone.

Silver Stars Parachute Team

Duke of Gloucestershire Barracks, Cirencester
01285 868259
www.silverstars.org.uk

This military organisation opens its doors
to members of the public at the weekend,
offering tandem parachute jumps for those
over 16yrs.

HORSE RIDING

Gordano Valley Riding Centre

Moor Lane, Clapton in Gordano, Bristol, BS20 7RF
01275 843473

Lessons, rides and lead-outs for everyone
from 5yrs+. Children's birthdays are catered
for. There are holiday clubs offering a range of
activities including riding and grooming.

Kingsweston Stables

Lime Kiln Cottage, Kingsweston Rd, Lawrence
Weston, Bristol, BS11 0UX
0117 982 8929
Classes and hacking: £12 per ½ hour, £17 per hour

Riding lessons and hacking for all ages.
Pre-booking required, please call for details.

Tynings Trekking Centre

Charterhouse, Blagdon, Bristol, BS40 7XU
01934 742501
www.tynings.halvor.co.uk

Rides, lead-ons and treks. Magical Mendip
scenery, all rides off-road and lessons are
available.

Urchinwood Manor Equitation Centre

Urchinwood Manor, Congresbury, Bristol, BS49 5AP
01934 833248
www.urchinwoodmanor.co.uk

Teaching centre, offering lessons for all
ages and stages, including working towards
competitions and exams.

KITE FLYING

Avon Kite Flyers

01275 875 342
www.avonkiteflyers.org.uk
£10 per family per year

This club is popular with families. The club is
a meeting point and information source for
local kite flyers of all abilities. There are fly-ins
at Ashton Court on the first Sunday of the
month. Benefits include 10% discount at local
kite shops and use of club kites.

ORIENTEERING

Bristol Orienteering Klub

0117 975 6545
www.freenetpages.co.uk/hp/bristolklub

A family club for all ages, part of a national network of clubs. Orienteering involves walking or running around a designated area, visiting control points along the way. You can compete against your own age group.

PAINTBALL

Bristol Outdoor Pursuits Centre

Hamburger Hill, Common Wood, Hunstrete, Nr Pensford, Bristol, BS39 4NT
0800 9803980
www.bristoloutdoor.co.uk

Hamburger Hill is a huge woodland paintball site with 20 game zones. There is also pulse ranger, quad bikes and laser sport.

Combat Zone

33 Hopps Rd, Kingswood, Bristol, BS15 9QQ
0117 935 3388
www.combatzone.co.uk
info@combatzone.co.uk

Junior paintball (AKA Young Guns) is available for young people aged 12-16yrs, including parties and even parents Vs kids!

Ministry of Paintball

www.ministryofpaintball.com
0870 724 6822
£10 per person for first 100 paintballs

This national paintball chain has three sites in the Bristol area: Thornbury, Henbury and one near Bristol Airport. You must be over 11yrs at Henbury and over 12yrs at the other two venues. Sessions last all day and you can come as a group or as an individual.

Paintball Adventures

Brockley Coombe Woodland, Backwell, BS48
0117 935 3300
www.paintball-adventures.co.uk

If your idea of heaven is a shoot out in the woods with paint splurge guns, then this is the place for you. Minimum age 12yrs.

Skirmish Paintball Games

Coast Rd, Portishead, Bristol, BS20
0800 107 6250
www.skirmishbristol.co.uk
Also: Skirmish Bath at Norridge Woods, BA12 7RZ

Eleven game zones in woodland terrain. Helicopter, armoured cars, cowboy town, medieval castle, great food, officers mess, base camp. No fighting or bad language. Also clay pigeon shooting, quads and karting. Junior days for ages 12-18yrs are held regularly. Over 16s can join any group. Turn up and join in on Saturdays and Sundays. Midweek, you'll need to be part of a group of 12.

SAILING & CANOEING

Baltic Wharf Sailing Club

Baltic Wharf, Cumberland Rd, Bristol, BS1
07860 209410, 0117 962 4224
adrian@bevholmes.co.uk

A friendly sailing club in the heart of Bristol, offering the chance to improve your skills, sail with others, borrow boats and race. As well as sailing in the harbour, there are trips to Clevedon and further afield. Annual membership for adults is £25 and there are discounts for young people.

Bristol Avon Sailing Club

Mead Lane, Saltford, BS31 3ER
01225 873472
www.bristol-avon-sailing.org.uk
enquiries@bristol-avon-sailing.org.uk

This family-friendly club offers reasonable membership rates for families and juniors and the chance to sail on a mile-long stretch of the River Avon. Royal Yacht Association accredited courses for beginners are run every spring.

Bristol Canoe Club

Baltic Wharf, Bristol Docks, BS1
0117 965 3724
www.bristolcanoeclub.org.uk
Apr-Dec: Thu, 6pm at the docks
Dec-Mar: Wed 7pm, pool sessions

This club, which has a youth section for keen paddlers, is active in white water trips, slalom, polo and surfing. They offer occasional formal beginners courses.

Bristol Sailing School

0117 926 0703
www.bristolsailingschool.co.uk

Sailing lessons for all ages in Bristol Harbour. Also powerboat courses for young people aged over 15yrs. Courses are usually held during school holidays and last from 1-3 days.

Bristol Water Ski Club

0117 987 9575
www.bwsf.co.uk
Summer: every other Sat, 8.30am-12.30pm
Winter: every other Sat, 9am-1pm
£20 per session

Water skiing in the harbour is available to all ages. Bring your own wetsuit. You don't have to be a strong swimmer as you wear buoyancy aids. Bristol Water Ski Club is an Approved Ski Boat Driver Award Test Centre.

Chew Valley Lake Sailing Club

01275 482948
www.chewvalleysailing.org.uk

Sailing and wind surfing for club members including courses. There's junior and family membership but there is a waiting list.

Portishead Yacht and Sailing Club

Sugar Loaf Beach, Belton Rd, Portishead, BS20
01275 847049
www.pysc.org.uk

The club offers the full spectrum of dinghy sailing, from tuition for beginners to top-class racing. Annual Try Sailing weekends allow anyone to come along and have a go with the help of club members. There are also family fun days and a Docks Regatta at Portishead Quays.

Thornbury Sailing Club

Oldbury Pill, Oldbury-on-Severn, BS35
www.thornburysc.org.uk
enquiries@thornburysc.org.uk

The club offers sailing courses and is a recognised RYA Sail Training establishment.

Weston Bay Yacht Club

Uphill Beach, Links Rd, Weston-super-Mare
01934 413366

SCUBA DIVING

Aqua Turtle

Trevor: 0117 967 6190
www.aquaturtle.co.uk

Regular scuba diving, PADI and snorkelling courses and one-off training sessions (£15) held at Kingswood Leisure Centre. Aqua Turtle also offers powerboat courses in the harbour.

Badminton Pool

0117 962 7972

Four-day intensive courses in diving, snorkelling and octopush (like underwater hockey!) run three times a year in April, July and December.

Extreme Marine

6 Harbury Rd, Henleaze, Bristol, BS9 4PL
0117 962 3363
www.extreme-marine.co.uk

Scuba diving courses with PADI instructors are offered through this long-established shop. Training for juniors starts with the Bubblemakers courses for ages 8-12. Qualified juniors of 10 and above can dive in open water to a depth of 12 metres as long as they are accompanied by a certified adult diver. You can become a fully qualified diver at 16yrs. Training courses take place at Clifton College Pool on Saturday evenings. Once you are qualified, there are trips every weekend.

SKATEBOARDING

50:50

16 Park Row, Bristol, BS1
0117 914 7783
www.5050store.com

Top skate shop, 50:50 has its own highly
successful team. Membership is by invitation.

Apex Leisure and Wildlife Park

Marine Drive, Burnham-on-Sea, TA8
www.sedgemoor.gov.uk

This 42-acre site has a great skate park.
Floodlit, it has half and quarter pipes and a
box ramp with grind and curb rails.

Dreamfields

The Exchange, Hamilton Rd, Taunton, Somerset
01823 325308
www.dreamfields.org.uk

Helmets, knee pads and wrist guards must be
worn. Parties available.

Motion Ramp Park

74-78 Avon St, St Phillips, Bristol, BS2 0PX
0117 972 3111
www.motionramppark.co.uk
Every day, 12pm-12am £6 per rider per day

A competition-level indoor ramp complex for
skateboards, bikes and blades. For beginners
up to extreme, including mini ramps, vert
walls, sub-boxes and the brand new Jersey
Barrier. The Motion Shop offers board
and bike repairs and upgrades as well as
Motionwear urban clothing.

Skate Parks In Bristol

www.sk8m8.com

The sk8m8 website has details of hundreds
of skate parks. In the Bristol area, there are
lots of venues, including: Dame Emily Smythe
Park, Bedminster; St George's Park; Filwood
Park, Hengrove; Withywood Skatepark;
Southey Park, Kingswood; Keynesham
Memorial Park; Emersons Green, Bradley
Stoke; Patchway; Warmley and Portishead.

The Epic Centre

582 Moseley Rd, Moseley, Birmingham, B12 9AA
0121 442 2425
www.epicskateparks.com

Epic by name, epic in proportion, this is said to be one of Europe's biggest skate parks. Recommended by 50:50 in Bristol, the park is based in an old bus depot and it boasts a vert ramp. There's also a climbing centre in the same building.

SKIING, TOBOGGANING & SNOWBOARDING

Gloucester Ski & Snowboard Centre

Robinswood Hill, Matson Lane, Gloucester, GL4 6EA
08702 400375
www.gloucesterski.com
Every day 10am-10pm,
except Thu, Sat/Sun until 6pm
For prices, call for more details

Kids Adventure Club for those that can ski recreationally, up to 16yrs. Private & group lessons for all ages and snowboarding from 12yrs. Tubing sessions for all ages, £5 a session. Adapted equipment available for disabled customers.

The Action Centre

Lyncombe Drive, Churchill, N Somerset, BS25 5PQ
01934 852335
www.highaction.co.uk
9.30am-10pm
Costs vary according to activity (Start at £4.50 for tobogganing)

Floodlit dry ski slope open all year. Any age permitted providing they can snowplough, stop, turn & use button drag lift, booking not necessary. Lessons available for all abilities. Also tobogganing, snow blading for established skiers and snowboarding from 7yrs (dependent on height). Activity days run by a qualified instructor, teaching skiing, archery and rifle shooting. Also quad biking, power kiting and mountain boarding. Booking essential for all activities except recreational ski-ing. Party bookings taken.

SURFING

Bristol Nomads Windsurfing Club

www.bristolnomads.org.uk

Friendly club, currently with members aged 16yrs+. The focus is on recreational windsurfing rather than racing.

Bristol Surfing Club

22 Church Lane, Clifton, Bristol, BS8 4TR
07771 902373
www.bristol-surf-club.co.uk

Bristol Surfing Club brings together everyone from enthusiastic beginners to qualified instructors, with trips to beaches in North Devon every weekend in search of the best waves. U18s are very welcome, although the weekly Thursday club meeting is currently held in a pub. However, full details of the weekend plans are posted on the club's website and tuition is available to beginners.

Point Breaks

07776 148679
www.pointbreaks.com

Surfing school at Croyde Bay, North Devon. All instructors fully qualified with the British Surfing Association.

Simon Tucker's Surfing Academy

Porthcawl, Mid Glamorgan
07815 289761
£25/2hr session

Former British champion, Simon Tucker coaches the Welsh U16s team and his academy teaches beginners who can swim 100 metres. Many pupils come from the Bristol area.

Surf South West

01271 890400
www.surfsouthwest.com
darren@surfsouthwest.com

Surf school offering courses at Croyde and Saunton, North Devon, from half days to full weeks and weekends.

RACES & CHALLENGES

Bristol Half Marathon

www.bristol-city.gov.uk/halfmarathon

A popular autumn event for runners looking for an endurance challenge.

Bath Half Marathon

www.bathhalfmarathon.co.uk

Another popular event held in the spring. Applications accepted in September.

Bristol Bike Fest

www.bristolbikefest.com

A 12 hour team endurance event. See picture above!

Bristol Biggest Bike Ride

www.bristol-city.gov.uk/bristolbikeride

Five different routes from 9 to 40 miles. Fun, traffic-free cycling. Event concludes at Brunel Picnic Park.

Cancer Research Race for Life

0870 513 4314
www.raceforlife.org

5km women-only charity race, held on the Downs every May. Men and boys get to race in the afternoon — Run for Moore.

Triathalon

www.sped-web.pwp.blueyonder.co.uk

This website lists many Triathalon events in the West as well as offering advice and links to local clubs.

INTERESTS & CLUBS

Rachel Miller

CONTENTS

INTRODUCTION

Are you mad about dance? Or perhaps you are a budding DJ or you long to go on the stage? Are you a real foodie that wants to learn how to be a professional chef? Maybe you're in a band and you want to record your songs. Or are you keen on archaeology or chess or even circus skills?

Whatever your interests, there are hundreds of clubs and after-school courses in Bristol where you can indulge your passion, learn new skills and meet like-minded people.

We've also listed all the action clubs and groups, everything from guides and scouts to the boys' and girls' brigades, all offering a chance to have real adventures and challenges. In addition, there are some great youth clubs in the city where you can hang out with friends. And there are a host of after-school and holiday clubs to help keep you occupied!

ANIMATION & CARTOONS

UWE Bristol School of Art, Media and Design

Bower Ashton Campus, Kennel Lodge Rd, BS3 2JT
0117 328 4810
www.uwe.ac.uk/amd
amd.shortcourses@uwe.as.uk

Animation courses for 12-17yrs and for 7-11yrs on Saturday mornings over six weeks. Also week-long summer courses in animation and drawing.

ARCHAEOLOGY

Archaeology websites

www.britarch.ac.uk
British Archaeology magazine has a great website with a searchable directory of organisations involved in British archaeology.

www.greenvolunteers.com/arkeo
A guide to archaeological and heritage volunteering.

Bath & Bristol Young Archaeologists Club

0117 914 1811
joannamellors@blueyonder.co.uk
£3pp and £5 family

The club meets once a month at venues across the West. Meetings include dig visits, survey work, studying original documents and aerial photographs. There are also events such as the Mediaeval Bristol trail, reconstruction drawing, a gladiator school workshop and a roman picnic.

Bristol & Avon Archaeological Society

www.digitalbristol.org/members/baas

Meetings are held in Cotham on Wed evenings. Events include walks, field trips and lectures.

Chedworth Roman Villa

Yamworth, Cheltenham, Glos, GL54 3LJ
01242 890256
chedworth@nationaltrust.org.uk
Tue-Sun, March-mid Nov

Holds archaeological activities, living history events, craft days and re-enactments.

Young Archaeologists Club

www.britarch.ac.uk/yac
8-16yrs

See their website for activities and details of your nearest branch.

ARCHITECTURE

The Architecture Centre

Narrow Quay, Bristol
0117 922 1540
www.architecturecentre.co.uk

Membership is open to anyone with an interest in architecture. Events include lectures, trips and exhibitions.

ARTS & CRAFTS

B Delicious

2 Triangle South, Clifton, Bristol, BS8
0117 929 1789

This little gem, tucked away in the far corner of the Triangle, offers you the opportunity to be creative with beads. Make yourself some jewellery or a decorative frame, hairband, belt or tiara. You can be as imaginative as you like, with or without the expert help of staff.

Bristol City Museum & Art Gallery

Queens Rd, Clifton, Bristol, BS8 1RL
0117 922 3571
www.bristol-city.gov.uk/museums

Arts and crafts-based holiday activities and workshops, also on first Sunday of the month, from mask-making to painting.

Orchard Workshops

Kingswood Foundation, Britannia Rd, Kingswood, Bristol, BS15 8DB
0117 967 0799

Sat am arts and crafts club. Each class is a self-contained session focusing on one craft, such as metalwork, woodwork, jewellery-making, silversmithing, glass or photography. Fully inclusive for able and disabled children from 8-15yrs. Book in advance. Janet also runs summer holiday workshops.

Recreating

01454 414915
elizabeth@vooght.com

Arts and crafts workshops held in the school holidays including half terms. Based in Thornbury and aimed at ages 8-14yrs. Based on small groups, so it gets booked up very quickly but Elizabeth can be booked for additional sessions.

CHESS

Bristol & District Chess League

www.chessit.co.uk

This league has some 17 clubs in Bristol and Bath. See website for more details.

Downend & Fishponds Chess Club

Downend Cricket Club, Downend Rd, Bristol
0117 937 3761
Tue 7.30pm

This club is part of the Bristol and District League. It welcomes junior players of all abilities.

CIRCUS SKILLS

Circomedia

St Paul's Church, Portland Square, Bristol, BS1
0117 935 3260
www.circomedia.com

Regular circus skills sessions during term time and during the holidays.

Circus Maniacs

Office 8A, The Kingswood Foundation, Britannia Rd, Kingswood, Bristol, BS15 8DB
0117 947 7042
www.circusmaniacs.com

A fantastic opportunity to get physical by learning skills such as trapeze, tight-wire, acrobatics, juggling, unicycling & stilt-walking. Taster sessions available.

COOKERY

Quartier Vert

85 Whiteladies Rd, Bristol, BS8
0117 904 6679
www.quartiervert.co.uk

This creative cookery school offers workshops and summer holiday courses for all ages.

The Bertinet Kitchen

12 St Andrew's Terrace, Bath, BA1 2QR
01225 445531
www.thebertinetkitchen.com

A purpose-built cookery school that offers cookery courses for all ages. There are half day classes for the over 10s and survival cooking for the 17s and over who are about to leave home for the first time.

DANCE

344 Dance School

Alexandra Pk, Fishponds, Bristol, BS16 2BG
0117 965 5660
www.dancestation.org.uk

Ballet, modern jazz, tap, drama, singing, Irish dancing & shows for all ages, including classes for teenage beginners. Sessions take place on weekdays after school and Sat. Also summer schools. Full-time dance college for ages 16 and over. Dancewear and tuck shop. Branches at: Bradley Stoke, Long Ashton, Wick, Knowle and Fishponds.

Annette Adams School of Dance

0117 968 4879
www.theannetteadamsschoolofdance.co.uk

Classes are held at Horfield Methodist Church and the Kelvin Players Drama Studio, both on Gloucester Road. Ballet, modern, jazz and tap. Classes held after school and Sat am. Working towards RAD and ISTD exams.

Ashley's Rise Morris Dancing

0117 940 1566
ashleyrisemorris@aol.com
Tue 6.15pm-7.15pm, Horfield United Reform Church

A performing English morris team for ages 8-16yrs. Mainly Border and some Cotswold dancing. And if that doesn't mean anything to you, don't worry, absolute beginners are positively encouraged. The first session is free and you can pay termly or weekly. There are regular performances at fêtes and fairs in the summer and at Seasonal Customs. All costumes provided, apart from black trousers.

Bollywood Dance

0117 931 4443
www.bollywooddance.co.uk
info@bollywooddance.co.uk

Classes for all ages, held in Hotwells, Easton and Bradley Stoke. Workshops can also be arranged. Call for further details.

Bristol Academy of Performing Arts

The Tobacco Factory, Raleigh Rd, Southville, BS3
0117 963 0966
www.baparts.co.uk

Practical sessions in musical theatre styles, dance and ensemble singing. Also, full-time courses in music theatre for ages 16+.

Bristol Community Dance Centre

Jacobs Wells Rd, Hotwells, Bristol, BS8 1DX
0117 929 2118
www.bristolcommunitydancecentre.co.uk ·

You'll find every type of dance class on offer at this fantastic centre, including flamenco, hip hop, breakdance, Bollywood and African dance. There are also classes in yoga, pilates and jitsu defence.

Dance Bristol

0117 915 0185

Dance Bristol provides funding and support for all kinds of dance in Bristol. It's the place to go if you are serious about a career in dance as it can help with career and professional development. There are also grants available for young people that want to do a two-year dance programme which includes the chance to work with leading dance companies.

Danceblast @ the Tobacco Factory

Tobacco Factory, Raleigh Rd, Southville, BS3 1TF
0117 964 6195
www.danceblast.co.uk
Sat/Sun, up to 18 yrs
£5 per session

All types of dancing: ballet, jazz, lyrical and hip hop as well as some singing and acting included, working towards an annual show. Drop-in sessions for 3-13yrs on Saturdays and for 14-18yrs on Sundays, lasting 1½ hrs.

Footwork

0117 963 3029
www.footwork.org/medea
medea@footwork.org

Middle Eastern dance classes held at a dance studio in Southville.

Funk It Up Dance Company

07816 498774
www.funkitupdance.com
info@funkitupdance.com

Hip hop and street dance for all ages and abilities, every evening from Monday to Thursday, ages 7yrs to adult.

Henleaze School of Dancing

0117 962 3224
Mon-Fri

Ballet & tap for ages up to 11yrs. Held at St Peters' Church Hall, Henleaze and at Stoke Bishop Village Hall.

Kuumba

0117 944 7504
www.kuumba.org.uk
7-11yrs: Thur 6pm-7pm. 11-16yrs: Thur 7pm-8pm

Weekly classes in all kinds of dance from R&B and dance hall to ragga, working towards performances. Summer courses also available.

Southville Youth Dance Project

Southville Centre, Beaulieu Rd, Bristol, BS3 1QG
07786 153857
southvilledance@hotmail.com
Wed 5.30pm-7pm, drop-in, term time

Contemporary and funky dance for girls aged 11-16yrs, working towards performances in the summer.

Stagecoach

68 Raymend Rd, Bristol, BS3 4QW
0117 986 2500
www.stagecoachbristol.co.uk
info@stagecoachbristol.co.uk

See listing in Drama, pg 39.

Stages Dance

0117 903 1297

Bristol City Council runs the Bristol Arts and Music Service, which works with Bristol schools to put on Stages dance performances at Colston Hall and the Hippodrome. Talented dancers get to work with Bristol's leading youth dance group, Kinesis.

Stapleton School of Dancing

01453 834211
From £25 per term
Venues:
Begbrook Primary School, Stapleton.
Christ Church Hall, Quaker Rd, Downend.
The Ridgewood Community Centre, Yate
Minchinhampton Youth Centre.

Ballet, modern, tap and jazz. A summer
school runs in the last week of July.

Stepping Out School of Dance

Baptist Church Hall, Station Rd, Shirehampton
01454 615463/07971 099706

Classes for all ages, including ballet, tap,
jazz and pop. Regular performances, no
set uniform. Drop-in classes take place on
Wednesdays, Fridays and Saturdays.

Street Vibes Dance

The Sanctuary Church, 55 High St, Staple Hill, BS16
07980 509461
streetvibesdance@blueyonder.co.uk

Sessions are drop-in and aimed at 7-18yrs.
Breakdancing classes for "Boyz", Wed at
5.45pm. "Girlz" learn everything from hip hop
to street dance, Thu at 6.30pm.

Westbury Park Dance Centre

79 Bell Barn Rd, Stoke Bishop, Bristol, BS9 2DF
0117 968 3682
westburyparkdancecentre@hotmail.com
After school & Sat at St Albans Church Hall,
Westbury Park, BS6

Classes following RAD Ballet and ISTD Jazz/
Modern/Tap syllabuses. For all ages, working
towards occasional shows.

Wingfield School of Ballet

The Pembles, Fishpool Hill, Brentry, BS10 6SW
0117 950 3916
wingfieldschool@brentry.freeserve.co.uk

Ballet, tap and modern dance classes for all
ages to adults. Prepares dancers for RAD
& ISTD examinations, shows & Eisteddfod.
Classes are held after school in: Patchway,
Little Stoke, Thornbury, Almondsbury &
Brislington and Sat am in Bradley Stoke.

Youth Dance

Bristol Community Dance Centre, Jacobs Wells Rd,
Hotwells, BS8 1DX
0117 377 1063

Creative and contemporary dance classes held
at Bristol Community Dance Centre for
11-15yrs. Summer schools also available.

DJ COURSES

Access to Music

309 Central Pk Ind. Estate, Petherton Rd, Hengrove
0800 281842

State-of-the-art music studios giving budding
musicians the chance to access professional
recording equipment. There are free courses
for vocal artists, DJs and producers, 16-19yrs.

DJ Academy

01905 22551
www.djacademy.org.uk
office@djacademy.org.uk

Eight-week courses for budding DJs held at
Club Fiesta Havana on Mon evenings. Aimed
at 13-18yrs, discounts for U17s. All the core
DJ skills taught including beat mixing and
scratching and how to be a top club DJ.

The Mark Davis DJ Academy

07770 940 930
djmarkdavis@yahoo.co.uk

Mark Davis runs DJ courses at over 40 venues
across the South West. Most are held in
schools but Mark also offers some evening
classes and private lessons.

Remix

0117 922 4276
www.remix-music.org.uk

The Bristol Youth Music Action Zone, provides
a wide range of music-making opportunities
for U18s, including DJ workshops. It has
established more than 20 music workshops
across the city, helping hundreds of young
people from diverse communities develop
their skills. If you are interested in singing,
song-writing, being a DJ or MC give 'em a call.

DRAMA

The Big Act

0870 881 0367
www.thebigact.com

Classes in acting, singing and dancing for children up to 18yrs. There are no auditions, places are offered on a first-come first-served basis. New students can come for a free trial lesson. Students regularly perform shows in Bristol. There are three venues in Bristol:

The Tobacco Factory, Southville
Fridays 5-7pm (8-18yrs)

Gate C, Knorr Bremse Ind Park, Douglas Rd, Kingswood, BS15 8NL
Sundays, 1.45pm-3.45pm (8-18yrs)

Bradley Stoke
New venue, call for further details.

Bigfoot Drama Academy

0870 011 4948
www.bigfoot-theatre.co.uk

Offering a special approach to drama. Starting with a topic, the work that is produced is student-led and is all about building confidence and improving empathy and communication. Currently sessions run in Bath for ages 8-11yrs and 12-14yrs. More classes and holiday workshops opening soon.

Bristol Academy of Performing Arts

The Tobacco Factory, Raleigh Rd, Southville, BS3
0117 963 0966
www.baparts.co.uk

Practical sessions in musical theatre styles, dance and ensemble singing. Also, full-time courses in music theatre for ages 16+yrs.

Bristol Musical Comedy Club

07799 717695
www.bmcc.org.uk

One of Bristol's foremost amateur theatrical clubs, BMCC puts on two or three performances a year and young people aged 16yrs+ are very welcome. Rehearsals are usually held on Mon and Fri nights.

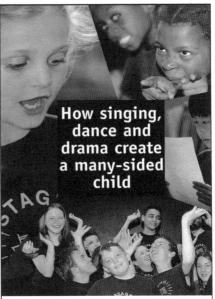

Bristol Musical Youth Productions

St Ursula's School, Brecon Rd, Henleaze, BS9 4DT
01275 842563
Fri 7.30pm-10pm
12-16yrs

BMYP puts on two major productions every year. Auditions take place regularly to recruit new young people. A high level of parental involvement is expected, from making costumes to selling tickets.

Bristol Old Vic Theatre School

2 Downside Rd, Clifton, Bristol, BS8 2XF
0117 973 3535 ext 253
Holiday courses, Mon-Fri 10am-4pm
£125 for a week

The Theatre School offers Easter and summer holiday courses for young people aged 11-20. These Skills Weeks take place at the Theatre School and are led by professional practitioners, covering everything from acting, voice training and role play to singing, dancing and stage combat.

Bristol Old Vic Youth Theatre

King St, Bristol, BS1 4ED
0117 949 3993 Ext 226
www.bristol-old-vic.co.uk

The Youth Theatre offers young people (7-21yrs) the chance to develop a wide range of practical theatre skills. It has over 400 members from across the South West. Sessions take place once a week on weekday evenings and on Saturday mornings and cost £35 or £40 per term, depending on age. There is a long waiting list. At 15, Youth Theatre members are offered an audition to join the Youth Theatre Company. Two week summer courses are also available for ages 11-18yrs. There are also workshops for all members of the community.

Bristol School of Performing Arts

Elmgrove Centre, Redland Rd, Cotham, BS6 6AG
01278 434 081
2-hour sessions, Thu and Sat, term time
£95 for 10 weeks

Drama classes for all ages up to 16yrs. Sessions last two hours. Holiday workshops. Lamba examinations are available.

Bristol Youth Theatre Studio

0117 951 4432

In its 46th year, this theatre group meets on Saturdays at 4.30-8.30pm in Westbury-on-Trym. Admission is by audition and it's aimed at ages 13-21yrs. The group performs two major and two minor shows every year (at theatres such as the Redgrave and QEH) and tours every two years during the summer.

Centre Stage

01454 851938
www.centrestage.bizland.com

Two-hour drama sessions with the emphasis on improving confidence, including dance, drama, singing and movement, with all ages (7-18yrs) working together. No auditions, opportunities for all and regular workshops from professionals, on everything from stage fighting to African dance. Sessions take place on Saturday mornings at Winterbourne and on Monday evenings in Yate.

Drama Queens

Southville Centre, Beaulieu Rd, Bristol, BS3 1QG
07977 681954
Weds, 5.30pm-6.30pm 8-11yrs;
6.30pm-7.30pm 11+yrs

Creating ideas, producing stories, learning stage and life skills, showing off, dressing up and having fun.

Helen O'Grady Drama Academy

0117 924 4944
www.helenogrady.co.uk
alison.mazanec@btinternet.com
Sessions after school and at weekends.
Venues: Frampton Cotterell, Keynesham, Bishopston, Redland, Portishead, Westbury-on-Trym, Almondsbury and Kingswood.
Upper primary (9-12yrs)

Youth theatre (13-17yrs)

The programme offered at the academy aims to provide confidence and skills in verbal communication through drama. Working towards summer performances. Phone for more information on the youth theatre.

ITV West Television Workshops

ITV West, Bath Rd, Bristol, BS4 3HG
0117 972 2497
www.itv.com
adam.fresco@itv.com
5-26yrs
Sessions at weekends, after school and in holidays, according to age

ITV West offers drama and production workshops training young people in performance, presenting and production for tv, theatre, radio and film. There are regular performances and you could get to make your own short films. Unsurprisingly, there is a waiting list but it's worth filling in an application form online to get your name down. The workshops also act as a casting resource for tv and film. Previous students have appeared in Charlie and the Chocolate Factory, Harry Potter and Casualty.

Ivy Arts Theatre School

Torwood House, Durdham Park, Redland, BS6 6XE
07748 983 436
Sat 10am-12pm and 12.30pm-2.30pm.
From £10 per session

Qualified teachers offer a broad range of theatre crafts, performing, singing, movement and dance for children up to 14yrs.
Pre-booking is essential. Children are split into age-related groups, but also spend some time integrated together. Working towards one major musical every summer. Workshops held during Easter and summer holidays.

Kick Off Youth Theatre

The Hope Chapel, Hope Chapel Hill, Hotwells, BS8
0117 929 1883
Mon 5pm-6.30pm (7-11yrs)
Mon 6.30pm-8pm (12-18yrs)
£3 per session £2 concessions, payable half termly

An opportunity to learn skills such as acting, voice, mime, masks and perform shows. Members must be prepared to have fun and show commitment to attend.

The National Association of Youth Theatres

01325 363330
www.nayt.org.uk

Information on drama clubs and regional youth theatre.

The National Youth Theatre

020 7281 3863
www.nyt.org.uk

Open to all young people, 13-21yrs, subject to audition.

QEH Youth Theatre

QEH Theatre, Jacobs Wells Rd, Bristol, BS8 1JX
0117 914 5805
www.qehtheatre.co.uk
7-11yrs, Mon 4pm-5.30pm
£5.50 per session payable in advance

Youth theatre with sessions for all ages from 7-16, held at the QEH theatre — movement, sound, art and craft, games, storymaking and telling, improvisation, role-play, mime and plays. New sessions planned for ages 11-13yrs and 14-16yrs, phone for details.

Stagecoach

www.stagecoachbristol.co.uk
bristolsouthwest@stagecoach.co.uk

Offers part-time training in drama, singing and dance to all ages up to 16yrs. There are no auditions. Their ethos concentrates on confidence and self-esteem. See advertisement on pg 39.

Ashton/Portishead 0117 953 2500

Keynesham 0117 330 5953

Cotham 0117 953 2500

Winterbourne 0117 959 3995

Totterdown 01225 484785

SWADA

Filton College, WISE Campus, New Rd, Stoke Gifford
0117 919 2659
Sat 10.30-12.30
£55 for 10-week course

The South West Academy of Dramatic Arts (SWADA) offers creative drama for young people aged 10-15yrs. No auditions required and there are end of term performances. You can come for a session to see if it's for you with no obligation.

The Tobacco Factory

Raleigh Rd, Southville, Bristol, BS3 1TF
Box office 0117 902 0344
www.tobaccofactory.com

The Tobacco Factory is a mecca for those interested in the creative arts. It has a great theatre with a varied programme of plays, including many for young people. The café/bar is open to U18s until 9pm. There are regular events and workshops as well as a thriving market on the third Sunday of every month. The Tobacco Factory is the home of The Big Act, Bristol Academy of Performing Arts (BAPA) and DanceBlast — see their separate entries in this section. Other activities at The Tobacco Factory include the following:

Tai Chi

Mary Leonard: 0117 977 5193.
www.bristoltaichi.org

Middle Eastern Dance Classes

Karine Butchart: 01373 466015
arabic.souldance@btinternet.com
Monday classes for 14yrs+ (£4-6)
Beginners 6.30pm
Improvers/intermediates 7.30pm
Intermediates/advanced 8.45pm

Transparent Youth Theatre

07737 379971
transparenttheatre@hotmail.co.uk
Held at: Bristol Foyer, 2a Victoria St, Bristol Bridge
Mon 5pm-7pm

An open theatre group for ages 16+. Experimenting with making performances that are issue-based. Free to attend. Can lead to paid acting opportunities with their theatre.

Travelling Light

0117 377 3166
www.travlight.co.uk

A youth theatre which meets on Thursday evenings at Barton Hill. There are workshops for ages 8-12yrs, 12-14yrs and 14-16yrs. Regular performances of original material created by the groups themselves.

University of Bristol Department of Drama

Cantocks Close, Woodland Rd, Bristol, BS8 1UP
0117 954 5471
www.bris.ac.uk/drama/lifelearn

Short courses in drama and film are offered at the University of Bristol department of drama — the place where Little Britain's Matt Lucas and David Walliams learnt their craft. These courses are available to young people aged over 16 and include everything from voice workshops and presentation skills training to puppetry and the Can Can.

FILM

Bath Film Festival

01225 401149
www.bathfilmfestival.org

Annual event held every autumn, with film-making workshops for 14-18yrs.

Brief Encounters

The Watershed, 1 Canon's Rd, Harbourside, BS1
0117 915 0185
www.brief-encounters.org.uk

Annual international showcase for short films held every November.

CEED Multimedia Centre

97-107 Wilder St, St Pauls, Bristol
0117 942 9555
www.ceed.co.uk

Part-time courses for those aged 16yrs and over in everything from radio and video production to advanced music technology.

Cinekids @ The Watershed

1 Canon's Rd, Harbourside, Bristol, BS1 5TX
0117 927 5100
www.watershed.co.uk
Adults £3.50, children £2

Cinekids is aimed at children aged 8-12yrs. It's a once-a-month event, with a film showing and workshop or talk afterwards. To get advance notice of the next events by email, call the box office or send an email to: kids@watershed.co.uk.

GEOGRAPHY

Bristol City Museum & Art Gallery

Queens Rd, Clifton, Bristol, BS8 1RL
0117 922 3571
www.bristol-city.gov.uk/museums

Regular sessions on rocks, fossils and minerals.

Young Geographers

Royal Geographical Society, 1 Kensington Gore, London, SW7 2AR
020 7591 3000
www.rgs.org
14-24yrs or in full time education

You will need a Fellow of the RGS or a head of department to sign your application form to become a member. Alternatively, see if your school or college has Educational Membership.

MUSIC

37th Kingswood Drum & Bugle Corps

0117 961 4607
www.37th.co.uk
rec37@yahoo.co.uk
Seniors (12-25yrs) Tue and Sun evenings
Cadet Corps (8-15yrs) Fri evenings
Subs: £2.50-£5 a week

This award-winning corps plays around the country and even further afield during the summer season. Practice sessions take place in Kingswood. Beginners to experienced musicians welcome, newcomers will be taught to read music and given the chance to try a range of instruments. Instruments and uniforms are provided.

Access to Music

309 Central Pk Ind. Estate, Petherton Rd, Hengrove
0800 281842

State-of-the-art music studios giving budding musicians the chance to access professional recording equipment. There are courses for vocal artists, DJs and producers which are free to those aged 16-19yrs.

Bristol Arts & Music Service

0117 903 1370

Informal auditions are held in June and July at various locations across the city. Successful musicians and singers will join one of the following five centres:

West Music Centre

Portway School
Mon 7.30pm-9pm
West Bristol concert band and big band, Grade 5 and over.

South Music Centre

Hengrove School
Sat 9.30am-12.30pm
Wind and string orchestra band and ensembles for Grades 1-2+.

Choral Centre

Redland Park United Reform Church, Whiteladies Rd
Fri 6pm-8pm Senior Girls' Chamber Choir, 12-18yrs
Fri 7.30pm-8.30pm Boys Changed Voice Choir, U18s

Open to all interested singers with enthusiasm and commitment.

Senior Music Centre

Henbury School
Sat 9.30am-12.30pm

Bands and orchestras for Grade 1+. Chamber orchestra for advanced strings, Grade 7+.

Percussion centre

Henbury School

Individual lessons for senior pupils.

CEED Multimedia Centre

97-107 Wilder St, St Pauls, Bristol
0117 942 9555
www.ceed.co.uk

Part-time courses for those aged 16yrs and over in everything from radio and video production to advanced music technology.

Christchurch Choir & Music Group

Christchurch, Clifton Down Rd, Clifton, BS8
0117 973 2011
Free — call for details.

Two weekly choirs, for ages 7-11yrs and 11-18yrs.

City of Bristol Brass Band

07977 137646
www.cobbb.co.uk
steve@cobbb.co.uk
Fri 6pm at St Bonaventure's School, Bishopston

This thriving youth band is primarily aimed at 7-12yrs, and there are opportunities to join the main band. Regular performances include events such as the Harbour Festival. There is a subscription but newcomers can try for free for three months, instruments are provided.

The Crotchet Factory

1 Edward St, Eastville, Bristol, BS5 6LW
0117 951 8015
max@crotchet-factory.co.uk

Music workshops. Also holiday and private sessions available, including tuition in piano, keyboard, guitar, flute, violin and recorder.

Great Western Chorus

07092 392729
contact@singbristol.com

This 50-man close harmonies choir has been performing and winning competitions since 1974. The Chorus sings popular songs from the past 100 years, including Sinatra, show tunes and sacred songs. U18s are very welcome, the youngest member is currently 9!

Hum & Drum

28 Dublin Crescent, Henleaze, Bristol, BS9 4NA
0117 962 1328/924 3159
penraw@aol.com

Piano, violin & recorder lessons after school (up to 18 yrs). Music theory and aural lessons for all ages, leading up to examinations. Also, tutoring for GCSE and A-Level music.

Music teachers

www.ism.org

Finding a good music teacher can be difficult, whether you play an instrument or are looking for singing lessons. A good place to start is the website of the Incorporated Society of Musicians. It offers a search facility which enables you to select your own region and instrument and it provides a suitable list of names and contact details.

You could also try musical instrument shops which often have details of local teachers.

North Somerset Music Service

01934 832395
Operates the North Somerset Centre for Young Musicians as well as the South West Youth String Camerata and the South West Youth Wind Symphonia.

North Somerset Centre for Young Musicians

Congresbury
Sat am

Intermediate orchestra, training orchestra and junior windband, along with improvision and musicianship.

Clevedon Centre

Sat am

North Somerset Symphonia, silver and swing, concert band and Vivace.

Evening Ensembles

St Andrews School, Congresbury
Mon-Fri evenings

Percussion, clarinet. flute, and brass ensembles as well as a jazz orchestra.

Opus Music

486 Wellsway, Bath, BA2 2UD
01225 460 209 (24 hr)

Individual and group piano tuition, for all ages up to 18yrs.

Remix

0117 922 4276
www.remix-music.org.uk

Remix, the Bristol Youth Music Action Zone, provides a wide range of music-making opportunities for U18s, from DJ workshops to jazz sessions. Remix has established more than 20 music workshops across the city and has successfully helped hundreds of young people from Bristol's diverse communities to discover and develop their musical interest and skills. If you are interested in singing, song-writing, or being a DJ or MC, then check out the Remix website. And if you've got a band of your own, Remix offers supervised rehearsals with advice on equipment and how to arrange songs.

South Gloucestershire Music Service

01454 863147

Kingswood Area Music centre

Kingsfield School

Sat 9.30am-12pm: Strings and concert band, intermediate band.
Mon 7.30pm-9.15pm: South Gloucestershire Youth Jazz Orchestra

Thornbury Area Music Centre

Marlwood School

Sat 9.30am-12pm: String groups, wind band and orchestra.

Yate Area Music Centre

Brimsham Green School

Sat 9.30am-12pm: String groups and wind bands.

Little Stoke

Thurs 7pm-9pm: Senior strings.
Thurs 7pm-8.15pm: Reed-up.

Ridings High School

Fri 4.15pm-5.15pm: Two flute ensembles

Studio 7

Kings House, 14 Orchard St, Bristol, BS1 5EH
0117 905 5019
www.studio-7.org
admin@studio-7.org
Tue and Thur, 6pm-9pm

Aimed at gifted and talented young people aged 8-21yrs, covering everything related to the music industry, from song-writing to dealing with stage fright. You need to be referred by your school or you can do an audition. There are regular performances and the training counts towards OCN acreditation. Sessions take place at the Lakota nightclub, 6 Upper York Street, BS1.

The Unsigned Guide

www.theunsignedguide.com

Calling all musicians and bands, this guide to the UK music industry boasts all the key industry information and contacts as well as a realistic take on the industry from the perspective of an unsigned or emerging artist, band, manager or producer.

OPERA

Bristol Amateur Operatic Society

Rooftop Studios, Feeder Rd, Bristol, BS2
07803 931986

The Bristol Amateur Operatic Society Juniors section is aimed at young people aged 12-18yrs. You must audition but the club has an easy-going ethos. There are two performances a year and practice takes place on Friday evenings and Sundays.

CLUBS

ACTION

2442 Squadron ATC

Westbury College, College Rd, Westbury-on-Trym,
Bristol, BS9 3EJ
0117 373 5971
www.2442squadron.fsnet.co.uk
lowndes@blueyonder.co.uk
Tue, Thu and Fri evenings
£6 per month

Cadets in 2442 Squadron enjoy flying and
gliding as well as lots of other activities,
adventures and sports. Aimed at ages 10-18,
the Squadron is 50:50 boys and girls.

Manor Farm Boys' Club

Wellington Hill, Horfield, Bristol, BS7 8ST
0117 924 0560
Tue-Thur 6pm
8-18yrs

Sports and activities are on offer. The club is
affiliated to the National Association of Clubs
for Young People.

Sea Cadets

HMS Flying Fox, Winterstoke Rd, BS3 2NS
0117 953 1991 (South West Office)
www.sea-cadet.org

The Sea Cadet Corps (SCC) is a voluntary
nautical youth organisation for boys and
girls aged 12-18yrs. Its aim is to help young
people towards responsible adulthood by
encouraging valuable personal attributes and
high standards of conduct, using a nautical
theme, based on the customs of the Royal
Navy. Nationally, there are just under 400
Units, with 82 in the South West, of which
four are based in Bristol at Shirehampton,
Knowle, Filton and Cumberland Basin. There
are also units at Bath, Weston-super-Mare
and Thornbury. Further details can be found
on the website.

Sea Cadets featured in photo above.

The Boys' Brigade

01442 231 681 (UK Headquarters)
www.boys-brigade.org.uk

One of the largest Christian Youth
Organisations in the UK, providing a
programme of activities for young people.

The Girls' Brigade

01235 510425
www.girlsbrigadeew.org.uk

International Christian charity offering girls
the chance to develop in confidence, ability
and friendship, venues across the West.

Woodcraft Folk

13 Ritherdon Rd, London, SW17 8QE
020 8672 6031
0845 458 0169 South West organiser
www.woodcraft.org.uk

National progressive educational organisation
designed to build self-confidence and
increase awareness of issues such as the
environment. Aimed at all ages, Woodcraft
Folk meet weekly for drama, discussion,
games, crafts, singing and dancing. There are
also opportunities for camping and hostelling
weekends and even international camps and
exchanges.

SCOUTING MOVEMENT

The Scout Association UK

Gilwell Park, Chingford, Essex, E4 7QW
0845 300 1818
www.scouts.org.uk

Scouting has been around for nearly a century and over that time has evolved into an international organisation offering young people adventurous activities, social awareness and the chance to grow in confidence and independence. It is hugely popular with both boys and girls making waiting lists long. Some forward-planning may be needed if you want to take part.

The Scouting Association is constantly looking for potential new leaders, helpers and fundraisers — calling all mums and dads if you have a few hours to spare!

Avon Scouts

Woodhouse Park, Almondsbury, BS32 4LX
01454 613 006
www.avonscouts.org.uk

Cubs

For 8-10½yrs
1½ hrs per week

Fun, activities, games, challenges and badges. The outdoors is emphasised with camps which can be for a weekend or longer if planned during the holidays.

Scout Troop & Explorer Unit

Scout Troop 10½-14yrs
Explorers 14-18yrs

All sections run structured programmes. At each level, the responsibility and teamwork increases as does the level of adventure which includes the Duke of Edinburgh award scheme. Many of the activities are outdoor pursuits like climbing, kayaking, sailing, gliding and caving along with international camps linking up Scouts from all over the world. Some Scouts take their involvement into adulthood with Network Scouts 18-25yrs.

GIRLGUIDING UK

Girlguiding UK

0800 169 5901
www.girlguiding.org.uk

An offspring of Scouting, initiated at the beginning of the last century by Baden-Powell's sister. It too has developed into a worldwide movement. It offers young people the chance to make friends outside school, learning teamwork and an awareness of the community they live in. There are opportunities for new experiences and adventure. And, like Scouting, it's about developing confidence, self awareness and respect. Below is an overview of the various stages in Girlguiding, however if you want more information, visit their excellent website or call the number above.

Brownies

Brownies 7-10yrs

They take part in indoor and outdoor activities that challenge them. Packs often go away on holiday, to camp or an overnight sleepover.

Guides

Guides 10-14yrs

Guides belong to a group, learn new skills and consequently make new friends often by helping others outside the group. There are personal goals which make up part of an on-going programme with an opportunity to work for a variety of badges. Guides work together in Patrols of between four and eight girls. They elect their own Patrol Leader. Together, Patrols plan their activities and make decisions.

Senior Section — Girlguiding

Senior Section 14-25yrs

This is the all-embracing term for Girl Guides of this age. They may belong to Ranger Guides, Young Leaders or Young Guiders. They take part in a programme called Look Wider which has eight areas covering topics such as creativity, fitness, community action, personal values and independent living.

LOCAL AUTHORITY YOUTH GROUPS

Local Authority Youth Groups

0117 353 2277
www.bristol-city.gov.uk

Bristol City Council runs a countywide programme of projects, activities and events accessed mostly through 16 youth projects it has in the city. Youth Club members may also get involved with the City of Bristol Young People's Forum (0117 903 1330). Projects also involve Bristol's twin cities and international youth work, giving members experience in another country.

For details of youth groups outside Bristol:

Bath and NE Somerset 01225 396980

North Somerset 01934 644075

South Gloucestershire 01454 868593.

YOUTH CLUBS

Ashton Vale Club for Young People

Silbury Rd, Ashton Vale, Bristol, BS3
0117 951 4752

Open to all for ages 8-21yrs, this club meets in the evenings three times a week. Activities include pool, computer games, table tennis, basketball and trips at weekends offering orienteering and kayaking. There are canteen facilities and floodlit tennis courts.

Harry Crook Youth Activities Centre

Moorlands Rd, Fishponds, Bristol, BS16 3LF
0117 965 6948
www.youth-club.co.uk
£5 a year membership

A club for 8-22yrs targeting mainly teenagers. Activities include: archery, arts and crafts, badminton, basketball, disco and karaoke, netball, tennis, table tennis, watersports, pool and snooker, photography and self defence. The Centre is also home to the Bristol 5 Football Club, see p 8.

Duke of Edinburgh Award

01753 727 400
southwest@theaward.org

Most people do their D of E award through school or a local youth or activity club. There are three stages: Bronze (14yrs+), Silver (15yrs+) and Gold (16rs+). You are required to learn a new skill, provide a service to the community or take up a physical activity. It's a great way to meet new people, learn new skills and gain a qualification.

Powerhouse Youth Club

The Sanctuary Church, 55 High St, Staple Hill, BS16
0117 956 3300
www.powerhouse-youth.co.uk
Fri 7.30pm

A huge range of activities for 11-16 yr-olds, from football, badminton, hockey, volleyball and pool to computer games and dance.

Southmead Adventure Playground

Doncaster Rd, Southmead, BS10 5PP
0117 950 3607
After school care Tue-Fri 3.30pm-6.45pm in winter and 3.30pm-7.45pm in summer
Sat & sch hols 10am-12.45pm & 2pm-5.45pm
Free

A variety of activities for U16s including sport and craft. Facilities include an all-weather pitch and a climbing area.

St Anne's Youth Project

281 Wick Rd, Brislington, Bristol, BS4 4HU
0117 983 7797

Youth project providing activities for young people aged 13-19yrs. Two sessions a week with pool, table tennis, PlayStation, IT suite, coffee bar, ball court and special workshops on issues such as drugs and sexual health.

The Mill Centre

Lower Ashley Rd, Easton, Bristol
0117 951 0188

This youth project is targeting young people aged 13-19 and has everything from IT, music and DJing to football and weight training.

AFTER SCHOOL GROUPS

After School Clubs

www.bristol-city.gov.uk

There are too many after school clubs to mention individually. The best place to find a suitable club close to you is on the Bristol City Council website. Go to Sports, Clubs and Centres and then click on the Local Organisations Database. There is a comprehensive list of after school clubs there.

HOLIDAY CLUBS & CAMPS

BHP Childcare Magic

The Whitehouse Centre, Fulford Rd, Hartcliffe, BS13
0117 954 1884

A 32-place holiday play scheme for ages 5-14yrs. Activities include cooking, crafts and sports plus trips.

Café Culture

Redland Parish Church, Redland Green, Redland, BS6
0117 946 4690
www.redland.org.uk
£40 for a week

Activity week for children in school years 7 and 8, held in the first full week of the summer holidays. Christian teaching, trips and sports such as tennis, swimming and climbing.

Clifton College Holiday Activities

Clifton College Services, 2 Percival Rd, Clifton, BS8
0117 315 7666
www.cliftoncollegeuk.com
From £23 per day, £13 half day.

Runs a range of holiday activities suitable for 4-16 yrs which include a mix of football, tennis, water sports, cookery, drama, arts and crafts. It also runs a programme of weekly courses suitable for 12-16 yrs. These cover tennis coaching, horse riding, sailing, hockey and drama. The courses have become very popular, so book in advance.

King's Camp, Bristol

King's Camp, Badminton School, Westbury-on-Trym
0870 345 0781
www.kingscamp.org
From £85 (4 days)

Part of a national scheme of activity day camps in the Easter and summer holidays for up to 17yrs. Activities have a sports emphasis but there are also arts and crafts, games and team building excercises. Camps are registered with Ofsted.

Kingswood Foundation

20 Old School House, Britannia Rd, Kingswood, BS15
0117 947 7948
www.kfl.org.uk

Kingswood Foundation is a charity focusing on innovative arts-based youth work for 8-19 year olds. Its regular summer school, in early August, offers street dance, circus skills and instant music (made with old tins and cardboard) culminating in an impressive show on the Saturday after a week of activities. There are other regular holiday schools throughout the year.

Torwood House

Durdham Park, Redland, BS6 6XE
0117 973 5620
Open 8am-6pm
£24/day, £14/½ day for ages 5-11yrs

Offers holiday care for children up to 11 yrs. Activities include PE, games, drama, music, cookery, arts and crafts, trips and outings.

OUT & ABOUT IN BRISTOL

Lindsey Potter
Alex Reed

CONTENTS

INTRODUCTION

Whether you live in the city or outside, it is easy to forget how much is going on your doorstep. Sometimes when you discover a new venue or activity, you wonder why it took so long to catch on to its existence.

Let us help you. Listed here is everything you need to know about going out in Bristol. There's the tourist trail, ideas for going out with friends or family and inspiration for getting out in the fresh air. There's also a guide to watching sport in the city, whether you are into football, rugby or cricket.

When it comes to going out in the evening, it can be extremely difficult for under 18s to find places that will let them in. However, there are clubs and concert venues that admit under 18s or hold special nights for this age group and we've got all the details here. We've also got the lowdown on all the cinemas and theatres that Bristol has to offer.

BE A TOURIST

VISITOR INFORMATION CENTRE

Bristol has an excellent tourist information office, known as Destination Bristol. Their website has excellent coverage of seasonal events. There are four visitor information points with the harbourside centre being the largest. They offer advice, accommodation booking, maps, guides, leaflets and brochures.

Bristol Visitor Information Harbourside

Wildwalk-At-Bristol, Harbourside, Bristol, BS1 5DB
0906 711 2191 (50p/min)
www.visitbristol.co.uk
Mon-Fri 10am-5pm, Sat-Sun & sch hols 10am-6pm

Bristol Visitor Information City Centre

Travel Bristol Centre, 11 Colston Ave, BS1 4UB
Mon-Fri 10.30am-5.30pm, Sat 10am-1pm

Self-serve terminal, booking hotline, leaflets and brochures.

Bristol Visitor Information Points

Ground Floor, The Mall Galleries &
Bristol City Museum & Art Gallery, Queens Rd, Clifton

Bristol City Sightseeing Tour

0870 4440654 information hotline
www.bristolvisitor.co.uk, www.city-sightseeing.com
Easter-Sep: 10am-5pm
Call for prices, one child free per adult passenger

Tickets can be bought on the bus or from Bristol Tourist Information Centre and the Travel Bristol Information Centre. This open-top, live guide sightseeing bus takes in all the major attractions: At-Bristol, Bristol Zoo, ss Great Britain, Clifton Village and the British Empire and Commonwealth Museum. There are discounts on a number of attractions on presentation of your bus ticket. You can hop on and off the bus at any of the 20 stops en route. See advertisement in the Colour Reference Section, pg 190.

LANDMARKS

Bristol Cathedral

College Green, Bristol, BS1
0117 926 4879
www.bristol-cathedral.co.uk
Daily 8am-6pm
Free (donations welcome)
P WC ♿

Bristol Cathedral welcomes visitors young and old, and a look-in holds more than you might first expect. The awesome size of the building is impressive and the animals, stained glass windows and gruesome gargoyles provide plenty of entertainment. There are guides and the cathedral staff encourage young visitors to draw many of the features and they also hold regular brass rubbing events and other workshops, including music, drama, environmental science and craft.

Cabot Tower

Brandon Hill Park, off Park St, Bristol, BS1
Daily 8am-½hr before dusk
Free

At over 32.4 metres high on top of a high hill, this tower offers one of the best panoramic views of Bristol. It was built in 1897 to celebrate John Cabot's voyage to America in 1497. There is a winding staircase that takes you to the top.

Clifton Suspension Bridge

0117 974 4664
www.clifton-suspension-bridge.org.uk
Guided tours from £2.50 pp

One of the world's greatest bridges and it's on our doorstep. It was designed by the Victorian engineer Isambard Kingdom Brunel, although he never lived to see it finished in 1864. Its spectacular setting over the Avon Gorge has made it the symbol of Bristol and the subject of many school projects! Bridge tours for groups are available by arrangement.

Concorde at Filton

Location 09L, Airbus UK, Filton, BS34 7AR
0870 3000 578 booking line
0117 936 5485 visitor centre
www.concordeatfilton.org.uk
Wed-Sun 4 guided tours each day
£12.50 adult, £7 child 5-14yrs, children must be accompanied

Concorde 216 flew home to Bristol on November 26th 2003. It's on loan from British Airways but the hope is that a permanent visitor centre can be funded to celebrate this piece of aviation history. Guided tours must be booked in advance. Parking at BAWA then a coach will take you through the Airbus site.

Doors Open Day

www.bristoldoorsopenday.org

This annual event held in the autumn is your chance to see, for free, inside some of Bristol's most architecturally and historically important buildings, many of which are not normally open to the general public.

THE DOCKSIDE

This is a fascinating and lively area of Bristol with cafés on both sides of the harbour. The city has a long maritime history which is well represented at the Industrial Museum and the ss Great Britain. This largely traffic-free area is ideal for walking and cycling. Parking is located at both museums.

Bristol Harbour Railway

Princes Wharf, Wapping Rd, Bristol, BS1 4RN
0117 925 1470
Apr-Nov selected w/e's
£1 single, £2 rtn, £3.50 family

This train steams along the dockside from the Bristol Industrial Museum to the ss Great Britain. Locally built engines (Henbury or Portbury) pull the wagons which once ran at the Avonmouth Docks.

Bristol Industrial Museum

See Museums' section in this chapter, pg 55.

Brunel's ss Great Britain

Great Western Dock Yard, Gas Ferry Rd, BS1 6TY
0117 929 1843 information line
0117 926 0680 enquiries & bookings
www.ssgreatbritain.org
Apr-Oct: 10am-5.30pm, Nov-Mar: 4.30pm
£9 adult, £5 child, £25 family ticket (2+2)

Brunel's masterpiece of ship design has been restored throughout and appears to float in her original dry dock. Go "under water", to stand below the ship's impressive hull and propeller. Step back in time in the Dockyard Museum and try your hand at preparing the ship for sail, steering her on a westerly course, or climbing to the crow's nest.

On board, explore cabins and quarters and try controlling the ship's massive recreated engine. Audio guides bring the ship to life. Holiday activities and private function hire available. See advertisement, pg 182.

The Matthew

A replica of the ship built in the 15th century in which John Cabot sailed from Bristol across the Atlantic to discover Newfoundland in 1497. It tours around the British Isles so is not always birthed alongside the ss Great Britain.

FERRIES

The Bristol Ferry Boat Company

MB Tempora, Welsh Back, Bristol, BS1 4SP
0117 927 3416
www.bristolferryboat.co.uk
Daily 10.30am-6.10pm (charters can run later)

This friendly company operates a waterbus service from the city centre which runs every 40 minutes, covering the middle and western end of the harbour. During Apr-Oct and in the school holidays the service covers the middle and eastern end of the harbour up to Temple Meads Station. There are many stops allowing access to tourist attractions along with cafes, restaurants and pubs. Chartered trips which go beyond the harbour to the river and gorge run Apr-Oct.

The Hotwells Ferry

Daily 10.30am-6.10pm
Single £1.50 adult, £1.20 child,
Round trip £4.30 adult, £2.80 child

The Hotwells Ferry is in operation around the harbour between Hotwells and the city centre. The 40 minute round trip includes the ss Great Britain.

The Temple Meads Ferry

Apr-Sept Sat-Sun/daily during the school holidays
Round Trip £4.30 adult, £2.80 child, £12 family
(2+2) shorter fares available

Operates between Temple Meads and the City Centre. This is a 60-minute round trip that includes the ss Great Britain and Castle Park.

Bristol Packet

ss Great Britain car park, Wapping Wharf, BS1 6UN
0117 9268157
www.bristolpacket.co.uk
Open all year, daily in school holidays, weekends
only during term-time

Bristol Packet offers a variety of educational-
based river adventures on one of their
four boats. These include city dock tours
with commentary, trips under the Clifton
Suspension Bridge and lunch and afternoon
tea cruises to pubs and Beese's tea gardens.

ZOO

Bristol Zoo Gardens

Clifton, Bristol, BS8 3HA
0117 974 7399
www.bristolzoo.org.uk
Daily 9am-5.30pm, 4.30pm winter
£11 adult, £7 child 3-14yrs
There are Gift Aid Visitor prices which include a
voluntary contribution of approx 10% above normal
admission prices. Good annual membership deals.
Follow the brown tourist signs from the M5 J17 or
from Bristol city centre

New for summer 2006, there's Monkey Jungle,
featuring "meet the lemurs". This offers an
immersive forest experience where monkeys
mingle with gorillas and visitors enjoy close-
up, walk through, encounters with lemurs.
It promises to fill the senses with the sights,
sounds and smells of the forest.

There is also the award-winning Seal &
Penguin Coasts where you come face-to-face
with seals and penguins through transparent
underwater walkways. Discover other
favourites including Gorilla Island, Twilight
World, Bug World and the Reptile House.

From the smallest and rarest tortoise in the
world, to the largest ape, there are over 400
exotic and endangered species to experience
at Bristol Zoo and there are regular animal
encounters every day, if you fancy holding a
tarantula in your hand!

MUSEUMS & GALLERIES

Arnolfini

16 Narrow Quay, Bristol, BS1 4QA
0117 917 2300
www.arnolfini.org.uk
Open daily, galleries & bookshop 10am-8pm,
Café/bar & cinema 10am-11pm
Entry to galleries, bookshop and exhibitions are free

This is Bristol's centre for the contemporary
arts. It has recently undergone refurbishment
and an ever-changing programme provides
lots to see including exhibitions, live art and
performance, dance and cinema. There are
regular events, activities and workshops.

At-Bristol

Anchor Rd, Harbourside, Bristol, BS1 5DB
0845 345 1235
www.at-bristol.org.uk
Daily 10am-5pm, 6pm weekends & sch hols
From £6.50 adults, £4.50 child, £19 family ticket,
various ticket combinations available
Membership includes free entry to Explore and
Wildwalk and £1 off each IMAX film.

Explore-At-Bristol

Experience the everyday and the
extraordinary in this interactive science and
discovery centre. You can make a programme
in a TV studio, experience a walk-in tornado
or watch a computer-generated film on the
journey of a sperm!

Wildwalk-At-Bristol

A fascinating journey through the plant and
animal kingdoms. Now with a new live events
area and People and the Planet exhibition.

IMAX Theatre-At-Bristol

Showing 2D, 3D and some feature films on
a screen that is four storeys high, this is the
ultimate film experience!

Blaise Castle House Museum

Blaise Castle Estate, Henbury Rd, BS10 7QS
0117 903 9818
Sat-Wed 10am-5pm
Admission free

Social history collections, exhibiting domestic
furnishings, costumes, textiles and toys.

Bristol City Museum & Art Gallery

Queens Rd, Clifton, BS8 1RL
0117 922 3571
www.bristol-city.gov.uk/museums
Daily 10am-5pm
Admission free

The region's largest museum and art gallery
has interesting and varied exhibits. The
permanent collections include displays of
fossils, minerals, wildlife, the South West's
geographic formation and a freshwater
aquarium. There are also collections of
Eastern Art, ceramics, silver and glassware.

Paintings on display range from old masters to
modern art. They have some excellent touring
exhibitions. There are workshops, holiday
activities, arts and craft sessions and lectures.

Bristol Industrial Museum

Princes Wharf, Wapping Rd, Bristol, BS1 4RN
0117 925 1470
Sat-Wed: 10am-5pm
Admission free

The first floor chronicles Bristol's aerospace
and maritime history, including a thought-
provoking section on the slave trade. At
weekends, there are activities such as
traditional printing, or you could climb on
a steam crane, ride on the tug, Pyronaut
fireboat and harbour railway.

British Empire & Commonwealth Museum

Clock Tower Yard, Temple Meads, Bristol, BS1 6QH
0117 925 4980
www.empiremuseum.co.uk
Daily 10am-5pm
£6.95 adult, £3.95 child, £16 family
Paying full price on your admission ticket allows you
free entry for 12mths

Housed next to Temple Meads Station, the
museum charts the 500-year history of the
British Empire. A visit includes entry to the
hands-on Pow Wow exhibition, plus a range of
exciting school holiday activities.

A new tour in celebration of the 200th
anniversary of the birth of Isambard Kingdom
Brunel will be available twice a month on

Sundays (until 10/06). The tour includes the original railway buildings adjacent to the current station. An expert guide will take you through the passenger sheds, cavernous vaults and the mock-Gothic railway boardroom. There have been ghostly sightings of Brunel so watch out! Pre-booking required.

Clifton Observatory and Caves

Clifton Down, Bristol, BS8
0117 924 1379
Mon-Fri 11.30am-5pm summer only,
Sat-Sun 10.30am-5pm can be closed due to adverse weather, phone first
£1 adults, 50p children
(£2 and £1 for both Obscura and caves)
Access from the Clifton side

The Observatory houses a Camera Obscura installed in 1829 with a rotating mirror in the roof which reflects the panorama outside. From the Observatory a steep stepped passage through the rock leads to a viewing platform which give splendid views of the bridge and gorge. Not for vertigo sufferers!

CREATE Environment Centre

Smeaton Rd, Bristol, BS1 6XN
0117 925 0505
www.bristol-city.gov.uk/create
Mon-Fri 9am-5pm, along with occasional w/e's and evenings for special events

A riverside centre, focusing on ecology and the environment, in particular recycling. The recycling exhibition demonstrates what happens to waste material. It also has an Ecohome (open weekdays 12pm-3pm) full of information and ideas about eco-living and building. There's an art gallery, recycling exhibition and café. CREATE encourages the use of public transport and is serviced by the no. 500 bus and harbour ferry.

Georgian House

7 Great George St, Bristol, BS1 5RR
0117 921 1362
Apr-Oct: Sat-Wed 10am-5pm Admission free

The lovely Georgian House was built in 1790.

Red Lodge

Park Row, Bristol, BS1 5LJ
0117 921 1360
Apr-Oct: Sat-Wed 10am-5pm Admission free

Elizabethan house with a Tudor knot garden.

Royal West of England Academy

Queens Rd, Bristol, BS8 1PX
0117 973 5129
www.rwa.org.uk
Mon-Sat 10am-5.30pm, Sun 2pm-5pm
Ground floor free, 1st floor £3 adult, free U16s

🅿 ♿ 🔧 ✂ 👶 🚻

The RWA welcomes young people. The exhibitions on the first floor change six times a year. Those on the ground floor change monthly. There are gallery tours and educational worksheets.

GOING OUT

There is so much going on in the city, from live performances to art house celluloids. If you are planning to get together with your friends, there is loads of interactive fun with bowling, laserquest and ice skating. If music is your buzz, there is everything from classical to big name bands. And when it comes to festivals, Bristol and the West Country know how to put on a good show, see pg 185. For seasonal fixtures and events, check out the following great sources of information:

Venue Magazine
www.venue.co.uk

Evening Post
www.thisisbristol.com

Bristol Tourist Information
www.visitbristol.co.uk

The Bristol Magazine
Free at libraries and through your door if you live in the right post code!

GWR Radio
www.gwrfmbristol.co.uk

Star Radio
www.starbristol.co.uk

BBC Radio Bristol
www.bbc.co.uk/bristol

THEATRES

Bristol Ticket Shop

The Arcade, Broadmead, Bristol, BS1
0117 929 9008/0870 4444 400

The place to get fairly-priced tickets for concerts in Bristol and beyond, including gigs at the Anson Rooms and Bristol University. They'll also sell unwanted tickets for you too.

Want to tread the boards?

There are masses of opportunities to learn all the skills you could need from dance, drama and circus skill to singing. See pg 36.

Bristol Old Vic

King St, Bristol, BS1 4ED
0117 987 7877
www.bristol-old-vic.co.uk
From £4 child, concession and seasonal family
tickets available

P WC X ⊞ 🚌 ♿

A varied and critically-acclaimed theatre
programme. Telephone the box office or visit
the website for details of the current season's
productions. Apart from their broad range
of shows they also run an excellent youth
theatre, see Interests & Clubs pg 40.

Back stage tours

Fri & Sat at 11.30am

Take a tour of the oldest continually-working
theatre in the country. Booking required.

Colston Hall

Colston St, Bristol, BS1 5AR
0117 922 3686
www.colstonhall.org, www.remix-music.org
boxoffice@colstonhall.org

P WC X

Bristol's largest concert hall. The Colston Hall
Education Project organises workshops for
young people and family days (from classical
to reggae). It also attracts well-known
musicians who encourage enjoyment of,
and interaction with, music for youngsters.
Colston Hall is connected to REMIX, the Bristol
Youth Music Action Zone, which provides
music-making opportunities for U18s, from DJ
workshops to jazz sessions.

QEH Theatre

Jacob's Well Rd, Bristol, BS8 1JX
0117 930 3082
www.qehtheatre.com

The QEH Theatre is currently closed for
refurbishment but reopens in autumn 2006.

Redgrave Theatre

Percival Rd, Clifton, Bristol, BS8 3LE
0117 3157 666
www.cliftoncollege.uk
For details of upcoming performances take a look at
the school's website or phone for details

A purpose-built school theatre attached to
Clifton College that stages productions by
school groups and local performing groups.
Seasonal shows for a younger audience and
productions from Clifton upper school, prep
school and pre-school. The Old Vic Theatre
School also performs at the Redgrave.

The Bristol Hippodrome

St Augustine's Parade, Bristol, BS1 4UZ
0117 3023333 (enquiries) 0870 607 7500 (bookings)
www.getlive.co.uk/bristol

The Hippodrome is Bristol's west end
theatre. Its large stage allows for spectacular
productions and is the place to see bands,
West End musicals, ballet and opera. Online
booking service. Parking at NCP car park.

The Tobacco Factory

Raleigh Rd, Southville, Bristol, BS3 1TF
0117 902 0344
www.tobaccofactory.com
tickets@tobaccofactory.com

The Tobacco Factory has an excellent
reputation as an innovative contemporary arts
venue with high quality theatre, music, dance,
opera and comedy. It has its own in-house
productions, nationally-acclaimed Shakespeare
and UK and international touring productions.

CONCERT VENUES

Anson Rooms

Bristol University Students' Union, Queens Rd, Bristol
0117 954 5830
www.ansonrooms.co.uk

This great venue has a wide range of live acts
and is open to young people aged 14+yrs. At
the same venue is little bro, AR2, where many
just-breaking and local bands play. Tickets can
be bought at Replay Records and the Bristol
Ticket Shop or go direct to the Union on
Queens Road to get non-commission tickets.

Cardiff International Arena

Mary Ann St, Cardiff
029 2022 4488

Okay it's not in Bristol but until Bristol gets its
own arena, this is the nearest stadium-sized
venue where all the big names in music play.

Carling Academy

Frogmore St, Bristol, BS1
0117 927 9227

A big name venue as well as a club, Bristol
Academy is open to the over 14s on gig
nights, about once or twice a week. A wide
variety of bands and singers perform on
the huge stage and there's a large dance
floor which can get very crowded. A crew
of stewards ensures a strict door policy and
alcohol is only sold with photo ID.

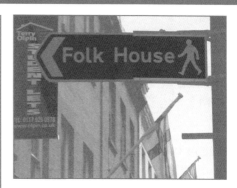

Colston Hall

Colston St, Bristol, BS1 5AR
0117 922 3686
www.colstonhall.org

The place to see big name bands and comedy.

Folk House

40 Park St, Bristol, BS1
0117 924 5170

Gigs at this cosy venue welcome over 16s.

St Bonaventure's

St Bonaventure's Parish Hall, Egerton Rd, Bishopston
01452 524950
www.crhmusic.com

When it comes to Americana and country, you can hear living legends and new talent here.

St George's

Great George St, off Park St, BS1 5RR
0845 40 24 001
www.stgeorgesbristol.co.uk
Ticket prices vary, family passes available

Famous for its exceptionally fine acoustic, St George's attracts leading musicians from around the world, everyone fom Sir Simon Rattle and John Williams to Elvis Costello and Bjork. Their family concerts offer a great introduction to music.

The Prom

26 Gloucester Rd, Bishopston, BS7
0117 942 7319
www.theprom.co.uk

This music bar and café is a popular venue for teenagers before 8pm only.

CINEMAS

Arnolfini

16 Narrow Quay, Bristol, BS1 4QA
0117 917 2300
www.arnolfini.org.uk

Broadmead Odeon

Union St, Bristol, BS1 2DS
0117 929 0884 Cinema office,
08712 244 007 Bookings
www.odeon.co.uk
Family Tickets £14 anytime (2+2 or 3+1)

Cineworld the Movies

Hengrove Leisure Park, Hengrove, Bristol, BS14 0LH
0871 220 8000
Kids Club Sat 10am, U11s must be accompanied

Cube Microplex

Dove St, nr Kings Sq, BS2 8JB
0870 4444 400 (Bristol Ticket Shop)
0117 942 2222 (Here Shop, Stokes Croft)
www.cubecinema.com

Presenting film and music in all its forms. It is best to buy your tickets in advance.

IMAX At-Bristol

Harbourside, Bristol, BS1 5DB
0845 345 1235
www.at-bristol.org.uk

The only IMAX screen in the South West, it's a massive 21 metres wide and 15 metres tall. You feel like you're in the middle of the action. Showing 2D and 3D documentaries along with some feature films.

Eating out

There are some great cafés and restaurants across the city to suit almost any budget. Some offer live music and even Karaoke, check out pg 79.

Odeon Cinema

Union St, Bristol, BS1 2DS
0871 224 4007
www.odeon.co.uk

Orpheus Cinema

7 Northumbria Drive, Henleaze, Bristol, BS
017 962 3301 cinema office, 0845 1662381 film info
www.reeltime-cinemas.co.uk

Great independent cinema and you can even hire it for your own private screening. Discount tickets cost £2.80 on Mondays.

Showcase Cinema

Avon Meads Leisure Park, St Philips Causeway, Bristol, BS2 0SP
0871 220 1000
www.showcasecinemas.co.uk

Vue

The Venue, Cribbs Causeway Leisure Complex
And at: Aspect Leisure Park, Longwell Green
www.myvue.co.uk
08712 240 240 booking & information

Multiplex cinemas, next to restaurants such as TGI Friday and Bella Pasta (Cribbs) and Eastern Eye (Longwell Green). Tickets can be booked online to avoid queues.

Watershed

1 Canon's Rd, Bristol, BS1 5TX
Tickets: 0117 927 5100
www.watershed.co.uk

Three screens and a great café. See also Cinekids, screenings and special events for 8-12yr olds, on pg 43.

DVD HIRE

20th Century Flicks
3 Richmond Terrace, Clifton, BS8 1AB
0117 974 2570
www.20thcenturyflicks.co.uk
Enormous stock of arty and epic films to hire on video and DVD from independents to blockbusters.

DVD Hire by Post
www.amazon.co.uk
www.blockbuster.co.uk
www.sainsburysdvdrental.co.uk
Get the latest DVDs delivered to your door.

CLUB SCENE

Bristol has a vibrant club scene, however much of it's restricted to over 18s. There are some venues which cater for younger people and it is worth checking the local press for one-off events.

Bristol Bierkeller

The Pithay, Broadmead, BS1
0117 926 8514

Most gigs and comedy nights are for over 18s only but there are occasional U18s nights.

Stormparty @ The Baja Club

Cannon's Rd, Watershed, Bristol, BS1 5UH
0117 922 0330
www.bajabristol.co.uk

New U18s club nights in Bristol. Stormparty offers a fab night out for teenagers with top name bands and DJs for 15-18 yr-olds. There's no alcohol or smoking.

The Works

15 Nelson St, Bristol, BS1
0117 929 2658
£8 in advance, £9 on the door, tickets include cloakroom fee and unlimited soft drinks

Once a month, this club holds a 13-17s night from 7pm-12am. The night features R&B, pop and chart music plus a live act. Their special foam parties are popular, if messy! The club operates a strict door policy including breath checks. No alcohol, soft drinks including fruit cocktails are included in the ticket price.

Internet & chat rooms

You should be aware of the dangers associated with the internet. Online chat rooms are especially risky because you don't know who you're talking to. However, some services are safer than others.

MSN Messenger and Yahoo Messenger, for instance, allow you to talk to your friends and have total control over who can talk to you. Alternatively, online "blog" sites are also good, where you can keep a diary and post photos online. Only your friends can view it, so it's secure. Examples of these are www.bebo.com or www.myspace.com.

Skype www.skype.com is a programme that allows you to call your friends from computer to computer, for free, as long as they have Skype too. You will need a microphone and headphones. It's a great way to keep in touch (and your parents won't hassle you about phone bills anymore!).

INTERNET CAFÉS

Bristol Life

27-29 Baldwin St, Bristol, BS1 1LT
0117 945 9926
£2/hr or £1/hr for members. Membership is £3 for three months. 50p to check email for 10 mins.

Café Eden

24 High St, Portishead, Bristol, BS20 6EN
01275 847673
U16s 70p/half hour; over 16s £1.20/half hour.

Easton Internet Café

137 Lawrence Hill, Bristol, BS5 0BT
0117 955 8996
50p per half hour; half hour free if you spend £5

Surf N Play

14 High St, Westbury-on-Trym, Bristol, BS9 3DU
0117 950 8833
wwwsurfnplay.co.uk
£3/hr or 5p a minute; can buy time in bulk,
Membership schemes for gaming or internet only.

The Lan Rooms

6 Cotham Hill, Bristol, BS6 6LF
0117 973 3886
£2.50/hr; £1 for 24mins,
£10 a year (gives 5 hours of free gaming)

BOWLING

Bowlplex

Aspect Leisure Park, Longwell Green, BS30 7DA
0117 961 0000
www.bowlplex.co.uk
Open daily from 10am
Special offers at off-peak times

Hollywood Bowl

Avonmeads Retail Park, St Philips Marsh, Bristol, BS2 0SP
0117 977 1777
www.hollywoodbowl.co.uk
Open daily
Special offers available after school. Children go free with a full paying adult on Sundays before 12pm. Call for further details of prices and offers.

Hollywood Bowl at Cribbs Causeway

The Venue, Cribbs Causeway, Bristol, BS10 7TT
0117 959 2100
www.hollywoodbowl.co.uk
Open daily
Special offers available after school. Children go free with a full paying adult on Sundays before 12pm. Call for further details of offers and prices.

Megabowl

Brunel Way, Ashton Gate, Bristol, BS7
0117 953 8538
www.megabowl.co.uk
Open daily
Family hour for up to six people £14.50,
Mon-Fri 12-6pm and w/e's 10am-1pm

The Time Out Club is available to youth or social groups who register with Megabowl and then can play for £2 per person per game.

LASER GAMES

Laserquest

The Old Fire Station, Silver St, Bristol, BS1 2PY
0117 949 6688
www.laserquest.co.uk
Mon-Fri 12pm-10pm, Sat 10am-10pm,
Sun 10am-8pm
Times may vary during school holidays

ICE SKATING

Bristol Ice Rink

Frogmore St, Bristol, BS1 5NA
0117 929 2148
www.jnll.co.uk
Session times vary, call for details
From £5.50 including skate hire

Skating and disco sessions for all abilities.

Christmas Ice Rinks

There are rinks at Castle Park, the Mall, Cribbs Causeway and in Bath, late Nov to early Jan.

SPECTATOR SPORTS

CRICKET

Gloucestershire County Cricket Club

The County Ground, Nevil Rd, Bristol, BS7 9EJ
0117 910 8010 ticket office
www.gloscricket.co.uk
Ticket prices from £10 adult, £5 child

The cricket season starts in April and ends in late September. There are several games to watch: the Pro 40 league, the C&G Trophy, the County Championships and Twenty20 matches. The latter is a popular evening event with families. There is an active supporters club, see website or press for fixtures.

RUGBY

Bristol Rugby Football Club

The Memorial Stadium, Filton Ave, Horfield, BS7 0AQ
www.bristolrugby.co.uk
0871 208 2234
Ticket prices from £18 adult, £5 U16s
Season tickets available

Sharing the grounds with Bristol Rovers means that games are played on Sundays.

FOOTBALL

Bristol City Football Club

Ashton Gate Stadium, Bristol, BS3 2EJ
0117 963 0619
www.bcfc.co.uk

This family-friendly club has its own Family Enclosure. Prices start at £5 for U16s. You can also apply for free tickets for U11s (when accompanied by an adult) under the Fans of the Future scheme. Call the Football in the Community department on 0117 963 0636.

Bristol Rovers Football Club

The Memorial Stadium, Filton Ave, Horfield, BS7 0BF
0117 909 6648
www.bristolroverssc.co.uk

Young Pirates is aimed at young people aged up to 16. Membership is £5 per season and the benefits include: priority on all-ticket matches; discounts on souvenirs, fun days and away travel; the chance to meet the players; an invitation to an exclusive Christmas party; access to the Young Pirates room at Memorial Stadium; and the chance to become a ball boy or ball girl. For those aged 16-18yrs in full-time education, Senior Pirates allows you to save money on matchday tickets. U11s can see some matches for free if accompanied by a full-paying adult. Tickets must be bought in advance, call for details.

FRESH AIR

PARKS & GREEN SPACE

Bristol City Council Parks, Estates and Sport

Department of Culture and Leisure Services, Colston House, Colston St, BS1 5AQ
0117 922 3719
www.bristol-city.gov.uk/parks

Call the above number for information about your nearest park or play area.

Park events

The parks service runs a programme of events and activities, many taking place during the school holidays. See their news and events guide produced twice a year called Park Life. It can be obtained in local libraries, the museums or by phoning the above number. Also take a look at the website. Examples of activities include wildlife discovery events, deer feeding rambles and sports activities. If you would like to organise your own community event in one of Bristol's 200 parks, call the Events Team: 0117 922 3808.

Ashton Court Estate

Long Ashton, BS41 9JN
0117 9639174
2 entrances off the A369, one at Kennel Lodge Rd and one at Clifton Lodge (opp. Bridge Rd). Third entrance off A370 at Church Lodge (opp. Long Ashton)

Ashton Court Estate is a huge heritage estate with woodland, grassland and meadowland to explore. For more information, visit the Ashton Court Visitor Centre, in the Stable Court Yard of Ashton Court Mansion.

Other attractions are the keeper's deer feeding rambles (phone for details), two pitch-and-putt courses, two 18 hole golf courses (pay and play), orienteering (maps at the visitor centre), mountain bike and horse trails. A small café and toilets are available at the golf kiosk.

Many large events such as the Bristol International Balloon Fiesta, International Kite Festival and, of course, the Ashton Court Festival take place on the estate, see Annual Events and Festivals, see pg 185.

Blaise Castle Estate BS10

0117 3532266
Entrance and car park off the B4057 Kingsweston Rd

You will find the largest play area in North Bristol at Blaise. It attracts young people of all ages from all over the city. There is a café which has toilets. The spacious grass areas are great for picnics and ball games. There are some resurfaced paths through the woodland valley. The Castle Folly is open on most summer Sunday afternoons. Also take a look in the museum, see pg 56.

Brandon Hill BS8

Entrances on Great George St (off Park St), Jacobs Wells Rd, Upper Byron Place and Queens Parade

Climb Cabot Tower's many steps and see superb views across the city. The opening times vary, normally 8am until half an hour before dusk. From the tower, there is a network of pathways and steps with waterfalls, ponds and trees. Toilets are on the middle terrace and further down the hill is a small play area.

viewpoint on the Sea Walls and at the Water Tower/The Downs Tea Room (see pg 73).The Downs usually hosts annual events such as the Children's Festival, circuses and a superb fireworks display in November.

Avon Gorge & Downs Wildlife Project
c/o Education Department, Bristol Zoo Gardens, Bristol, BS8 3HA
0117 903 0609
www.bristolzoo.org.uk/conservation/avongorge

In partnership with several groups, this project works to protect the wildlife and nature of the Avon Gorge and Downs. Holiday activities include wildlife trails and the popular Gorgeous Wildlife Family Fun Day, held each summer. For further information, pick up leaflets from the Downs Tea Rooms or at the Zoo.

Canford Park BS10

Entrance on Canford Lane, Westbury-on-Trym.

This is an attractive well-kept park, with a play area. The park itself has a large, flat lawn, excellent for ball games and picnics. There is also a sunken rose garden with a pond. Tennis courts for hire by the hour.

Clifton Down BS8

Off the Suspension Bridge Rd

This is an unfenced play area with a good mixture of assault course style climbing equipment. Nearby are natural rock faces, slippery when wet, slide at your own risk!

Cotham Gardens BS6

Entrance on Redland Grove, nr Redland train station

A small friendly park. Spacious fenced play area and grass for ball games and picnics.

The Downs BS8

Park anywhere along Ladies Mile

The Downs are made up of Clifton Down and Durdham Down. They are Bristol's most famous open space with grassland and some wooded areas. They are very popular with footballers, joggers, kite flyers and dog walkers. The Circular Road offers dramatic views of the Gorge and the Suspension Bridge. Toilets can be found near the

Easton Park BS5

Main entrance on Chelsea Rd next to The Mission

This playground has the usual kit plus an amazing seesaw suitable for all ages. There is an all-weather 5-a-side football pitch. The Bristol-Bath cycle path runs alongside.

Eastville Park BS16

Alongside Fishponds Rd(A432) & adjacent to M32 J2

A large area of grassland ideal for ball games. There are two playgrounds, a lake and woodland walks. The path along the river leads to Oldbury Court.

Hengrove Play Park BS14

01275 836946
Entrance off Hengrove Way

Next door to the leisure park. It features the innovative play dome, a 12-metre high domed frame with enclosing chutes and walkways. There is a skateboard/BMX zone, a café and toilets. Staffed during the day.

Monks Park BS7

Entrances off Lyddington Rd, Kenmore Crescent and Biddestone Rd.

Two equipped play areas for children of all ages and plenty of green open space.

Oldbury Court Estate & Snuff Mills BS16

Entrances: Oldbury Court Rd & Riverview, Broom Hill

A large park that extends from Snuff Mills to Frenchay, with the River Frome in its grounds. There is a large play area with a 9.6m high tower unit with tubular slides. Toilets and a café by the Broom Hill entrance.

Redcatch Park BS4

Main entrance on Redcatch Rd and Broadwalk

A quiet park with a play area and tennis courts which can be hired by the hour.

Redland Green BS6

Entrances on Redland Green Rd and Cossins Rd

Lovely green with a play area. If it snows, the valley area is great for tobogganing.

Shirehampton Park BS11

Entrance off Shirehampton Rd

Open parkland and wooded areas with walks to Penpole Wood and Kingsweston Down.

Good views of both Severn Bridge crossings and of Kings Weston House.

St Andrews Park BS6

Entrances on Effingham Rd, Leopold Rd, Maurice Rd, Somerville Rd and Melita Rd

Good play area and lots of grass. During hot weather the attraction of the paddling pool makes the park very crowded. It hosts Music or Cinema in the Park in June, a fun family afternoon but they're having a break in 2006.

St George Park BS5

Entrances on Church Rd (A420), Park Crescent and Park View, with a car park off Chalks Rd

A large park with a lake and a wheel park for skateboarding, roller-skating and BMX biking.

Victoria Park BS3

Entrances from Fraser St, Somerset Terrace, Nutgrove Ave, Hill Ave, St. Luke's Rd, Windmill Close

Views over Bristol, a playground, a basketball backboard and a planned multi-sport facility off St Luke's Rd.

WALKS

There are some great walks all over the city. Below are a few of our favourites. However, if you are looking to discover new places, check out the websites of the organisations below or your local book shop for family walking guide books. For walks further afield, see pg 122.

Forest of Avon

Ashton Court Visitor Centre, Bristol, BS41 9JN
0117 953 2141
www.forestofavon.org.uk

This is an excellent website giving an extensive guide to local woodlands within the Forest of Avon.

Avon Wildlife Trust

32 Jacobs Well Rd, Bristol, BS8 1DR
0117 917 7270
www.avonwildlifetrust.org.uk

This charity is dedicated to protecting wildlife. It has two centres, one at Folly Farm, Chew Valley and one at Willsbridge Mill, Keynsham. They offer activities and walks for families.

Ashton Court Estate

Ashton Court Estate Office, Long Ashton, BS41 9JN
0117 963 9174
Two entrances off the A369, one at Kennel Lodge Rd and one at Clifton Lodge (opp. Bridge Rd). Third entrance off A370 at Church Lodge

Ashton Court Estate is a huge heritage estate with woodland, grassland and meadowland to explore. Footpaths link to the Community Forest path, Long Ashton and Abbots Leigh. For more information, visit the Ashton Court Visitor Centre in the Stable Court Yard of Ashton Court Mansion.

Blaise Castle Estate

Henbury Rd, Henbury, Bristol, BS10 7QS

Park at Blaise Castle Estate car park on Kings Weston Road. Pleasant wooded walks through the grounds, leading up to the castle folly and into Coombe Dingle. See parks, pg 65.

Eastville Park

Opposite the Royate Hill Turn off on the A432, Fishponds Rd

Once in the park, descend the hill to the lake, turn right and continue along the banks of the Frome for 1½ miles to Snuff Mills. See Oldbury Court Estate in Parks, pg 67.

Floating Harbour Walk

This walk can be combined with a ferry trip, see The Dockside, pg 53. You can walk a circuit around the Floating Harbour, taking in the ss Great Britain, Industrial Museum, Arnolfini, Watershed, At-Bristol and the skateboarders! Start from the car park at the ss Great Britain. The Floating Harbour extends beyond Prince St Bridge, along Welsh Back towards Temple Meads.

Kings Weston Wood & House

Kings Weston Lane, Shirehampton, BS11 0UR
0117 938 2299
www.kingswestonhouse.co.uk
7 mins walk to house from the car park opposite Shirehampton Golf Course

Paths through the woods lead to the grotto and to Kings Weston House, a Palladian mansion built in 1710. There is a tea room open Mon-Fri: 9am-5.30pm, Sat-Sun and bank holidays 10am-4pm.

Leigh Woods

The National Trust, Valley Rd, Leigh Woods, BS8 3PZ
0117 9731645
leighwoods@nationaltrust.org.uk
Open all year round
From Clifton, take A369 towards Portishead, after the traffic lights there is a large old archway on the right, take right turn almost immediately after this, car park ½km on the left

The waymarked Purple Trail begins and ends at the car park and is a 2½ km circular route, hard-surfaced, mostly level and suitable for wheelchairs. There are other hard-surfaced paths leading from the Purple Trail which are marked on the board in the car park and on a free leaflet available from the Reserve Office on Valley Road. However, not all are waymarked on the ground. Don't miss the bluebells in April and May.

Willsbridge Mill

Avon Wildlife Trust, Willsbridge Hill, Bristol, BS30 6EX
0117 932 6885
www.avonwildlifetrust.org.uk
Nature Reserve open all year, mill seasonal
Free admission
A431 Bristol to Bath Rd, turn into Long Beach Rd, car park on left

A converted mill with wildlife and conservation displays. It's only open when schools are visiting, but there is plenty to do outside. The Valley Nature Reserve includes a Heritage Sculpture Trail, a Wild Waste Garden and sculptural seating areas for picnics. Pond dipping equipment is available for hire. Most of the paths are suitable for wheelchairs.

Cycling

There are some excellent cycling routes in and around Bristol. See pg 174. Also look out for Bristol Bike Fest and Bristol's Biggest Bike Ride, see pg 187.

CITY FARMS

Visiting farms is a great family day out, whatever your age and, having visited a farm recently with teenage nephews, we found they loved the outdoors, animals, hay barns and death slides! In addition, some of these farms have opportunities for teenagers to help with animal care and conservation work.

Avon Valley Country Park

Pixash Lane, Bath Rd, Keynsham, BS31 1TS
0117 986 4929
www.avonvalleycountrypark.co.uk
Apr-Oct: Tue-Sun, B/Hs 10am-6pm, daily in sch hols
£5 adult, £4 child
Winter w/e's: play barn £3.50 per child
A4 towards Bath, follow brown signs

Farm trail leads through several fields of farm animals and rare breeds. Other attractions include bottle feeding the lambs in the spring, a large adventure playground, a barn with impressive slides, quad bikes for any age, a small lake with boat hire and a river walk.

Hartcliffe Community Farm

Lampton Ave, Hartcliffe, Bristol, BS13 0QH
0117 978 2014
Daily 9.00am-4.30pm
Admission free (donations welcome)
Signposts from Bishport Ave

The main site is 35 acres of pasture with a collection of the usual farm animals plus an aviary with canaries, cockatiels and peacocks.

HorseWorld

Staunton Lane, Whitchurch, Bristol, BS14 0QJ
01275 540173
www.horseworld.org.uk
Easter to Oct & school holidays: daily 10am-5pm
Oct to Easter: Tues-Sun 10am-4pm
£5.75 adult, £4.75 child, £19.50 family ticket (2+2)
Access: Just off the A37

Horseworld is an equine welfare charity. Learn about rescue, rehabilitation and re-homing and meet the horses, donkeys and ponies.

Lawrence Weston Community Farm

Saltmarsh Drive, Lawrence Weston, BS11 0ND
0117 938 1128
Tue-Sun 8.30am-5.30pm, winter 4.30pm
Admission free (donations welcome)

A city farm with some rare breeds. There is a bee-keeping club, educational projects and a volunteer programme.

St Werburgh's City Farm

Watercress Rd, St Werburgh's, Bristol, BS2 9YJ
0117 942 8241
Daily 9am-5pm (summer) 9am-4pm (winter)
Admission free (donations welcome)

A small community farm with lots of animals, a pond and farm shop selling plants and organic produce. Teens (13-19yrs) can learn community farm skills by joining their environmental youth work programme. There is a café (closed Mon/Tue) and a children's homeopathic clinic, see Healthcare, pg 250.

Windmill Hill City Farm

Philip St, Bedminster, Bristol, BS3 4EA
0117 963 3252
www.windmillhillcityfarm.org.uk
Tue-Sun: 9am-dusk
Admission free (donations welcome)

Well laid-out paved farmyard with animal enclosures. Wide paths lead to paddocks, a nature reserve and gardens. There's an adventure playground and holiday activities and events.

EATING OUT

Diana Beavon

Jo Smart

CONTENTS

INTRODUCTION

This chapter highlights some of Bristol's best places to eat, whether you want a sandwich and a smoothie, a pizza or something a bit spicy. The city has a fantastic choice of restaurants and cafés, with every type of cuisine under the sun.

We've catered for absolutely everyone with this selection — there are lots of great cafés where young people can meet and eat with their mates, there are some lovely places to go out as a family and there are plenty of recommended pubs and eateries further afield to sustain you when you are out for the day.

We've sought out the places that offer good value for money — both to ensure that the cafés and restaurants featured are affordable for the average teenage wallet and also to cater for families eating out together — let's face it, now that kids' portions are a thing of the past, the bill for a family meal out can come as a shock!

CAFÉS

2-3-2

232 Gloucester Rd, Bishopston, BS7 8NZ
0117 924 9736
Tue-Sat 9am-10pm

Café bistro serving breakfast from 9am-12pm, with a lunchtime menu of home-cooked meals salads, burgers and toasties from 12pm-3pm. It also serves sandwiches and cakes until 6pm. In the evening, it becomes a bistro.

Aruba

6 Clifton Down Rd, Clifton Village, BS8 4AD
0117 974 4633
Mon-Fri 8am-4.30pm, Sat 9am-4pm,
Sun 10am-2.30pm

Licensed café with friendly and helpful staff serving homemade food. Spacious patio area for al fresco dining.

Avon Gorge Hotel

Sion Hill, Clifton Village, BS8 4LD
0117 973 8955
Mon-Sun 11am-11pm

Based in the Avon Gorge Hotel, the White Lion has the advantage of a large sun terrace with magnificent views of the Suspension Bridge. Open daily for cakes and coffees from 11am, hot bar food served from 12pm-10pm.

Bar Chocolat

19 The Mall, Clifton Village, BS8 4NS
0117 974 7000
www.bar-chocolat.com
(online shop ordering available soon)
Mon-Sat 9am-6pm, Sun 11am-5pm

Café and shop selling handmade cakes and chocolates. A relaxed atmosphere in which to enjoy a drink and a treat. An ideal place to buy a chocoholic friend an unusual gift.

Big Banana Juice Bar

Units 21-22, The Glass Arcade, St Nicholas Market
0117 927 3274
www.thebigbananajuicebar.co.uk
Mon-Sat 9am-5pm

Serves a great selection of juices and smoothies. Start with the fairly healthy fruit and ice-cream smoothies and work your way up to 100% healthy pure vegetable juices. Popular with students.

Blaise Tea Rooms

Blaise Castle Estate, Henbury Rd, Henbury, BS10
0117 904 1897
Mon-Sun 8.30am-7pm, closes 4pm winter

Adjacent to the children's play area, the café serves hot drinks and snacks.

Blue Juice

39 Cotham Hill, Cotham, BS6 6JY
0117 973 4800
Mon-Fri 8am-4pm, Sat 9am-4pm

Excellent juice bar with a good range of light snacks to eat in or take away.

Bristol Old Vic

King St, City Centre, BS1 4ED
0117 987 7877
www.bristol-old-vic.co.uk
Mon-Sun 10am-7pm

A galleried area overlooking the main foyer. Good value menu.

Boston Tea Party

75 Park St, Clifton, BS1 5PF
0117 929 8601
www.thebostonteaparty.co.uk
Mon-Wed 7am-7.30pm, Thu-Sat 7am-10pm,
Sun 9am-7.30pm

Relaxed café with terraced garden and upstairs room with lots of sofas to sink into. As well as great coffee, it serves fresh rustic food including an all-day breakfast, paninis, soups, salads and daily specials.

Coffee #1

157 Gloucester Rd, Bishopston, BS7 8BA
0117 942 9909
Mon–Fri 8am-6pm, Sat 9am-6pm, Sun 10am-6pm
And at: 33 Princess Victoria St, Clifton Village, BS8
0117 923 8021
Mon-Fri 8am-6pm, Sat 9am-6pm, Sun 10am-6pm

Attracting a wide clientele, this non-smoking café serves smoothies, coffees, cakes and paninis with great fillings. The Bishopston café has a garden at the rear.

Café Delight

189 Gloucester Rd, Bishopston, BS7 8BS
0117 944 1133
Mon-Sat 9am-5.30pm, Sun 9.30am-4pm,
Tue-Sat open evenings

Laid-back café serving snacks and Medi-themed home cooking with great specials.

Café Iguana

113 Whiteladies Rd, Clifton, BS8 2PB
0117 973 0730
Mon-Sat 12pm-3pm, 6pm-12pm;
Sun 12pm-10.30pm

A bustling little piece of Mexico, ideally located in the midst of Whiteladies. Café Iguana prides itself on providing more colour than the human eye can stand — but does have a great atmosphere and offers good food.

Café Unlimited

209 Gloucester Rd, Bishopston, BS7 8NN
0117 924 0035
Mon-Sat 9am-4.30pm

This fair trade café has a large downstairs room popular with families and there's a more sophisicated space upstairs with sofas. It also offers gluten and dairy-free options. The premises can be hired out for parties.

Caffé Gusto

5 Queens Rd, Clifton Village, BS8 1QE
0117 925 0868
And at: Unit 3, Clifton Down Shopping Centre,
Whiteladies Rd, BS8
0117 974 7277
Mon-Sun 7am-6pm

Coffee bar selling sandwiches, baguettes and cakes as well as lovely fruit smoothies.

Danby's Café

Queens Rd, Clifton, BS8 1RL
0117 922 3571
Sun & Mon 10.30am-4.30pm, Tue-Sat 10am-4.30pm

Based in Bristol City Museum and Art Gallery, this is a good place to stop and grab a sandwich. It serves hot snacks, cakes and jacket potatoes as well.

Downs Tea Room

Stoke Rd, Durdham Downs, BS8
0117 923 8186
Mon-Sun 8.30am-5pm

On the Downs near the large Water Tower, this pleasant café is open daily for breakfasts, cakes and coffees and serves a great lunchtime menu. Lots of tables outside.

Fresh & Wild

The Triangle, 85 Queens Rd, Clifton, BS8 1QS
0117 910 5930
Mon-Fri 8am-8pm, Sat 9am-7.30pm,
Sun 12pm-5.30pm, winter Sun 11am-4.30pm

Organic supermaket with great café serving salads, sandwiches, soups and juices, plus great cakes and muffins.

Friary

9 Cotham Hill, Cotham, BS6 6LD
0117 973 3664
Mon-Sat 9am-7pm, Sun 10am-3pm

Serving the best breakfasts, this café serves great food in casual and friendly surroundings. Most dishes cost less than a fiver — choose from curries, chillies, casseroles, good vegetarian options, all made on the premises.

Halo Restaurant & Bar

141 Gloucester Rd, Bishopston, BS7 8BA
0117 944 2504
Mon-Fri & Sun 12pm-11pm, Sat 10am-11pm

Popular café/bar, serving breakfasts till 4pm, also snacks, salads and burgers. The large garden is a great sun trap.

Havana Coffee

37a Cotham Hill, Cotham, BS6 6JY
0117 973 3020
Mon-Fri 8am-5pm, Sat 9am-5pm, Sun 10am-5pm

Popular café serving fair trade coffees, herbal teas and juices, plus light South American inspired bites, English breakfasts and wraps.

Juice Café

12 Park Row, Bristol, BS1 5LJ
0117 925 0700
Mon-Fri 8am-6pm, Sat 9am-5pm
www.juice-cafe.com

New café tucked away on Park Row offering freshly made juices and light snacks.

Madisons

1 Princess Victoria St, Clifton Village, BS8 4BX
0117 973 4790
Mon-Fri 8am-5.30pm, Sat 8am-6pm, Sun 10am-4pm

Airy café serving light snacks including paninis, toasties and good cakes.

Oasis Café

Southville Centre, Beauley Rd, Southville, BS3 1QG
0117 923 1039
www.southville.org.uk
Mon 9.30am-5.30pm, Tue-Fri 9.30am-3.45pm

Based in the Southville centre, popular, spacious community café serving wholesome inexpensive menu. Not open at weekends.

Pieminster (take away)

24 Stokes Croft, BS1 3PR
0117 942 9500
Mon-Sat 11am-7pm, Sun 12pm-4pm

Bristol's award-winning, famous pie shop! Loads of choice, from traditional fillings to the more exotic, and a few veggie options too.

Primrose Café & Bistro

1 Boyces Avenue, Clifton Village, BS8 4AA
0117 946 6577
Mon-Sat 10am-5pm, Sun 10.30am-3pm

Great place to people watch from their outside tables. Great sandwiches, paninis and soup. Also open in the evenings.

Rainbow Café

10 Waterloo St, Clifton Village, BS8 4BT
0117 973 8937
Mon-Sat 10am-5.30pm

Small, friendly café, serving homemade whole-food lunches, snacks and teas.

Rocotillos

1 Queens Row, Clifton, BS8 1EZ
0117 929 7207
Mon-Thu 8am-5pm, Fri-Sat 10am-6.30pm,
Sun 10am-5pm

Small, popular fifties-style American diner complete with booths or counter seating serving Mexican and American dishes, along with intriguing milkshakes. Now caters for the heath-conscious with newly opened juice bar serving freshly squeezed juices.

Shaken Stephens

88 Park St, Clifton, BS1 5LA
www.shakenstephens.co.uk
Mon-Fri 7.30am-7.30pm
Sat 10am-6pm Sun 12pm-6am

This milkshake and smoothie bar is hugely popular and it is not surprising with its 123 different flavoured shakes and 30 smoothies. Check out their Banana Pie, Mango Madness, Coconutty 'nana and if you're feeling crook try their Health and Healing. There are no additives and they can cater for vegans or those on gluten or lactose-free diets.

Splinters Coffee House

66 Clifton Down Rd, Clifton Village, BS8 4AD
0117 973 4193
Mon-Sat 8am-6pm, Sun & B/Hs 10am-5.30pm

Traditional-style café with friendly staff. All food homemade and theres a spacious patio.

St Werburgh's City Farm Café

Watercress Rd, St Werburgh's, BS2 5YJ
0781 395 4933
Wed-Sun 10am-5pm, Fri 7pm-10pm

Lively and unusual tree house café serving locally produced food. It offers 15-minute internet access sessions from 5pm.

The Stables Café

Ashton Court Visitor Centre, Ashton Park, BS41 9JN
0117 963 3438
Mon-Sun 10am-5pm, winter Mon-Sun 11am-4pm

Courtyard café in the old stables of Ashton Court Visitor Centre. Serves hot food and light snacks, eat inside or alfresco.

Subway

15 Queens Rd, Clifton Village, BS8 1QE
0117 925 6164
Mon-Thu 8am-12am, Fri & Sat 8am-3am,
Sun 9.30am-12am

This branch of Subway is popular with skaters and students who love their man-sized deli subs. Healthy, reasonably priced food.

Windmill Hill City Farm Café

Philip St, Bedminster, BS3 4EA
0117 963 3252
Tue-Sat 9am-5pm, Sun 10am-6pm, Fri closes 7pm
Tue-Thu hot food until 2pm, Fri-Sun hot food all day

Nice café serving healthy, organic food, open to all, whether you visit the farm or not.

Woodes

18 Park St, Clifton, BS1 5NA
0117 926 4081
Mon-Sat 7am-6.30pm

A popular café serving sandwiches and soup, with a few tables outside where you can watch the world go by.

York Café

1 York Place, Clifton, BS8 1AH
0117 923 9656
Mon-Sun 9am-4pm (3pm in summer)

An award winning café, popular with students. Famous for its fry-ups which start at 99p (before 11am Mon-Fri), York Café also serves roasts, curry and other traditional favourites.

RESTAURANTS

Bocacina

184c Wells Rd, Lower Knowle
0117 971 3377
www.bocacina.co.uk
Mon-Thu 9am-10.30pm, Fri-Sat 9am-11pm,
Sun 10am-10pm

A café and deli described in their own words,
"A place to absorb an atmosphere of fresh
coffee, bosanova rhythms and indulge in
patisseries and home-made cakes". They
serve deli sandwiches, fresh Mediterranean
tapas, salads and soups during the day.
Pizzas, salads and tapas after 5pm and a lazy
Sunday breakfast (10am-3pm). Family friendly
with great service.

Browns Restaurant & Bar

38 Queens Rd, Clifton, BS8 1RE
0117 930 4777
www.browns-restaurant.com
Mon-Sat 12pm-11pm, Sun 12pm-10.30pm

Large attractive licensed refectory, popular
with families. Good extensive menu and it will
take bookings for parties of five or more.

Le Monde

The Pavillion, Triangle West, Clifton, BS8 1ES
0117 934 0999
Mon-Sat 12pm-10.30pm, Sun 12-4pm

Large airy restaurant serving a wide choice of
grilled meats or fish where younger children
can eat free Mon-Sat between 12pm-6pm.
On Sundays, there is a set price roast lunch.
Bookings accepted for eight or more.

Nando's

49 Park St, Clifton, BS1 5NT
0117 929 9263
Mon-Fri 12pm-11pm, Sat & Sun 12pm-12am
And at: Unit 208, Cribbs Causeway Retail Park
0117 959 0146
Mon-Fri 11am-9pm, Sat 11am-7pm, Sun 11am-5pm

Chicken restaurant serving great hot wings
and chips! Vegetarian options available. You
pay up front and help yourself to refills of
drinks and frozen yoghurts. Bookings only
accepted for parties of eight or more.

Tootsies

74 Park St, Clifton, BS1 5NX
0117 925 4811
www.tootsiesrestaurants.co.uk
Mon-Fri 12pm-11pm, Sat-Sun 10am-11pm

Family friendly restaurant, serving a great
char-grilled menu, with skewers, burgers and
veggie options.

Queen Square Dining Room & Bar

63 Queen Square, City Centre, BS1 4JZ
0117 929 0700
Mon-Sat 10am-11pm, Sun 10am-4pm

This is a large, airy and informal place to eat.
British and European dishes updated daily.
Recommended for family Sunday lunches with
a roast joint cooked and ready to carve at
your table (order joint by Fri 12pm). Popular
weekend brunch from 10am.

Walrus & Carpenter

1 Regent St, Clifton, BS8 4HW
0117 974 3793
Tue-Fri 12pm-2.30pm, 6pm-11pm,
Sat 12pm-2.30pm, 6pm-11pm, Sun 12pm-9.30pm

New to Bristol, this popular Bath bistro has taken over from Casa Caramba serving a range of home-made food using organic produce to offer great burgers, pastas, kebabs and numerous vegetarian dishes. Can offer a pick-up take away service.

HARBOURSIDE

Arnolfini

16 Narrow Quay, Harbourside, BS1 4QA
0117 917 2300
Mon-Sun 10am-11pm
Entry to galleries, bookshop and exhibitions are free

The café bar serves coffee and pastries from 10am, food from 12pm-9pm. It has a popular weekend brunch 10am-4pm and Sunday roast 12pm-4pm. Waterfront seating.

Bordeaux Quay

Canon's Rd, Harbourside, Bristol, BS1
www.bordeaux-quay.co.uk
Mon-Sun

Brand new food lovers' emporium with restaurant, bakery, deli and cookery school all in under one gastro-roof. Opening in summer 2006, it's the brainchild of Barny Haughton chef and owner of Quartier Vert. With support from the Soil Association, among others, this organic restaurant promises to source most of its ingredients from within 50 miles of Bristol.

Brunel's Buttery

Wapping Wharf, Harbourside, BS1 6UD
0117 929 1696
Mon-Fri 8am-4pm, Sat & Sun 8-5pm

Situated at the end of the old dock railway beyond the Industrial Museum, this café has become a Bristolian landmark, with fantastic bacon butties, chips and lots more.

Create Café

Create Centre, Smeaton Rd, Spike Island, BS1 6XN
0117 903 1201
Mon-Fri 8.30am-2pm
Serviced by the no. 500 bus and harbour ferry

Whether you want breakfast, lunch or just a coffee, you'll find a menu full of organic and fair trade options, reasonably priced. There are great river views and if you have time take a look at their art gallery and Ecohome.

Havana Café-Bar

3 Welsh Back, Harbourside, BS1 4SL
0117 930 4034
www.havanacoffee.net
Sun-Thu 10am-6pm Fri-Sat 10am-11pm

A bigger version of the Cotham favourite down by the waterside offering comfy sofas and the same great menu.

Olive Shed

Princes Wharf, Harbourside, Bristol, BS1 4RN
0117 929 1960
www.therealolivecompany.co.uk
Tue-Sat 11am-11pm, Sun 11am-5pm

This dockside deli and restaurant has tasty organic tapas and an à la carte menu featuring veggie dishes and fish.

Riverstation

The Grove, Harbourside, BS1 4RB
0117 914 4434
www.riverstation.co.uk
Mon-Thu 9am-10.30pm, Fri & Sat 9am-11pm,
Sun 9am-9pm

Two-storey bar and restaurant on the
waterfront with decking. The kitchen
downstairs now serves coffees and pastries,
including lovely chocolate brownies, from 9am
most days, with tapas/bistro food available
from lunchtime onwards. Upstairs, the
restaurant offers a variety of fresh food with a
brunch menu on Sundays.

Severnshed Restaurant

The Grove, Harbourside, BS1 4RB
0117 925 1212
Mon-Sun 12pm-3pm, 6pm-10.30pm

Buzzing harbourside restaurant with outdoor
seating serving an eclectic seasonal menu of
meat and fish. Great special offers, so eating
out needn't break the bank.

Mud Dock

40 The Grove, Harbourside, BS1 4RB
0117 934 9734
www.mud-dock.com
Mon-Sat 9am-11pm, Sun 10am-10pm

Ever-changing breakfast, lunch, tapas and
evening menus using fresh ingredients.
The atmosphere in this converted dockside
warehouse is relaxed in the day, vibrant at
night. Lunch and early evening meal deals are
listed on the website.

Watershed Café Bar

1 Canons Rd, Harbourside, BS1 5TX
0117 927 5101
www.watershed.co.uk
Mon 11am-11pm, Tue-Fri 9.30am-11pm,
Sat 10am-11pm, Sun 10am-10.30pm

Welcoming and popular, it serves good quality
snacks, main meals and drinks, at reasonable
prices. Great vegetarian selection. Warehouse
loft interior is airy with dockside views. Free
web access for customers.

AMERICAN & MEXICAN

Firehouse Rotisserie

Anchor Square, Canon's Marsh, BS1 5DB
0117 915 7323
www.firehouserotisserie.co.uk
Mon-Sun 12pm-3pm & 5pm-9.30pm

California-style cooking served in a casual
restaurant next to At-Bristol, with outside
tables. It accepts bookings for lunch and is
very popular on Sundays.

Henry Africa's Hot House

65 Whiteladies Rd, Clifton, BS8 2LY
0117 923 8300
Fri-Sun 12pm-11pm, Mon-Thu 4pm-11pm

Relaxed and friendly licensed contemporary
American restaurant offering lunchtime
express menu on Fri & Sat from 12pm-7pm.

Tequila Max

109 Whiteladies Rd, Clifton, BS8 2PB
0117 946 6144
Mon-Sat 5pm-11.30pm

Good food and great atmosphere.

TGI Friday's

The Venue, Lysander Rd, Cribbs Causeway, BS10
0117 959 1987
www.tgifridays.co.uk
Sun-Thu 12pm-10.30pm, Fri-Sat 12pm-11.30pm

Lively eaterie to suit all ages. American-style
menu with generous portions. They serve
a good selection of non-alcoholic cocktails.
Great for parties or after a cinema visit.

ASIAN

Beijing Bistro

72 Park St, Clifton, BS1 5NX
0117 373 2708
www.beijingbistro.co.uk
Sun-Thu 12pm-11pm, Fri-Sat 12pm-12am

Tasty oriental food served in trendy, relaxed
surroundings. Great for a quick lunch or a
longer meal, the portions are large and good
value (approx. £5-£6).

Budokan

31 Colston St, off St Augustine's Parade, BS1 5AP
0117 914 1488
Clifton Down, Whiteladies Rd, BS8 2PH
0117 949 3030
www.budokan.co.uk
Mon-Sat 12pm-2.30pm, 5.30pm-11pm

Recently voted best pan-Asian restaurant by The Times newspaper. Both restaurants offer good value, authentic Asian cuisine. Sociable, communal dining in trendy surroundings.

Krishna's Inn

4 Byron Place, Triangle South, Clifton, BS8 1JT
0117 927 6864
Mon-Thu/Sun 12pm-3pm, 6pm-11pm,
Fri/Sat 12pm-3pm, 6pm-12pm

Popular with families, this restaurant serves delicous Kerala cuisine.

New World Karaoke Bar & Restaurant

Unite House, Frogmore St, City Centre, BS1 5NA
0117 929 3288
www.newworldgroup.co.uk
Mon-Thu 12pm-2.30pm, Fri-Sun 12pm-2.30pm,
Evenings 6.30pm-12.30am

A freshly-prepared oriental feast served buffet-style, with more than 40 dishes including crispy aromatic duck. Buffet prices are very reasonable — £6.50 for lunch, £13.95 for dinner and £10.50 for Sunday lunch. And then there's the karaoke — it's your chance to sing in front of your friends or family and the whole restaurant via TV screens!

One Stop Thali Café

12 York Rd, Montpellier, BS6 5QE
0117 942 6687
Tue-Sun 6pm-11.30pm offering two sittings between 6pm-9pm or after 9pm

Popular vegetarian Indian restaurant serving a range of dishes upon a steel platter. Great place to eat with friends and try new dishes at bargain prices.

Teoh's

28-34 Lower Ashley Rd, St Paul's, BS2 9NP
0117 907 1191
Mon-Sat 12pm-3pm, 6pm-11pm
And at: The Old Tobacco Factory, North St,
Southville, Bristol, BS3 1TF
0117 902 1122
Mon-Sat 12pm-2.30pm, 6pm-10pm

Popular oriental-style eatery serving vast range of Thai, Japanese, Chinese or Malaysian dishes at low prices.

Wagamama

63 Queens Rd, Clifton, BS8 1QL
0117 922 1188
Mon-Sat 12pm-11pm, Sun 12pm-10pm

Pan-Asian style canteen where you can turn up and eat (if seats are available) a range of noodles and juices.

ITALIAN

Ask

51 Park St, Clifton, BS1 5NT
0117 934 9922
www.askrestaurants.co.uk
Mon-Sun, 12pm-11pm

A popular, up-market Italian chain.

Bar Celona

91 Regent St, Kingswood, BS15 8LN
0117 961 9311
Mon-Sun 11am-11pm

Friendly local restaurant offering a range of pizza, pasta and tapas.

Bella Italia

8-10 Baldwin St, City Centre, BS1 1NA
0117 929 3278
Mon-Thu 10am-11pm, Fri & Sat 10am-11.30pm,
Sun 10am-10.30pm

Formerly Bella Pasta. It offers a good choice of pizza and pasta dishes.

Karaoke

If you find yourself watching The X Factor or American Idol and think, "I could do better than that" then you need to try karaoke!

Many Bristol venues run regular karaoke nights in Bristol but there's only one that offers karaoke every night of the week, New World Karaoke Bar and Restaurant (see pg 79). Otherwise you could always host your own karaoke evening in the comfort of your own home by hiring your own machine. A word of warning though: make sure your parents are out, otherwise they'll hog the mic!

Bottelino's Restaurant

22 Bond St, Broadmead, BS1 3LU
0117 926 8054
Mon-Fri 11.30am-2.30pm, 5pm-11pm,
Sat 11.30am-11pm

Nice Italian restaurant with lunchtime fixed price offers Mon-Sat on pizza and pasta.

Cibo

289 Gloucester Rd, Horfield
0117 942 9475
www.cibo.co.uk
Mon-Sat Deli & Café Bar 9am-5.30pm,
Restaurant 6pm–11pm

From quick snacks, pizza and pasta to exotic evening meals, Cibo suits a wide range of tastes and wallets. The service and food never disappoint and the specials are always good.

Deep Pan Pizza

Unit 15, Silver St, Broadmead, BS1 2DU
0117 929 8014
www.deeppanpizza.co.uk
Mon-Sun 11.30am-9pm

A wide selection of pizzas and pasta dishes.

Pizza Express

31 Berkeley Square, Clifton, BS8 1HP
0117 926 0300
And at: Mon-Sat 11.30am-12am, Sun 11.30-11.30pm
2-10 Regent St, Clifton Village, BS8 4HG
0117 974 4259
Mon-Sat 11.30am-11pm, Sun 12pm-10.30pm

A firm favourite with families. Smart, lively and comfortable. Added attraction of watching the chefs make the pizzas.

Pizza Hut

23-25 St Augustines Parade, BS1 4UL
0117 925 2755

Clean efficient pizza chain.

Planet Pizza

83 Whiteladies Rd, Clifton, BS8 2NT
0117 907 7112
And at:187 Gloucester Rd, Bishopston, BS7 8BS
0117 944 4717
www.planetpizza.co.uk
Mon-Sun 11am -11pm

Non smoking, relaxed restaurant serving great pizzas and salads. Lunchtime special available every day and early evening offers Sun-Weds. Available for parties.

Zizzi

7 Triangle South, Clifton, BS8 1EY
0117 929 8700
Mon-Sun 12pm-11pm
And at: 29 Princess Victoria St, Clifton Village, BS8
0117 317 9842
Mon-Sun 12pm-11pm

Great Italian food.

VEGETARIAN

Café Maitreya

89 St Marks Rd, Easton, BS5 6HY
0117 951 0100
www.cafemaitreya.co.uk
Fri 11am-3pm, Sat & Sun 11am-3.30pm,
Tue-Sat 7pm-11pm

Good vegetarian food in light airy surroundings. Menus clearly marked to show vegan, wheat/gluten free and dairy free items.

FURTHER AFIELD

Finding somewhere for lunch when you are out for the day can be difficult. We've taken the pressure off, by recommending some pubs, cafés and restaurants that will satisfy the whole family.

Where possible there are map grid refernces on each entry to help you navigate, see maps on pgs 90 & 178.

BATH

Adventure Café

5 Princes Buildings, Bath, BA1 2EN
01225 462038
Mon-Tue 10am-5pm, Wed-Sun 10am-11pm

Seating inside and out. Enjoy milkshakes, smoothies, sandwiches and salads. In the evening, there are gourmet pizzas, nachos, dips and breads.

Ask

Royal York Hotel, George St, Bath, BA1 2AF
01225 789997
www.askrestaurants.com
Mon-Sun 12pm-11pm

A popular, up-market Italian chain, with lovely pizzas and pasta dishes.

Blackstones' Kitchen (take away)

10a Queen St, Bath, BA1 1HE
01225 338803
www.blackstonefood.co.uk
Mon-Fri 8am-6pm, Sat 9am-6pm

Centrally-located, these guys serve excellent, affordable, no-nonsense food. The menu is constantly changing and features organic local produce. The breakfasts get a big thumbs up. There is currently very limited seating so they are opening a restaurant over the road.

The Bridge Coffee Shop

17 Pulteney Bridge, Bath, BA2 4AY
01225 483339
Mon-Fri 9am-4.45pm, Sat 9am-6pm, Sun 9am-5pm

Popular cosy café in a great location. Eat in or take away. They do homemade soups and cakes, baguettes and pasties.

The Boathouse

Newbridge Rd, Bath, BA1 3NB
01225 482584
Mon-Sat 11am-11pm, Sun 12pm-10.30pm

Located on the edge of Bath by the river, a great pub to round off a day out. Open plan, modern styled bar restaurant. New menu with good range of home-cooked meals. No bookings necessary.

California Kitchen

The Podium, Northgate St, Bath, BA1 5AL
01225 471471
Mon-Sun 9am-9pm

Burgers, steaks, chicken, huge range of salads, nachos, club sandwiches, hot dogs, melts, BLTs — choosing what to order is going to be tough with this selection of mouth-watering grub!

Cornish Bakehouse (take away)

11a The Corridor, Bath, BA1 5AP
01225 426635
Mon-Sat 9am-5.30pm, Sun 10am-5pm

If you are looking for something on the move, check out their award-winning pasties. They also do great sandwiches, baguettes, wraps and salads. Finish it all off with a bit of Cornish fudge.

Green Park Brasserie & Bar

Green Park Station, Green Park Rd, Bath, BA1 2DR
01225 338565
Mon-Sat 10.30am-11pm exc Mon closes 3pm

Beautifully situated in an old train station only ten minutes' walk from the city centre. Relaxed and friendly with outdoor seating in summer. Enjoy a non-alcoholic cocktail or check out their home-made burgers, paninis and cakes. There is live jazz three evenings a week and an internet café in their library.

Kindling Coffee Company

9a Claverton Buildings, Widcombe, Bath, BA2 4LD
Mon-Fri 8am-4.30pm, Sat 10am-4.30pm, Sun 10am-2pm
01225 442125
www.kindlingcoffee.co.uk

Two minutes' walk from the station, you will find this friendly café serving local, organic and fair trade food. Homemade soups, cakes and sandwiches. There is a terrace outside and cosy seating inside.

Martini Restorante

9 George St, Bath, BA1 2EH
01225 460818
www.martinirestaurantbath.co.uk
Mon-Fri & Sun 12pm-2.30pm, 6pm-10.30pm
Sat 12pm-10.30am

With Bath's Roman connections why not go Italian? This popular centrally-located restaurant has a reasonably-priced menu, two course lunches from £8.95, with loads to choose from — pizzas, pasta, fish, antipasti, homemade breads and risottos. They asked us to mention the nice-looking waiters but we'll let you be the judge of that!

Pizza Express

1 Barton St, Bath, BA1 1HG
01225 420119
Mon-Sat 11.30am-12am, Sun 12pm-11.30pm

This family favourite is conveniently located next to the theatre. This branch seems to have a particularly friendly team. Doors slide open to outdoor eating — there's a great atmosphere.

The Regency Tea Rooms

40 Gay St, Queens Sq, Bath, BA1 2NT
01225 442187
Mon-Sun 10am-5pm

On the second floor above the Jane Austen Centre with view across Bath's roof tops. This wonderful period tea room offers light snacks, Mrs Bennet's lemon drizzle cake and hot Belgian chocolate. If you're lucky, you may see Mr Darcy!

Royal Pavillion

Royal Ave, Royal Victoria Park, Bath
01225 448860
Mon-Sun 8am-5pm

Conveniently situated in Victoria Park, with outside seating in summer. Offering light lunches, homemade soups and cakes. Carvery available on Sundays. Will cater for parties from £5pp. Popular with party bookings using the adventure golf, see pg 98.

Sally Lunn's

4 North Parade Passage, Bath, BA1 1NX
01225 461634
www.sallylunns.co.uk
Mon-Sat 10am-9.30pm, Sun 11am-9.30pm

Go on, be a tourist! The building dates back to the late 15th century, the cellar museum even has evidence of Roman foundations. There are three refreshment rooms where you can have just a coffee or three course meal. The menu is based around the Sally Lunn Bun, check out the Trencher.

Schwartz Brothers (take away)

Walcot St, Bath, BA1 5BG
01225 463613
Saw Close, Bath, BA1 1EY
01225 461726
Mon-Sun 12pm-late

Recommended as having the best burgers in town, with chicken and vegetarian options. Good quality, so worth paying a bit more for.

Shakeaway

3 Beau St, Bath, BA1 1QY
01225 466200
Mon-Sat 9am-5.30pm, Sun 10.30am-5pm

Unbelievable! Here you can order any one of their 150 milkshakes. Try cucumber, Oreo cookie, Refresher or Flying Saucer. That's it though, no food but who needs food with shakes like these?

BARROW GURNEY

Dundry Inn

Church Rd, Dundry, BS41 8LH
0117 964 1722
Mon-Thu 12pm-3pm, Fri-Sun 12pm-11pm
See map on pg 90, C4

Quiet local pub with garden. Friendly staff and an excellent menu.

Fox & Goose

Bridgwater Rd, Barrow Gurney, BS48 3SI
01275 472202
Mon-Sat 11am-11pm, Sun 12pm-11pm
See map on pg 90, C4

Family-friendly pub with special Sunday menu including a roast. Best to book. Large garden and deck.

BERKELEY

Salmon Inn

Wanswell, Berkeley, GL13 9SE
01453 811306
Mon-Sat 11am-11pm, Sun 12pm-10.30pm
See map on pg 90, D1

Oak-beamed village pub with a few nooks and crannies, bare floorboards and a piano. A large section of the pub is given over to diners. The front garden seems to double up as the village green. There is a kid's tuck shop in the garden where you can purchase reasonably-priced crisps and drinks.

BRADFORD-ON-AVON

The Lock Inn Café

48 Frome Rd, Bradford-on-Avon, BA15 1LE
01225 868068
www.thelockinn.co.uk
Mon-Sun 8.45am-6pm, Tue-Sat until 9.30pm

Situated on the popular Kennet & Avon Canal, a great stop-off on your cycle ride. Try the famous Boatman's Breakfast or a leisurely coffee. Also hires out bikes, see Cycle Hire in Transport chapter, pg 174.

BURNHAM-ON-SEA

Fortes Ice Cream Parlour

213 Pier St, Burnham-on-Sea, TA8 1BT
01278 782 651
Mon-Sun 9am-6pm (Summer 9pm)
Located just off the seafront
See map on pg 90, A5

Near to the Tourist Information Office. Extensive menu offering delicious home-made ice cream and other treats.

The Goat House Restaurant

Bristol Rd, Brent Knoll, Burnham-on-sea, TA9 4HJ
01278 760 995
Wed-Sun 11.30am-2.30pm, Sun 12pm-2.30pm
See map on pg 90, A5

Open from Wednesday to Sunday serving a seasonal menu using locally-sourced produce at lunchtime and in the evenings.

CHEW MAGNA

Carpenter's Arms

Stanton Wick, Nr Pensford, Somerset, BS39 4BX
01761 490202
www.the-carpenters-arms.co.uk
Mon-Sat 11am-11pm, Sun 12pm-10.30pm
Off the A368, about ¾ mile from Jct with A37
See map on pg 90, C4

17th century miners' cottages overlooking the Chew Valley, converted into a pub with outdoor seating, log fires and two restaurants (booking advisable at weekends).

Chew Valley Lake Tea Shop

Chew Valley Lake Picnic Area, Chew Stoke, BS40 8TF
01275 333345
www.bristolwater.co.uk
Mon-Sun 10.30am-4.30pm
See map on pg 90, C4

Overlooking the lake, this friendly tea shop serves light snacks and main meals. Hot meals until 2.30pm. There are nature trails, a picnic area, visitor centre and shop.

The Blue Bowl

Bristol Rd, West Harptree, BS40 6HJ
01761 221269
Open all day, every day.
Mon-Sat 11am-11pm, Sun 12pm-10.30pm
See map on pg 90, C4

Next to Chew Valley Lake, this family-friendly pub offers a great menu.

CHIPPING SODBURY

Chatties

16B Horse St, Chipping Sodbury, BS37 6DB
01454 321121
Mon-Sat 9.30am-5pm
See map on pg 90, E3

A comfortable coffee shop offering tasty snacks and inexpensive meals.

Codrington Arms

Wapley Rd, Codrington, BS17 6RY
01454 313145
Mon-Sat 11.30am-3pm & 6pm-11pm,
Sun 12pm-3pm & 6pm-10.30pm
See map on pg 90, E3

A comfortable, unspoilt family country pub with a large attractive garden. Food outside until 8pm. Book indoor tables at weekends.

The Dog Inn

Badminton Rd, Chipping Sodbury, BS37 6LZ
01454 312006
Open all day, every day
Mon-Sat 12pm-11pm, Sun 12pm-10.30pm
See map on pg 90, E3

A busy pub with a large garden.

CLEVEDON

The Little Harp Inn

Elton Rd, Clevedon, BS21 7RH
01275 343739
Mon-Sat 11am-11pm, Sun 12pm-10.30pm
See map on pg 90, B3

Good restaurant pub on the seafront. There
are outside tables or sit in the conservatory.
Blackboard menu, with a carvery on Sundays.

The Moon and Sixpence

15 The Beach, Clevedon, BS21 7QU
01275 872443
Mon-Sat 12pm-11pm, Sun 12pm-10.30pm
See map on pg 90, B3

Pleasant pub, set back off the road near the
pier, with a few tables outside. There's a roast
option on Sundays, it can take bookings.

The Old Inn

Walton Rd, Clevedon, BS21 6AE
01275 790052
Mon-Sat 7.30am-11pm, Sun 8am-11pm
See map on pg 90, B3

Near Clevedon Court, this popular pub
offers traditional home-cooked food. Open
for breakfast from 7.30am and on Sundays
bookings are advised for the roast lunch
served from 12pm-2.30pm.

CLUTTON

Hunter's Rest

King Lane, Clutton Hill, BS39 5QL
01761 452303
Mon-Sat 11.30am-2.30pm, 6pm-11pm,
Sun 12pm-4pm, 6pm-10.30pm
Take A37 south from Bristol, follow brown signs
See map on pg 90, D4

A real gem, this 18th century country inn
with conservatory à la carte restaurant is
worth a visit. During the summer holidays,
children eat free on a Wednesday night.
Booking advisable, special offers available.
Large family garden with famous miniature
steam railway (third of a mile) on summer
weekends, weather permitting.

Warwick Arms

Upper Bristol Rd, Clutton, nr Shepton Mallet, BS39
01761 452256
Mon-Sat 11am-11pm, Sun 12pm-11pm
See map on pg 90, D4

Busy pub offering good food with a popular
garden. It gets busy at the weekend, so it is
advisable to book a table.

COMPTON MARTIN

Ring O'Bells

Main St, Compton Martin, BS40 6JE
01761 221284
Mon-Sat 11.30am-2.30pm, 6.30pm-9.30pm,
Sun 12pm-2.30pm

A cosy country pub with tables in the garden.

CONGRESBURY

Cromwells

2 Kent Rd, Congresbury, BS49 5BE
01934 833110
Mon-Sun 12pm-11pm
See map on pg 90, B4

New Civil War-themed 80-seater bar/
restaurant with family room serving food all
day including a carvery and fish.
Large garden.

CHURCHILL

Burrington Inn

Burrington Coombe, Burrington, Bristol, BS40 7AT
01761 462227
www.burrington.co.uk
Mon-Sun 10am-11pm
Next to garden centre, Burrington Coombe
See map on pg 90, B4

Nestled at the foot of the Mendip Hills in
picturesque Burrington Combe, open all year
round serving coffee, afternoon teas, snacks
or full meals plus ice cream parlour.

Langford Inn

Lower Langford, Nr Churchill, BS40 5BL
01934 863059
Mon-Sun 12pm-11pm
See map on pg 90, B4

Charming restored coaching inn with walled
garden and restaurant. Advisable to book.

FRAMPTON COTTERELL

The Golden Heart

Down Rd, Winterbourne, BS36 1AU
01454 773152
Sun-Thu 12pm-11pm, Fri-Sat 12pm-12am
See map on pg 90, D3

Quaint old pub with restaurant serving a
range of home cooked food. Large garden.

The Golden Lion

Beesmoor Rd, Frampton Cotterell, BS36 2JN
01454 773348
Mon-Fri 12pm-11pm, Sat 11am-12am,
Sun 12pm-10.30pm,
See map on pg 90, D3

Traditional, family pub, with extensive menu.

GLASTONBURY

Blue Note Café

2-4 High St, Glastonbury, BA6 9DU
01458 832907
Mon-Sun 9.30am-5pm
See map on pg 90, C6

An extremely busy, casual and alternative
licensed café serving vegetarian dishes.

LONG ASHTON

The Angel Inn

172 Long Ashton Rd, Bristol, BS41 9LT
01275 392 244
Mon-Fri 12pm-11pm, Sun 12pm-10.30pm
See map on pg 90, C4

Pleasant traditional village pub with good
range of food. Restaurant gets busy on
Sundays for the roasts, best to book.

NAILSEA

The Old Farm House

Chelvey Rise, off Trendlewood Way, Nailsea, BS48
01275 851 889
Mon-Fri 11.30am-3pm, 5.30pm-11pm,
Sat-Sun 12pm-11pm
See map on pg 90, C4

A traditional pub under new ownership using
fresh produce in extensive menu. Very popular
on Sundays when they serve a carvery
alongside the full menu, bookings advisable.

The Star Inn

Stone Edge Batch, Clevedon Rd, Tickenham, BS21
01275 858836
Mon-Fri 12pm-2.30pm, 5.30pm-11pm,
Sat 12pm-3pm, 6pm-11pm, Sun 12pm-10.30pm
See map on pg 90, C4

Large pub, serving traditional food with a large garden.

PILL

The Anchor

Ham Green, Pill, BS20 0HB
01275 372253
Mon-Sat 11am-11.30pm, Sun 11am-11pm
See map on pg 90, C3

A village pub with a separate family room. There is a garden and play area. Snacks available as well as main meals.

Rudgeleigh Inn

Martcombe Rd, Easton-in-Gordano, BS20 0QD
01275 372363
Mon-Sat 12pm-11pm, Sun 12pm-10.30pm
See map on pg 90, C3

Large country pub serving extensive pub menu all day. The Sunday carvery is very popular, so booking is advised.

The Priory

Station Rd, Portbury, Bristol, BS20 7TN
01275 378 411
Mon-Sat 11.30am-11pm, Sun 11am-10.30pm
See map on pg 90, C3

Family-friendly pub with a garden serving great food, with roasts on Sundays.

PORTISHEAD

Marine Lake Café

Lake Grounds, Portishead, BS20
01275 842248
See map on pg 90, C3

Friendly café, near children's play area and lake, serving snacks, fast food and ice creams.

SALTFORD & COMPTON DANDO

Compton Inn

Court Hill, Compton Dando, BS39 4JZ
01761 490 321
Mon-Fri 4pm-11pm, Sat 12pm-12am,
Sun 12pm-10.30pm
See map on pg 90, D4

A small, unspoilt traditional pub with a large grassy garden. Open all day at weekends

The Crown

500 Bath Rd, Saltford, BS31 3HJ
01225 872117
Mon-Sat 11.30am-11pm, Sun 12pm-10.30pm
See map on pg 90, D4

Family-friendly pub on the A4. There is a lounge bar with an open fire, a separate restaurant and a public bar, plus an outdoor play area. Food can be eaten anywhere in the pub and al fresco during the summer. At weekends, the kitchen is open all day.

The Riverside Inn

The Shallows, Saltford, BS31 3EZ
01225 873862
Open for food all day throughout summer.
See map on pg 90, D4

Adjacent to Kennet lock. The upstairs pub and restaurant is smart and there is a conservatory for families and garden overlooking the weir. Very comfortable with an extensive menu.

STROUD & TETBURY

Gumstool Inn

Calcot Manor, Nr Tetbury, Glos, GL8 8YJ
01666 890391
www.calcotmanor.co.uk
Sat-Sun 12pm-9pm, Mon-Fri 12pm-2pm & 7pm-9pm
On the B4135 Dursley-Tetbury, at the A46 jct

A gastropub that positively welcomes families. Part of the luxury Calcot Manor country hotel, the inn is situated in a former farmhouse set around a courtyard of lime trees. Eat inside beside cosy log fires or outside on the terrace. Booking advisable at weekends.

Hobbs House Bakery

4 George St, Nailsworth, Gloucestershire, GL6 0AG
01453 839396
www.hobbshousebakery.co.uk
Mon-Fri 7.30am-6pm (5pm Sat)

Unusual bakery-cum-café, an offshoot of the award-winning family-run bakery of the same name, located in Chipping Sodbury. A variety of freshly baked bread, including an organic range, as well as cakes, pastries, sandwiches and drinks to take away or eat-in the small café upstairs. As you enter, you walk right past the busy kitchen and can see the bakers at work.

Hunters Hall Inn

Kingscote, Tetbury, Gloucestershire, GL8 8XZ
01453 860393
www.huntershallinn.com
Mon-Sat 11am-11pm, Sun 12pm-10.30pm
2 miles west of A46 on the A4135 Tetbury-Dursley

Creeper-clad 16th-century coaching inn with several bars, a restaurant, beamed ceilings and open fires. Large garden with lots of tables. Convenient for lunch after the nearby Lasborough Park walk see pg 124. Booking advisable at weekends.

The Priory Inn

London Rd, Tetbury, GL8 8JJ
01666 502251
www.theprioryinn.co.uk
Mon-Sun 7am-10pm

Friendly hotel/gastropub serving teas, coffees and cakes. Lunch served from 12pm using local produce cooked in wood-fired oven. Lots of great walks around Tetbury, or you can while away the afternoon by the fire!

Woodruffs

24 High St, Stroud, Gloucestershire, GL5 1AJ
01454 759195
Mon-Sat 9am-5pm (no food service 11am-12pm)

Award-winning organic café with a largely vegetarian menu, occasional fish dishes and vegan options. Additional seating upstairs.

THORNBURY & ALMONDSBURY

Bowl Inn

Church Rd, Lower Almondsbury, BS32 4DT
01454 612757
www.theoldbowlinn.co.uk
Mon-Sat 5pm-11pm, Sun 12pm-10.30pm
See map on pg 90, D2

Traditional village pub with à la carte restaurant and bar menu, great for family meals out. It's very popular so book a table. On warmer days you can sit outside next to the pretty church.

Lamb Inn

Wotton Rd, Iron Acton, BS37 9UZ
01454 228265
Mon-Sat 12pm-11pm, Sun 12pm-10.30pm
See map on pg 90, D2

Quiet, cosy historic village pub with small family dining area. Attractive shaded grassy garden and covered patio. Large function room available for hire.

The Swan

Tockington Green, Tockington, BS32 4NJ
01454 614800
Mon-Sat 11am-3pm & 6pm-11pm,
Sun 12pm-10.30pm
See map on pg 90, D2

Atmospheric village pub, with large garden.

The White Hart

Littleton-on-Severn, Nr Thornbury, BS35 1NR
01454 412275
Mon-Fri 12pm-3.00pm & 6pm-11pm
Sat-Sun 12pm-11pm, Sun 10.30pm
See map on pg 90, D2

A lovely old country pub with great food. No bookings, so it's best to go early! There is a large garden.

WELLS

Cloister Restaurant

West Cloister, Wells Cathedral, BA5 2PA
01749 676543
Mon-Sat 10am-5pm, Sun 12.30pm-5pm
See map on pg 90, C5

A relaxed licensed restaurant in beautiful surroundings with homemade dishes and cakes. Central car park 10 mins.

The Crown at Wells & Antons Bistro

Market Place, Wells, BA5 2RP
01749 673457
www.crownatwells.co.uk
Mon-Sun 12pm-2.30pm and 6pm-9.30pm
See map on pg 90, C5

A medieval inn serving good food and fine wine in Wells marketplace, overlooking the Cathedral and Bishop's Palace. Has an outdoor café serving food all day throughout the summer. Free car park for residents only; central car park 10 mins.

The Fountain Inn & Boxer's Restaurant

1 St Thomas St, Wells, BA5 2UU
01749 672317
www.fountaininn.co.uk
Food Mon-Sun 12pm-2.30pm, 6pm-10.30pm
See map on pg 90, C5

Award-winning, family friendly gastro-pub.

The Good Earth Restaurant

4 Priory Rd, Wells, BA5 1SY
01749 678600
Mon-Sat 9am-5pm
See map on pg 90, C5

Simple, quality whole-food restaurant and gift shop, with vegetarian and vegan dishes.

WESTON-SUPER-MARE

Seven VII

Seven Beach Rd, Weston-super-Mare, BS23 1AS
01934 636969
www.viibar.com
Mon-Sun 12pm-8pm
See map on pg 90, A4

Large beach front bar/restaurant with conservatory serving a wide range of lunchtime snacks and evening meals.

The Crown

The Batch, Skinners Lane, BS25 5PP
01225 314864
Mon-Sun 11am-11pm, food served 12pm-2.30pm
See map on pg 90, A4

Close to the Mendips, this country pub serves farmhouse-style food using local produce including casseroles, chillis, jacket potatoes and a great beef sandwich.

WOTTON-UNDER-EDGE

McQuigg's

44 Long St, Wotton-under-Edge, Glos
01453 844108
Mon-Sat 9am-5pm, Fri-Sat 7pm-9pm
See map on pg 90, E2

Café serving light lunches and substantial specials. Tables in the small garden.

The Ark Coffee Shop

43 Long St, Wotton-under-Edge, Glos, GL12 7BX
01453 521838
Mon-Fri 9am-12pm, 12.45pm-4.15pm,
Sat 9.30am-12.30pm
See map on pg 90, E2

Ecumenical coffee shop selling fair trade products. Serve drinks, cakes and biscuits.

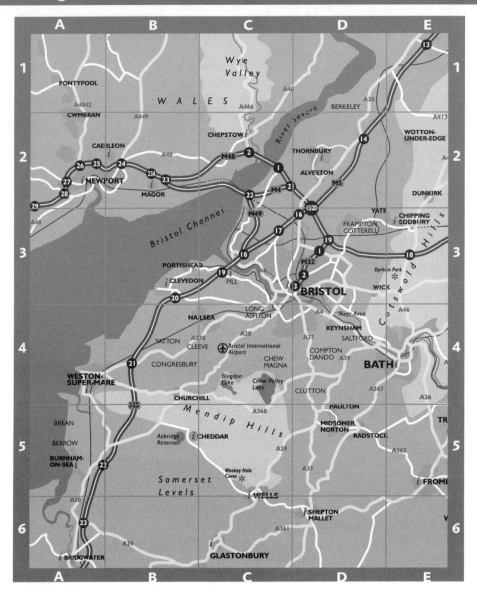

Map courtesy of Destination Bristol
www.visitbristol.co.uk

OUT & ABOUT IN THE WEST COUNTRY

Nicola O'Brien

Lindsey Potter

CONTENTS

INTRODUCTION

Bristol is incredibly well-placed for getting out at the weekends. Whether you like messing about on beaches, getting on your bikes or exploring museums, there is a wide choice of places to visit within an hour's drive of the city. There is something for everyone and many attractions are free.

The entries in the first part of the chapter are places of interest, listed by location, starting at Portishead, moving down the coast to Burnham, and then anticlockwise past Bath, up through Gloucestershire and ending up in Cardiff. The rest of the chapter lists attractions by type, such as castles, farms, Roman Britain and so on. Once you've picked your destination, don't forget to cross-reference chapters such as Eating Out to find a good spot for lunch or check out Farmers' Shops and Markets for other excursion ideas.

DAYS OUT & DESTINATIONS

PORTISHEAD

Twenty minutes from Bristol's city centre you will find this peaceful town on the edge of the Bristol Channel. There is a marina, a leisure centre and a wonderful open-air pool. The Lake Grounds are set in a spacious seafront park with boating lake and café. The nearby beach is fine for walking but you cannot swim, it's mud!

Portishead Open Air Pool

Esplanade Rd, Portishead, BS20 7HD
01275 843454
May-Sep

Heated open air swimming pool with sunbathing terraces.

CLEVEDON

This Victorian seaside town has a pleasant seafront promenade and the rocky foreshore is good for fossil hunting! At the opposite end of the promenade to the pier is Salt House. In season, there is crazy golf and a snack bar. There are various coastal walks around the area, see Walks pg 122.

Clevedon Tourist Information

Clevedon Library, 37 Old Church Rd, BS21 6NN
01275 873498
www.somersetcoast.com
Mon/Thu/Sat 9.30am-5pm, Tue/Fri 9.30am-7pm,
Wed/Sun closed

Clevedon Craft Centre

Moor Lane, off Court Lane, Clevedon, BS21 6TD
01275 872 149
Daily 10am-5pm, but most workshops closed on Mon
Admission free
M5 J20, follow brown signs, Court Lane is off B3130
(Tickenham Rd).

Craft studios demonstrating a variety of skills. Jewellery, pottery, illustrations, hand-carved leather goods and stained glass are just some of the items made and sold here. Refreshments are available.

Clevedon Heritage Centre

4 The Beach, Clevedon, BS21 7QU
01275 341 196
Daily 10.30am-4.30pm, seasonal variations
Admission Free

Photographic history of Clevedon.

Clevedon Pier

The Toll House, Clevedon Pier, Clevedon, BS21 7QU
01275 878 846
Mon-Wed 10am-6pm, Thu-Sun 9am-6pm
£1 adult, 50p child

Grade 1 listed pier, a fine example of Victorian architecture. Summer sailings to islands, see Severn Adventures and Boat Trips, pg 117.

WESTON-SUPER-MARE

Seaside town, offering a vast expanse of safe, flat, sandy beach. The tide is always in at Marine Lake at the North end of the seafront with rock pooling at Anchor Head. Seasonal crazy golf, putting green and other attractions. If it rains, check out the pier, the Helicopter Museum or, for train fanatics, the model train layout in Model Masters, see pg 150.

Weston-super-Mare Tourist Information

Beach Lawns, Weston-super-Mare, BS23 1AT
01934 888 800
www.somersetcoast.com
Daily exc Sundays in winter

North Somerset Museum

Burlington St, Weston-super-Mare BS23 1PR
01934 621 028
www.n-somerset.gov.uk/museum
Mon-Sat 10am-4.30pm
£3.75 adult, accompanied children free

Victorian dressing up clothes, interactive computers, passport trail and holiday events.

Seaquarium

Marine Parade, Weston-super-Mare, BS23 1BE
01934 613361
www.seaquariumweston.co.uk
Daily 10am-4pm
£5.50 adult, £4.50 child, £18 family (2+2)
Reduction of £1 on presentation of this book.

Built on its own pier, the aquarium has a wide variety of marine life and an underwater walkway. There are opportunities to handle Some of the sea creatures.

The Grand Pier

Marine Parade, Weston-super-Mare BS23 1AL
01934 620 238
www.grandpierwsm.co.uk
Feb-Nov: daily 10am-dusk
At north end of seafront

Covered amusement park over the sea, including bowling, dodgems, haunted house, ride simulators and fairground rides.

BERROW & BREAN

Berrow has a sandy beach and sand dunes which can be reached from the nature reserve (parking free). Brean's beach car park is inexpensive. At the North end, a steep climb will take you to Brean Down, a rocky National Trust headland with great views.

Animal Farm Country Park

Red Rd, Berrow, Nr Burnham-on-Sea, TA8 2RW
01278 751 628
www.animal-farm.co.uk
Daily 10am-5.30pm, closes 4.30pm in winter
£5.50 adults & child, bag of animal feed with presentation of this book
Annual: £19.50

P WC X 🏪 ⛱ ♿

Large variety of animals, including rare breeds, set in 25 acres of countryside. Opportunities to feed the animals. Huge indoor and outdoor play areas. Treasure hunts in the holidays.

Brean Down Tropical Bird Garden

Brean Down, Brean, Somerset, TA8 2RS
01278 751 209
www.burnham-on-sea.co.uk/brean_bird_garden
Mar-Oct: daily 10am-4pm
Nov-Mar: Sat-Sun 10am-4pm
Phone for school holiday openings
£1.95 adult, 95p child

P WC X 🏪 ♿

Located at the foot of Brean Down. Largest selection of tropical parrots in the West!

Brean Leisure Park

Coast Rd, Brean, Somerset, TA8 2QY
01278 751 595
www.brean.com
Mar-Oct, daily, some exceptions, phone for details
Pool complex £3/session,
£17.99 wrist band for unlimited rides 10yrs-adults, £9.99 U10s

P WC X 🏪 ⛱ 🚌 ♿

Fun park with over 40 rides and attractions including go-karts, laserquest and rollercoasters, some height restrictions apply. Indoor and outdoor pools (May-Sep) with water shutes. U12s must be accompanied by an adult.

BURNHAM-ON-SEA

Seven miles of sandy beach stretches from Burnham to Brean. Walking, kite flying, picnics and seasonal attractions. Swimming restrictions due to hazardous tides. Esplanade, pier and amusement arcade.

Burnham-on-Sea Tourist Information

South Esplanade, Burnham-on-Sea, TA8 1BU
01278 787 852
www.somersetbythesea.co.uk
Mon-Sat 9.30am-4.30pm (closed 1-2pm), open Sun in summer

Apex Leisure and Wildlife Park

Marine Drive, Burnham-on-Sea
Sedgemoor Parks Dept: 01278 435435

 WC

42-acre park, walks, birds, skate park, BMX biking (members only) and a play area.

STREET

Clarks Village is a great day out for shopaholics with an eye for a bargain. And there's fun stuff for the rest of the family too! See Shopping chapter.

Greenbank Outdoor Pool

Wilfrid Rd, Street, Somerset, BA16 0EU
01458 442468
www.greenbankpool.co.uk
May-mid Sept: Mon-Fri 12am-6.45pm term time
Sat-Sun 10am-6.45pm, summer hols 10am-6pm
£4 adult, £3 child.
Ring or see website for details of season tickets

P WC X 🏪 ⛱ 🚌 ♿

This pleasant heated outdoor pool surrounded by grass is less than five minutes' walk from Clark's Village. There's a new wet play area and refreshments.

The Shoe Museum

40 High St, Street, BA16 0YA
01458 842169
Mon-Fri 10am-4.45pm, Sat 10am-5pm
Sun 11am-5pm
Admission free

Traces the history of shoes and shoe making from Roman times to today.

BATH

Bath is a beautiful and compact city with lots to do whether you are looking for culture or just want to shop!

It takes only 15 minutes on the train from Temple Meads to Bath Spa. If driving, there are Park & Rides at Newbridge (A4) and Lansdown (A46) or the Charlotte Street car park in the centre is convenient if coming in from the A4. You can also cycle on the Bristol to Bath cycleway.

See also the Bath sections of the Eating Out and Shopping chapters which have lots of inspiration for a great day out.

Bath Tourist Information Centre
Abbey Chambers, Abbey Churchyard, BA1 1LY
0906 711 2000 (50p/minute)
www.visitbath.co.uk
Mon-Sat 9.30am-6pm, Sun 10am-4pm

CENTRAL BATH

Bath Postal Museum
8 Broad St, Bath, BA1 5LJ
01225 460333
www.bathpostalmuseum.org
Mon-Sat 11am-5pm, winter 4.30pm
£2.90 adult, £1.50 child, £6.90 family

The only museum in the country telling the story of the Postal Service. Have fun in a reconstructed 1930s post office weighing items, stamping forms and sorting letters. Educational videos, discovery trails and computer games. The museum is moving to the general post office (opposite the Podium) in summer 2006, check website for updates.

Bath Abbey
01225 422462
www.bathabbey.org
Apr-Oct: Mon-Sat 9am-6pm, Sun 1pm-2.30pm, 4.30pm-5.30pm
Nov-Mar: Mon-Sat 9am-4.30pm, Sun 1pm-2.30pm
Admission free
Donations of £2.50 adult, £1 child welcome

This magnificent building dates back to 1499 and is the last great gothic church in England.

Over the past ten years, the Abbey has been restored, revealing some elaborate heraldry and shields in the fan vaulted ceiling. There is an informative worksheet for young people filled with intriguing facts, one of which highlights some 400 year old graffiti! Enter the Heritage Vaults Museum from outside the Abbey, it houses archaeological remains, textiles and art (open daily 9am-4.30pm).

Bath City Boat Trips & Charters

9 York St, Bath, BA1 1NG
07974 560197
www.bathcityboattrips.com
Daily 11am-5pm (subject to weather conditions)
1 hr tour: £6.95 adult, £5.95 student, child £4.95
(longer tours available)
To find the moorings take the stairwell on North
Parade Bridge, turn right on to footpath, walk 200m

Full commentary on the historic sights of Bath
and the River Avon. Private charters available
for parties, with karaoke available for those
singing gondoliers!

Bath Open Top Bus Tour

Bath Bus Company, 1 Pierrepont St, Bath, BA1 1LB
01225 330444
www.bathbuscompany.com or
www.citysightseeing.co.uk for online sales
Daily 10am-5pm, reduced service in winter
£9.50 adult, £6 child (6-12), family discount

Tickets for this 45-min trip are valid for two
days and can be bought on the bus, at the
tourist office, online or from the train station.
Tours start on High St, Grand Parade.

Bizarre Bath Comedy Walk

01225 335124
www.bizarrebath.co.uk
Daily Apr-Sep 8pm
Depart Huntsman Inn, North Parade
£7 adult, £5 student & child

In 90 minutes, this entertaining walk mixes
comedy, street theatre and improvisation.
We've been told it's better to be in the tour
than a passer-by!

Museum of East Asian Art

12 Bennett St, Bath, BA1 2QJ
01225 464640
www.meaa.org.uk
Tue-Sat 10am-5pm, Sun & B/H's 12pm-5pm
£4 adult, £1.50 U12s, £9 family
Opposite the Assembly Rooms

This museum is situated in a restored
Georgian house and has a collection of
ceramics, jades, bronzes and other artifacts
from China, Japan, Korea and Southeast Asia.
They welcome young visitors of all ages and
there are fun activities such as Origami.

Museums of the Bath Preservation Trust

www.bath-preservation-trust.org.uk

The Trust works to save listed buildings from
demolition and to preserve the historic beauty
of Bath. It runs four museums which, due to
restrictive planning, do not allow for disabled
facilities. Three of the museums have fully
illustrated trails, £1.50 (also on the website).

Beckford's Tower

Lansdown Rd, Bath
01225 422212
Easter-Oct: Sat/Sun/B/H's 10.30am-5pm

This 120ft tower, two miles north of Bath, has
great views of the countryside.

Building of Bath Museum

The Countess of Huntingdon's Chapel,
The Vineyards, Bath, BA1 5NA
01225 333 895
Mid Feb-Nov: Tue-Sun & B/H's 10.30am-5pm
£4 adult, £2.50 child, £10 family (2+2)

This museum describes how the city of Bath
was designed and built.

Number 1 Royal Crescent

1 Royal Crescent, Bath, BA1 2LR
01225 428 126
Tue-Sun & B/H's 10.30am-5pm, winter 4pm
Dec-Feb closed
Open B/H's & Mondays of Bath Festival
£4 adult, £2.50 child, £12 family (2+2)

First house built on the Royal Crescent in
1767. Restored as a grand townhouse of the
period. See how people lived 200 years ago.

William Herschel Museum

19 New King St, Bath, BA1 2BL
01225 446865
www.bath-preservation-trust.org.uk
Mid Jan-Mid Dec: 1pm-5pm, Sat-Sun 11am-5pm
£3.50 adult, £2 child, £7.50 family (2+2)

For budding young astronomers. It was the
home of William Herschel, who discovered the
planet Uranus in 1781. An auditorium shows
programmes on space travel and astronomy.
You can follow the family trail or take an audio
guide. Part of Spaced Out UK, a large scale
model of the solar system built across the UK
with fantastic sculptures.

Roman Baths and Pump Room

Pump Room, Stall St, Bath, BA1 1LZ
01225 477 785
www.romanbaths.co.uk
Daily 9am-5pm, seasonal variations
£10 adult, £6 child, £28 family (2+4) Combined
tickets to costume museum and Roman Baths are
good value and valid for 7 days

One of the best-preserved Roman sites in
Northern Europe, this spa is a fine example
of ancient engineering. There is an excellent
audio guide and special school holiday events.

The spring produces over a million litres of
hot water a day. Taste it for yourself!

Theatre Royal

Sawclose, Bath, BA1 1ET
01225 448844
www.theatreroyal.org.uk

One of the oldest working theatres in the
country. An impressive range of performances
to suit all ages. Workshops in school holidays.

The Jane Austen Centre

40 Gay St, Queens Sq, Bath, BA1 2NT
01225 443000
www.janeausten.co.uk
Daily 10am-5.30pm, Nov-Feb 11am-4.30pm
£5.95 adult, £4.95 student, £2.95 child (6-16yrs)

The Jane Austen Centre celebrates the life
and times of this famous regency author. She
paid two long visits here towards the end of
the eighteenth century and lived in Gay Street
between 1801 and 1806.

Whether you are studying her work or are just
a romantic for the Regency era, this exhibition
will give you the opportunity to find out more
about Bath in Jane Austen's time and the
importance of this magnificent city to her life
and work. There are knowledgeable guides
and a gift shop where you may be tempted to
take up needle point! (Wheelchair access to
exhibition only.)

See also The Regency Tea Rooms in Eating
Out, pg 82.

The Museum of Costume

Assembly Rooms, Bennett St, Bath, BA1 2QH
01225 477789
www.museumofcostume.co.uk
Daily 11am-6pm, winter 5pm
£6.50 adult, £4.50 child, £18 family (2+4)
Combined tickets to museum and Roman Baths are
good value and valid for 7 days

Clothing from the late 16th century to today,
with interactive exhibitions, audio guide and
activity trolley. Activities during the holidays.
See photo pg 98.

Thermae Bath Spa

Bath St, Bath BA1 1SJ
01225 331234
www.thermaebathspa.com
Daily 9am-10pm
New Royal Bath: 2 hrs £19, 4hr £29, full day £45
Cross Bath: £12
Children from 12yrs welcome, each visitor U16 must
be accompanied by an adult

This long awaited spa will open as we go
to press so it's not tried or tested. However
if you are in need of a little pampering or
are tempted to swim in an open air roof-top
pool overlooking this wonderful city, let us
know your opinion. With your ticket price
you have access to jacuzzis, back massage
power showers, aromatherapy steam rooms,
four natural thermal baths and an array of
treatments (which cost extra). Then if you
are not too chilled, treat yourself in the café.
Discounts for BANES residents. This could be
a great Mother's Day present to win the odd
Brownie point! See photo pg 95.

Victoria Art Gallery

Pulteney Bridge, Bath, BA2 4AT
01225 477233
www.victoriagal.org.uk
Tue-Fre 10am-5.30pm, Sat 10am-5pm,
Sun 2pm-5pm, some B/H's
Free admission

Housing permanent works by 15th century artists, such as Gainsborough, along with others up to the present day. Two other galleries have exhibitions that change every two months. There are workshops, holiday activities and a full schools programme.

OUTSKIRTS OF BATH

American Museum

Claverton Manor, Bath, BA2 7BD
01225 460 503
www.americanmuseum.org
Museum: Mar-Oct Tue-Sun 12pm-5pm, some B/H's
Gardens & exhibitions 12pm-5pm
Nov/Dec: Tue-Sun 1pm-4pm, Wed 5.30pm-7.30pm
£6.50 adult, £3.50 child (all areas)
£4 adult, £2.50 child (gardens and galleries)
Take A36 Warminster road out of Bath, follow signs

Displays of American decorative art spanning 17th to 19th Century. Authentically furnished rooms showing the American way of life from colonial times to the eve of the Civil War. Beautiful terraced gardens. Museum re-opens for a few weeks during Nov/Dec with the rooms decorated according to the period they represent for Christmas. For seasonal exhibitions see website for details.

Bath Boating Station

Forester Rd, Bathwick, Bath, BA2 6QE
01225 312 900
Apr-Oct: daily 10am-6pm
£6 adult, £3 child
Follow A36 through Bath. Just after big roundabout at Sydney Gardens, Forester Rd is 1st on left

A couple of miles NE of the centre you'll find this Victorian boating station with rowing boats and punts for hire. They also operate boat trips to Bathampton taking one hour.

Great Western Maize Maze

Newton Farm, Newton, St Loe, Bath
0777 587 0728
www.greatwesternmaze.net
Jul-Sep daily 10am-6pm, phone for prices
A4 from Bristol, Globe roundabout

Whatever your age, getting lost in 6ft+ high Maize is made fun by a mad bunch of enthusiastic helpers. On hot days they have been known to throw ice pops from the lookouts to the sweaty lost souls.

Royal Victoria Park

Upper Bristol Rd, Bath
01225 477010
Take A4 into Bath, about a mile before city centre

Families tend to visit this park for its massive well-equipped playground for all ages, including skateboarders. There are also beautiful botanical gardens and a duck pond. See Pavilion Tea Rooms, pg 83.

Victoria Falls, Adventure Golf

Victoria Park
01225 425066
Daily 10am-dusk
£3.50 adult, £2.50 child, £3 concessions, £10 family 2+2, group discounts

Just below the Royal Crescent, this 18-hole adventure golf course is landscaped around rushing waterways and waterfalls. It comes highly recommended from kids, students and grandparents. Can you score a par on the 15th hole in the middle of the lake?

BRADFORD-ON-AVON & KENNET AND AVON CANAL

It only takes half an hour to get to this attractive old wool town by train from Temple Meads, but it feels a world apart from Bristol. The canal, which played such an important role 200 years ago allowing goods to be transported to and from London, has been restored and offers lots of recreational opportunities. The stretch between Bath and Devizes is one of the most attractive. Colourful narrowboats and waterside pubs make cycling, walking or boating fun for everyone. There is a car park at the station.

Bradford-on-Avon Tourist Information

50 St Margarets St, Bradford-on-Avon, BA15 1DE
01225 865797
www.bradfordonavontown.co.uk
10am-5pm, Sun 11am-3pm

This helpful office is situated in new premises in Westbury Gardens — look for the flag pole.

Barton Farm Country Park and The Tithe Barn

www.wiltshire.gov.uk
The Country Park is always open.
B3109 just out of town centre, past station

This park, created on land belonging to the ancient Manor Farm, is set in the wooded valley on the River Avon, stretching 1.5 miles between Bradford and the hamlet of Avoncliff. See walks on pg 127.

14th Century Tithe Barn

English Heritage
www.english-heritage.co.uk
Apr-Oct 10am-6pm, winter 4pm, admission free

On the edge of the park is this impressive barn, once used to store the Abbey's tithes. The granary and old cow byres have been restored as craftshops and galleries. There are also tea gardens and a play area.

Brass Knocker Basin

Brass Knocker Basin, Monkton Combe, BA2 7JD
01225 722292
www.bathcanal.com
Daily 8am-dusk, with seasonal variations
Take A36 south of Bath, at Monkton Combe turn left at lights onto B3108

This is a good point from which to orientate yourself whether you're walking, cycling or boating. The visitor centre here has displays and information about the canal. The Angelfish restaurant is a scenic option for lunch.

Kennet & Avon cycling & boating

The canal offers bike and canoe hire as well as relaxing narrow boat trips. See Lock Inn and Bath & Dundas Canal Co. in the Transport chapter, pg 174.

THE COTSWOLDS

The Cotswolds are within easy reach of Bristol and cover a large area. There are plenty of attractions, see Cheltenham Tourist Office which also has guides for family walks.

Butts Farm

Nr South Cerney, Cirencester, GL7 5QE
01285 862205
Easter-Oct: Wed-Sun 11am-5pm, daily sch holidays
£4 adult, £3 child
3 miles east of Circencester on the old A419 towards Swindon, follow brown tourist signs

Near Cotswold Water Park, this is a hands-on farm, which specialises in rare breeds. Geared to younger children but fun for all ages. Help milk goats, bottle-feed young animals and ride ponies. New farm shop selling local produce.

Cotswold Farm Park

Guiting Power, Nr Stow-on-the-Wold, GL54 5UG
01451 850307
www.cotswoldfarmpark.co.uk
Mar-Sep: daily 10.30am-5pm
Sep Oct: w/e's only (daily in autumn ½ term)
£5.50 adult, £4.50 chlid, £18 family (2+2),
Annual: £27.50 adult, £22.50 child
Follow brown signs from Bourton-on-the-Water.

Rare British breeds, informative animal audio guide, seasonal demonstrations of lambing, shearing and milking. There are animal feeding sessions and a battery-powered Tractor Driving School, but only for U12s. There are also woodland walks, nature trails, and an adventure playground. The campsite gives reduced rates to the park.

Cotswold Wildlife Park

Burford, Oxfordshire, OX18 4JW
01993 823 006
www.cotswoldwildlifepark.co.uk
Daily 10am-6pm, Oct-Feb 10am-dusk
£9 adult, £6.50 child
Annual: £45 adult, £32.50 child
Jct 15 M4, A419, A361, from Lechlade follow brown tourist signs.

Spacious enclosures with rhinos, zebras, leopards, emus, lions and more. Other attractions include adventure playground, a reptile house and animal encounters — feed the penguins, ducks and big cat.

Prinknash Bird and Deer Park

Cranham, Gloucestershire, GL4 8EX
01452 812727
www.prinknash-bird-and-deerpark.com
Daily 10am-5pm, 4pm winter
£4.40 adult, £3 child
M5 J11a, on the A46 between Cheltenham and Stroud, follow brown tourist signs

Set in the grounds of a working abbey, the bird park has aviaries housing exotic birds, and a lake. Many birds including ducks, mute swans, black swans, peacocks and cranes wander freely and will feed out of your hand, as will tame deer and pygmy goats. There is a tearoom and an 80-year-old 2-storey Tudor style wendy house.

Cotswold Water Park

Spratsgate Lane, Shorncote, Cirencester, GL7 6DF
01285 861459
www.waterpark.org
Keynes Country Park open daily 9am-5pm, with seasonal variations

Britain's largest water park with over 130 lakes. Water sports, walking, nature spotting or just relaxing on the beach.

Gateway Information Centre (and café)

01285 862962
At the A419 entrance to the park
For accommodation, family activities and eating out information.

Keynes Country Park

The larger of the two country parks. Here you will find: the millenium visitor centre and a bathing beach (Jun-Sep 1pm-5pm); two large play areas; lakeside walks and cycling; a boardwalk café and picnic/barbeque areas. Boats (pedalos to surfbikes) and bicycles can be hired here (phone 07970 419208)

Adventure Zone

01285 861459
or email: advzone@waterpark.org
Based at Keynes, the Adventure Zone, offers a range of activities for 8-16yrs including waterskiing, windsurfing, kayaking, sailing and horseriding. Pre-booking essential.

Waterland

01285 861202
An outdoor pursuit centre offering sailing, windsurfing, canoeing and kayaking, archery and raft building.

Neigh Bridge Country Park

Smaller park with picnic site, play area and lakeside walk.

Hobourne Cotswold Water Park

See Holidays & Weekends Away, pg 202.

BOURTON-ON-THE-WATER

Birdland Park and Gardens

Rissington Rd, Bourton-on-the-Water, GL54 2BN
01451 820480
www.birdland.co.uk
Apr-Oct: 10am-6pm, Nov-Mar: 4pm
£4.75 adult, £3 child, £14.50 family (2+2),
Annual: £19 adult, £11 child

Over 500 birds can be seen in a natural setting of woodland and gardens. The River Windrush runs through the park forming a natural habitat for flamingos, pelicans, storks and waterfowl. The colony of penguins is fun to watch at feeding time (2.30pm). Over 50 aviaries contain exotic birds. Nice picnic spots, play area and café (open w/e's only in winter).

Bourton Model Railway

Box Bush, High St, Bourton-on-the-Water, GL54
01451 820686
www.bourtonmodelrailway.co.uk
Apr-Sep: daily 11am-5pm
£2.25 adult, £1.75 child, £7 family (2+2)
Oct-Mar: Sat-Sun 11am-5pm only
Limited opening in Jan

Over 500 sq ft of scenic model railway layouts. 40 British and continental trains run through realistic and detailed scenery; some are interactive. There is a well-stocked model shop, with extended opening hours.

Bourton-on-the-Water

Visitor Information Centre: 01451 820211

Further attractions accessible from its main car park:

The Dragonfly Maze
01451 822251

Use clues found on journey through maze to help you find the golden dragonfly.

The Model Village
01451 820467
www.theoldnewinn.co.uk

Detailed replica of the village built from Cotswold stone in one-ninth scale.

Cotswold Motoring and Toy Museum
See Wheels and Wings, pg 118.

STROUD

A mixture of old and new, this is one of the larger towns in the Cotswolds and it has much to offer in terms of shops, cafés, restaurants and things to do. There's a cinema, leisure centre and a large park. Regular events include a farmers' market and the Stroud Fringe Festival, held in September.

Stroud Tourist Information Centre
The Subscription Rooms, George St, Stroud, GL5
01453 760960
Mon-Sat 10am-5pm

Museum in the Park

Stratford Park, Stratford Rd, GL5 4AF
01453 763394
www.stroud.gov.uk
Tue-Fri 10am-5pm, Sat-Sun and B/H's 11am, seasonal variations
Admission free
M5 J13, A419 follow signs to Stratford Park

Set in beautiful parkland, this family-oriented museum has interesting interactive displays. Displays include local history and a room devoted to childhood over the years. There are quiz trails, activity packs and holiday workshops. Free car parking at Stratford Park Leisure Centre (indoor and outdoor pools).

Owlpen Manor

Nr Uley, Gloucestershire, GL11 5BZ
01453 860261
www.owlpen.com
May-Sep, Tue/Thu & Sun
House 2pm-5pm
Restaurant & gardens 10.30am-5pm
£4.80 adults, £2 child (4-14yrs), £13.50 family
Gardens & grounds £2.80 adults, £1 child
1 mile east of Uley, off B4066 Dursley-Stroud road

A romantic Tudor manor house with formal terraced yew gardens set in a beautiful Cotswolds valley. Contains family portraits and collections, 17th-century wall hangings and Cotswold Arts and Crafts furniture. Grounds include medieval buildings, a mill pond and early Georgian mill. The Cyder House Restaurant offers light lunches, teas and dinners). The 300-year-old oak cider press in the corner was once used for cider feasts.

Stratford Park Leisure Centre

Stratford Rd, Stroud, Gloucestershire, GL5 4AF
01453 766771
www.leisure-centre.com
Outdoor pool end May-1st w/e Sept
Leisure Centre all year
£3.10 adult, £1.70 child, £5.60 family (2+2)

[P] [WC] [🏛] [✗] [⊞] [♿]

Set in 32 acres of parkland, this leisure centre provides indoor and outdoor facilities for a variety of sports. The outdoor pool is popular in summer, with grass sunbathing areas.

Stroud Farmers' Market

Cornhill Market Place, Stroud, Gloucestershire
01453 758060
www.madeinstroud.org/markets
1st & 3rd Sat every month: 9am-2pm

Award-winning farmers' market offering a wide range of local produce and local crafts. Entertainment from local musicians adds to the atmosphere. Seasonal events include Apple Day festivities in the autumn and Christmas activities in December.

Woodchester Park Mansion

Nympsfield, Stroud, Gloucestershire, GL10 3TS
01452 814213 park, 01453 861541 mansion
www.woodchestermansion.org.uk
Mansion: Easter-End Oct Sun 11am-5pm & 1st Sat's in mth, daily Jul-Aug & B/H w/e's
Park open all year 9am-dusk
£1.50 parking
Nympsfield Rd 300m from the junction with he B4066 Uley-Stroud. Car park is a mile from the mansion, with regular bus transfer

[P] [✗] [🛒] [🚻]

National Trust-owned park in a secluded Cotswold valley with trails through scenic woodland, parkland and around lakes. The Mansion, a Grade 1 listed building, was built in the 19th-century in the French Gothic revival style but never finished. Rare bats use the roof spaces in summer. See them from the observatory or join a bat-watching evening.

WOTTON-UNDER-EDGE

True to its name, this ancient wool town is still a settlement by a wood under the Cotswold Edge, and together with the surrounding villages and countryside, it has plenty to attract families. The characterful high street has a range of shops and cafés. There's a small swimming pool (open in summer), with a larger year-round pool at the leisure centre in nearby Dursley. The Heritage Centre in the Chipping is a tourist information point.

Under the Edge Arts
www.undertheedgearts.org.uk

Organises events and activities for young people.

Megamaze

Kingswood, Wotton-under-Edge, Gloucestershire
01453 843120
www.megamaze.co.uk
Mid Jul-Mid Sept: daily 10am-5pm
£4 adult, £3 child (up to 12yrs), £12 family (2+2)
About ½ mile out of Kingswood on the Hillesled Rd, go past the Dinneywicks pub and continue to the find the maze on the left-hand side just after the turn to Wortley (Nind Lane)

[P] [WC] [🏛] [⊞]

A seasonal maze with more than two miles of paths carved through five acres of maize. The maize reaches more than six feet in height and is harvested in early autumn. Also on site is a giant haystack for climbing, trampoline and pedal karts. There are outdoor and covered picnic areas, and refreshments.

Newark Park

Ozleworth, Wotton-under-Edge, GL12 7PZ
01453 842644
www.nationaltrust.org.uk
Apr-May: Wed/Thu 11am-5pm
Jun-Oct: Wed/Thu, Sat-Sun, B/H's 11am-5pm
£5 adult, £2.50 children, £13 family

National Trust property, high on a limestone cliff, with far-reaching views. It started life as a hunting lodge in the 1550s. You can stroll in the deer park and gardens, renowned for their snowdrops in spring, or follow a longer circular walk through the Lower Lodge Woods, see Walks pg 124.

The Tortworth Chestnut

Next to St Leonard's Church, Tortworth
Turn off the B4509 Tortworth-Wotton at the crossroads just east of Tortworth Primary School, following signs to Damery and Wick. The tree is on the right, about ¼ mile from the junction, in a field next to St Leonard's Church.

This sweet chestnut tree, at least 1,100 years old, has a huge, twisted main trunk and branches that have touched the ground and rooted, creating a mini-woodland.

Tortworth Estate Shop

Box Walk, Tortworth, Wotton-under-Edge
01454 261633
Mon-Sat: 9am-5.30pm, closed B/H's

Farm shop with locally produced foods.

Wotton Farm Shop

Gloucester Row, Wotton-under-Edge, GL12 7DY
01453 521546
www.wottonfarmshop.co.uk
Apr-Dec: Mon-Sat 9am-4.30pm, Sun 10am-1pm

Farm shop and pick-your-own. New facilities include a farm kitchen for take-away home-cooked food, picnic and play area.

GLOUCESTER

Gloucester Tourist Information

28 Southgate St, Gloucester, GL1 2DP
01452 396 572
www.gloucester.gov.uk/tourism
Mon-Sat: 10am-5pm, Jul/Aug: Sun 11am-3pm

There is also a tourist information point at the National Waterways Museum, see below.

Gloucester Folk Museum

99-103 Westgate St, Gloucester, GL1 2PG
01452 396 868
www.gloucester.gov.uk
Tue-Sat 10am-5pm
Admission free

One of the earliest folk museums in the country. It chronicles local history, crafts and trades in the city dating back to 1500 to the present day. There is an ironmonger's shop, wheelwright and carpenter's workshop.

The portal ICT gallery has quizzes for all ages. Free half-term and holiday activities, and free kids club Sat 11-3pm.

National Waterways Museum

Llanthony Warehouse, Gloucester Docks, GL1 2EH
01452 318200
www.nwm.org.uk
Daily 10am-5pm
£5.95 adult, £4.75 child, £17.50 family
M5 J12 follow brown tourist signs to Historic Docks

This award-winning museum is housed in a listed Victorian warehouse within the historic Gloucester Docks. Exhibits range from touch-screen computers to interactive pulleys to portray the history of canals and rivers in a hands-on way. Outside, you can watch a blacksmith at work or board historic boats.

Queen Boadicea II

From Easter to Oct: 12pm-4pm
£4.50 adult, £3.50 child

This Dunkirk little ship makes 45-minute trips along the canal.

Nature in Art

Wallsworth Hall, Main A38 Twigworth, GL2 9PA
0845 4500 233
www.nature-in-art.org.uk
Tue-Sun & B/Hs 10am-5pm
£3.60 adult, £3 child
M5 J11A, take A417 and A40 to A38 north.
Brown/green sign at entrance

This museum is full of art inspired by nature. Sculptures, tapestries, ceramics and paintings. Feb-Nov, visiting artists can be seen demonstrating skills ranging from oil painting to chainsaw sculpting. There is an activity room and activities takes place during school holidays, book in advance.

CHELTENHAM

Cheltenham Tourist Information

77 Promenade, Cheltenham, GL50 1PP
01242 522878
www.visitcheltenham.info
Mon-Sat 9.30am-5.15pm, Wed 10am,
B/Hs 9.30am-1.30pm

Cheltenham Art Gallery and Museum

Clarence St, Cheltenham, GL50 3JT
01242 237431
www.cheltenhammuseum.org.uk
Mon-Sat 10am-5.20pm, closed Sun & B/Hs
Admission free

The collections relate to the Arts and Crafts Movement with fine examples of furniture, silver, jewellery, ceramics and textiles. Other displays include oriental art, a history of Cheltenham, sparkling costume accessories, archaeology and natural history.

Sandford Parks Lido

Keynsham Rd, Cheltenham, GL53 7PU
01242 524430
www.sandfordparkslido.org.uk
Mid Apr-Sep: daily 11am-7.30pm
£3 adult, £4.20 family (1+1), £6.80 (1+2),
£8.20 (2+2)
M5 J11, A40 to Cheltenham then follow tourist signs.
It's next door to Gen. Hospital

Large heated outdoor pool set in landscaped gardens with spacious terraces for sunbathing and a café. Table tennis and basketball.

CHEPSTOW

Chepstow Racecourse

Chepstow, Monmouthshire, NP16 6BE
01291 622260
www.chepstow-racecourse.co.uk
On the A466 Chepstow to Monmouth road.

A day at the races is a great family day out. At Chepstow, there are some 29 meets a year, both with flat racing and jumps. All children under 16yrs are admitted free when accompanied by a paying adult and some race days are designated family days with extra entertainment laid on. However, do note, there is a dress code — no football or rugby shorts, ripped jeans, shorts or trainers.

THE FOREST OF DEAN

The Forest of Dean is one of the few remaining ancient oak forests. It covers 35 square miles between the Rivers Wye and Severn. From Bristol, it's less than an hour's drive, unfortunately public transport is not at its best in the area. The forest has a huge amount to offer young people, such as cycling, walking, orienteering, bird watching, archery, canoeing and climbing.

Coleford Tourist Information Centre

High St, Coleford, GL16 8HG
01594 812388
www.forestofdean.gov.uk
Mon-Sat 10am-5pm, some seasonal variations

Information on seasonal activities, places to stay, outdoor pursuits, walks and llama trekking!

Forest of Dean Forestry Commission

Bank House, Bank St, Coleford, GL16 8BA
01594 833057
www.forestry.gov.uk
Mon-Thu 8.30am-5pm, Fri 8.30am-4pm

Many useful leaflets and information on special events such as deer and bird spotting.

Outdoor pursuits in the Forest of Dean

There are all sorts of outdoor pursuits in the area, see pg 15-21

Cycling in the Forest of Dean

A great place to cycle with a 10-mile circular forest track, cycle hire available, see pg 174.

Beechenhurst Lodge

Speech House Hill, Near Coleford, GL16 7EG
01594 827357
www.beechenhurstlodge.co.uk
Daily 10am-6pm, winter 10am-dusk, Jan w/e's only
B4226 between Coleford and Cinderford

This is a good base to start familiarising yourself with the forest. There's plenty of parking (£2/day) and it's the starting point for The Sculpture Trail as well as a good place to pick up the circular 10-mile family cycle route. Next to the information centre, there is a café, picnic and BBQ area.

Forest of Dean Sculpture Trail

01594 833057
www.forestofdean-sculpture.org.uk
Open daily dawn-dusk
Admission free
B4226 between Cinderford and Coleford, follow brown tourist signs

This walk features sculptures, inspired by the forest, located along a trail through beautiful woodland. It has a magical feel with wonderful views. The route is about 3½ miles long, a shorter loop is possible.

Clearwell Caves

Near Coleford, Royal Forest of Dean, GL16 8JR
01594 832535
www.clearwellcaves.com
Feb-Oct & Dec: daily 10am-5pm
£4.50 adult, £2.80 child, £12.90 family,
Christmas special: £5.50 adult/child inc. gift for U14s
From Coleford take B4228 south for 1 mile, turn right at Lambsquay Hotel

These natural caves have had iron ore mined from them for thousands of years (by children as young as 6yrs). Nine caverns are open to the public and miners' tools and equipment are displayed. See website for special events.

Dean Heritage Centre

Soudley, Cinderford, Gloucestershire, GL14 2UB
01594 824024/822170
www.deanheritagemuseum.com
Daily 10am-5.30pm, 4pm winter
£4.50 adult, £2.50 child, £13 family (2+4)
B4227 between Blakeney and Cinderford

Did you know that during the Roman occupation, the Forest of Dean was a major industrial region? Learn more about its rich history, along with information on the geology, wildlife and social history of the area.

In the grounds there is a reconstructed Victorian foresters cottage with Gloucester Old Spot pig and chickens. Adventure playground with a hurdle maze and a BBQ area. There are accessible woodland walks and a café with deck overlooking the millpond.

Hopewell Colliery Museum

Cannop Hill, Coleford
01594 810706
www.hopewellcoalmine.co.uk
Mar-Oct: daily 10am-4pm, Dec: Santa Specials
Underground tours £3.50 adult, £2.50 child
On B4226 Cinderford to Coleford road, a mile west of Beechenhurst Lodge

Local miners will take you underground to show you around the old mine workings (45min trip). The descent into the mine is steep (as is the exit) but the route through it is level (just over ½ mile). Practical footwear and warm clothing recommended. There's a tea room, picnic and play area.

WYE RIVER

Symonds Yat Rock

Log Cabin Symonds Yat, Near Coleford
01594 833057
www.forestry.gov.uk
Log cabin: Mar-Oct 9.30am-dusk
Nov-Feb: limited opening
Take B4432 north of Coleford

Fantastic viewpoint high above the River Wye. Log cabin with snack bar, information, souvenirs and picnic area. Waymarked walks start from here. A pair of peregrine falcons nest on the nearby cliffs and from mid-April to August, staff from the RSPB (see below) can tell you all about the fastest birds in the world and hopefully help spot them with telescopes (10am-6pm). If you're walking, there are two useful hand ferries (seasonal) which run from The Olde Ferrie Inne on the west bank of the Wye to the base of the Rock, and from the Saracen's Head Inn on the east bank.

Royal Society for the Protection of Birds

The Puffins, New Rd, Parkend, Lydney, GL15 4JA
01594 562852
www.rspb.org.uk

The RSPB organises events in and around the Forest of Dean. These included badger watching, pond-dipping, evening bat walks and making nest boxes and bird feeders. They'll help you spot peregrine falcons at Symonds Yat rock (see above). You can also visit their two nature reserves at Nagshead and Highnam Woods, phone for details.

King Fisher Cruises

Symonds Yat East
01600 891063

If you'd like to see the area from the water but don't fancy paddling yourself along, take a 35 minute river trip

CARDIFF

45 minutes from Bristol Parkway to Cardiff Central, short walk to centre

Cardiff has undergone a complete transformation over the past 20 years. New landmarks such as Cardiff Bay, the Millennium Stadium and modern shopping centres alongside Victorian arcades make it a pleasant city to visit. If you're hoping to combine a visit to the city centre and Bay area, the Bay Xpress runs every 15 minutes between Cardiff Central station and the Bay. The Cardiff festival takes place in mid July with theatre, music and fairground entertainment. There is usually an outdoor ice rink outside City Hall during December and January.

CITY CENTRE ATTRACTIONS

Cardiff Gateway Visitor Centre

The Old Library, The Hayes, Cardiff, CF10 1ES
029 2022 7281
www.visitcardiff.info
Mon-Sat 9.30am-6pm, Sun 10am-4pm

Cardiff Open Top Bus Tour

01708 866000
www.citysightseeing.co.uk
Apr-Oct: Daily from 10am-4pm
Nov-Dec: Sat-Sun 10.30am-3.30pm
£7.50 adult, £3 child (5-15), £18 family (2+2)

Good for getting an idea of the layout of the main attractions, from the Millennium Stadium to the new Bay area with a pre-recorded commentary. Tickets, valid for 24 hours, can be bought from the driver, tourist info or online. Tour starts at Cardiff Castle and lasts about 50 minutes; local fares available.

Cardiff Castle

Castle St, Cardiff, CF10 3RB
029 2087 8100
www.cardiffcastle.com
Mar-Oct: daily 9.30am-6pm, Nov-Feb: 9.30am-5pm
£6.80 adult, £4.20 child, £22 family (2+3 or 1+4)

[WC] [⚡] [🏛] [⛲]

Situated in the town centre, Cardiff Castle spans a 2000 year history from its Roman remains, to the Norman keep and its opulent Victorian interior. Guided tours start at 10am and last 50 minutes. Large green for picnicking; peacocks and ducks wander freely.

Millennium Stadium

029 2082 2228
www.millenniumstadium.com
Mon-Sat 10am-5pm, Sun & B/Hs 10am-4pm.
Restaurant open event days only.
£5.50 adult, £3 child, £17 family (2+3)

[WC] [🏛] [⚡] [♿] [&]

All sports fans will enjoy a tour of this huge stadium and even the less sporty members of the family can't fail to be impressed by the largest retractable roof in Europe! The tour includes a chance to run down the players tunnel and sit in the Royal Box. Pre-booking advisable, no tours on match days.

National Museum and Gallery

Cathays Park, Cardiff, CF10 3NP
029 2039 7951
www.nmgw.ac.uk
Tues-Sun 10am-5pm & B/Hs
Admission free
Follow signs to Cardiff city centre, nr to University

[P] [WC] [🏛] [⚡] [♿] [&]

Superb range of art (best collection of Impressionists in Europe outside Paris), natural history and science. Exhibitions on the evolution of Wales, with life size dinosaurs and Ice Age creatures. The Glanely Gallery is an interactive area enabling you to touch items not normally on display.

CARDIFF BAY

Car Park: Stuart St, opposite Techniquest
From Central Station: Bay Xpress bus service

Cardiff was once the busiest coal exporting port in the world. The regeneration of 2,700 acres of docklands, and the construction of the barrage has created a new Cardiff Bay with its cultural attractions, restaurants, shops and summer Harbour Festival.

Mermaid Quay

029 2048 0077
A shopping and leisure complex.

Roald Dahl Plass

A large oval space used for outdoor events and performances. It's all pedestrianised.

The Norwegian Church Arts Centre

029 2045 4899
Originally built in 1868 as a mission for Scandinavian seamen, this has been restored as an arts and music centre with café. Roald Dahl was baptised here. Beyond here is:

The Goleulong 2000 Lightship

029 2048 7609
www.lightship2000.org.uk
Daily Mon-Sat 10am-5pm, Sun 2-5pm
Free
Originally positioned off the Gower coast to warn off ships. Explore the engine room, light tower and cabins and there's a café.

Cardiff Bay Visitor Centre

The Tube, Harbour Drive, Cardiff Bay, CF10 4PA
029 2046 3833
www.visitcardiff.info
Daily 9am-5pm summer, 10am-5pm winter
10 min walk for Mermaid Quay along waterfront

[P] [WC] [🏛] [⚡] [⛲] [♿] [&]

Recognisable award winning tubular design.

Cardiff Bay Barrage

Harbour Authority: 029 2087 7900
Open daily, summer closes 7pm, winter 4pm

One of the most ambitious engineering projects in Europe. The barrage, across the bay entrance is over 1km long. It provides a 500 acre freshwater lake. Visiting the barrage with its fish pass (allowing fish access from the sea to the rivers to spawn) is fascinating. Penarth Marina is on the other side.

Cardiff Barrage Road Train

029 2051 2729
www.cardiffroadtrain.com
April-Oct: daily 11am-5pm frm Stuart St.
Return ticket: £3 adult, £2 child
Leaves from behind Techniquest

It takes 20 minutes to reach the Barrage.

Cardiff Bay Water Bus

07940 42409
www.cardiffcats.com
Easter-Oct: daily 10.30am-6pm
Nov- Easter: W/ends only but daily in school hols
Summer return trip: £4 adult, £2 child.
Winter: £2 adult, £2 child, family discount available.

Cardiff Cats offer 40-minute cruises of the Bay with the opportunity to land at the Barrage, leaving from Mermaid Quay. Tickets can be bought from the quay information points.

Cardiff Bay Cruises

029 2047 2004
www.cardiffbaycruises.com
Seasonal cruises, phone for times
1hr cruise: £6 adult, £3 child.
½ hour cruise: £3 adult, £1.50 child

Cruise up the Taff, along the River Ely or around the Bay. Boats, including a restaurant boat, leave from the Pierhead building.

Bay Island Voyages

01446 420692
www.bayisland.co.uk
Run all year dependent on weather and demand
Fast Bay Cruise: £8 adult, £5 child U16s
Coastal blast: £15 adult, £10 child

Thrill seekers need look no further than a high speed trip on the Celtic Ranger travelling at up to 60mph! A 30-minute Fast Bay Cruise tends to be calmer. For those with strong sea-legs there are longer tours which go up the coast or around Flat Holm and Steep Holm.

Cardiff Bay Tours

029 2070 7882
www.cardiffbaytours.com
Easter-Oct: daily 10am-4pm
£4 adult, £1.50 child

Informative 1½ hour walking tours of the Bay starting at the Tube Visitors Centre and ending at St Davids Hotel.

Techniquest

Stuart St, Cardiff, CF10 5BW
029 2047 5475
www.techniquest.org
Mon-Fri 9.30am-4.30pm, Sat-Sun and B/Hols
10.30am-5pm, School Hols 9.30am-5pm.
£6.90 adult, £4.80 child, £20 family (2+3)

On the waterfront, this large Science Discovery Centre has over 150 hands-on exhibits and a Planetarium.

Craft in the Bay

The Flourish, Lloyd George Ave, Cardiff, CF10
029 2049 1136
www.makersguildinwales.org.uk
Daily 10.30am-5.30pm
Free admission
Five mins' from Mermaid Quay, Bay Xpress bus stop

Retail gallery set in old maritime warehouse displaying crafts made by members of the Makers Guild in Wales.

BEYOND THE CENTRE

St Fagan's Museum

St Fagans, Cardiff, CF5 6XB
029 2057 3500
www.nmgw.ac.uk
Daily 10am-5pm
Admission free
M4 J33, follow tourist signs, bus from city centre

A village chronicling the history of Wales. A whole day is needed to see everything. Over 40 buildings have been transported here from all over Wales and rebuilt in attractive parkland. They give a fascinating insight into how people lived, worked and spent their leisure time over the past 500 years. There is a row of ironworker's houses each furnished from a different decade, a Victorian classroom and a pottery where you can throw a pot. There is a large indoor museum, and a variety of places to eat.

WEST COUNTRY ATTRACTIONS

This section of the chapter lists attractions under themed headings. Where possible, we've provided grid references, see map on pg 90.

CASTLES

Berkeley Castle & Butterfly Farm

Berkeley, Gloucestershire, GL13 9BQ
01453 810332
www.berkeley-castle.com
Apr-Sep: Tue-Sat & B/H's 11am-4pm, Sun 2pm-5pm
Oct: Sun only, Nov-Apr: closed
£7.50 adult, £4.50 child
Garden only (avail Tue-Fri) £4 adult, £2 child
On A38 between Bristol and Gloucester.
See map on pg 90, ref D1

Twenty four generations of the Berkeley family have lived here since 1153 in what is England's oldest inhabited castle. It has been transformed over the years from a Norman fortress to a stately home full of paintings and treasures. Lawns and terraced gardens surround the castle. Admission price includes an optional 1-hour guided tour plus entry to the Butterfly Farm (Apr-Sep).

Caerphilly Castle

Castle St, Caerphilly, CF83 1JD
029 2088 3143
www.cadw.wales.gov.uk
Daily 9.30am-5pm, seasonal variations
£3 adult, £2.50 child, £8.50 family (2+3)
M4 J28 direction 'Risca' then A468 to Caerphilly
See map on pg 90, ref A2

P WC ♨ 🚻 🚌 ♿

This huge castle built in the 13th century is the second biggest in Britain after Windsor. It's a classic castle with high towers, moats, banqueting hall, working replica siege-engines and a leaning tower to make the people of Pisa green with envy! Excellent re-enactment days through spring and summer.

Caldicot Castle and Country Park

Church Rd, Caldicot, Monmouthshire, NP 26 4HU
01291 420241
www.caldicotcastle.co.uk
Mar-Oct: daily 11am-5pm
Castle: £3.50 adult, £2 child, £10 family (2+3)
Admissions to Country Park: free
M4 to M48 J2 for Chepstow then A48 twd Newport then B4245, follow signs
See map on pg 90, ref C2

P WC ♨ ✗ ♨ 🚻 🚌 ♿

Although founded during Norman times, the castle was restored in the Victorian period and inhabited until the 1960s. Adult and children's audio guide and discovery sheets. The country park has walking trails and a wildlife pond with dipping platform. There is an orienteering course in the grounds. The castle hosts events and re-enactments.

Castell Coch

Tongwynlais, Cardiff, CF15 7JS
029 2081 0101
www.cadw.wales.gov.uk
Apr-Oct: daily 9.30am-5pm, summer 9.30am-6pm
Nov-Mar: Mon-Sat 9.30am-4pm, Sun 11am-4pm
Jan-Feb: closed
£3 adult, £2.50 child, £8.50 family (2+3)
M4 J32, take A470 north, follow signs

P WC ✗ ♨ 🚻

Hidden in woodland, this fairytale castle, complete with conical roofed towers, working portcullis and drawbridge, looks convincingly medieval. It was, however, built in the late 19th century. The inside remains faithful to the Victorian era being richly furnished and decorated. Pick up a worksheet or audio guide from the shop.

Chepstow Castle

Bridge St, Chepstow, Monmouthshire, NP16 5EY
01291 624065
www.cadw.wales.gov.uk
Mar-Oct: daily 9.30am-5pm, summer 6pm
Nov-Mar: Mon-Sat 9.30am-4pm, Sun 11am-4pm
£3 adult, £2 child, £8.50 family (2+3)
M4 J21 to M48 J2, then A466 and follow signs
See map on pg 90, ref C2

P ♨ 🚌

One of Britain's first stone-built strongholds. Building started not long after the Battle of Hastings in 1066 and the castle was significantly extended over the following centuries. Today, the well-preserved ruins perch above the River Wye offering an insight into life in a Norman castle.

Farleigh Hungerford Castle

Farleigh Hungerford, Nr. Bath, BA2 7RS
01225 754 026
www.english-heritage.org.uk/farleighhungerford
Apr-Sep: daily 10am-5pm
Oct-Mar: Sun only, 10am-4pm
£3.30 adult, £1.70 child
3½ miles west of Trowbridge on A366
See map on pg 90, ref E5

P WC ♨ 🚻

Ruins of a 14th century castle and chapel with museum. Audio guide and events, including exhibitions, medieval pageants.

Sudeley Castle

Winchcombe, Cheltenham, GL54 5JD
01242 602308
www.sudeleycastle.co.uk
Mar-Oct: phone for details
Castle & Gardens: £7.20 adult, £4.20 child
£20.80 family (2+2), seasonal variations
M5 J9 take A46 then B4077 then to Winchcombe

P WC ♨ ✗ ♨ 🚻

The castle can boast many royal visitors, including Anne Boleyn, Queen Elizabeth I and Henry VIII. The Six Wives at Sudeley exhibition is popular with those needing material for a Tudor project. See photo.

STATELY HOMES

Bowood House & Gardens

Derry Hill, Calne, Wiltshire, SN11 0L2
01249 812102
www.bowood.org
Apr-Oct: daily 11am-6pm
£7.50 adult, £5 child (5-15yrs)
£3.80 child (2-4yrs), £22.50 family (2+2)
Off A4, Derry Hill, between Calne & Chippenham

Capability Brown designed the beautiful park in which Bowood stands. The huge grounds include a lake, waterfall, cave, Doric temple and ample space for games and picnics. There is a woodland garden of azaleas and rhododendrons (separate entrance off the A342), open for six weeks during the flowering season (May & June).

Bowood also has a superb outdoor adventure playground for U12s with high level rope-walks, giant slides, shutes and trampolines.

NATIONAL TRUST PROPERTIES

National Trust properties are becoming increasingly family friendly. There are often, trails, quiz sheets and activities on offer for older children. Around Bristol, we're spoilt for choice, the latest Trust acquisition being Tyntesfield.

The four listed below are all over an hour's journey from Bristol, but well worth a day trip:

Stourhead, Wiltshire (01747 841152) Superb landscaped garden and house, with temples and mature woodland set around large lake.

Avebury, Wiltshire (01672 539250) A huge megalithic stone circle encompassing part of the village of Avebury.

Dunster Castle, Somerset (01643 821314) Impressive castle atop a wooded hill set in attractive gardens.

Hidcote Manor Garden, Gloucestershire (01386 438333). A gorgeous garden designed as a series of outdoor rooms.

The National Trust
PO Box 39, Warrington, WA5 7WD
0870 458 4000
01985 843600 (Wessex branch)
www.nationaltrust.org.uk
Details of all the Trust's properties can be found on the website. Becoming a member of the National Trust can be cost effective if you plan to visit several properties during the year.

Clevedon Court

Tickenham Rd, Clevedon, N. Somerset, BS21 6QU
01275 872257
www.nationaltrust.org.uk
Apr-Sep: Wed/Thu/Sun & B/Hs 2pm-5pm
£5 adult, £2.50 child
B3130 1½ mile east of Clevedon
See map on pg 90, ref B3

This 14th-century manor house has been home to the Elton family since 1709. Eltonware pots and vases and a collection of Nailsea glass are on display. Attractive terraced garden.

Dyrham Park

Dyrham, nr. Chippenham, Gloucestershire, SN14 8ER
0117 937 2501
www.nationaltrust.org.uk
Park: daily 11am-5.30pm
House & Garden: Mar-Oct Fri-Tue 12pm-4pm
Phone for winter opening times
Garden and house: £9 adult, £4.50 child,
£22.50 family (2+3)
Garden and Park: £3.50 adult, £1.80 child,
£8 family (2+3)
M4 J18, take A46 towards Bath for 2 miles
See map on pg 90, ref E3

House and gardens built at the turn of
the 18th century, with most of the original
furnishings. Family activity pack and children's
guidebook available. Spacious grounds and
deer park. See photo top right.

King John's Hunting Lodge

The Square, Axbridge, Somerset, BS26 2AP
01934 732012
www.nationaltrust.org.uk
Daily Apr-Sept 1pm-4pm
Oct-Mar 1st Sat of mth
(coincides with Farmers' Market)
Free (donations welcome), not essential
See map on pg 90, ref B5

Immaculately restored Early Tudor wool-
merchant's house, home to a local history
museum run by Axbridge and District Museum
Trust. Upper floors accessed via steep spiral
staircases. Occasional walking tours of the
historic town of Axbridge start here.

Lacock Abbey, Fox Talbot Museum & Village

Lacock, Nr Chippenham, Wiltshire, SN15 2LG
01249 730459
www.nationaltrust.org.uk/lacock
Museum, cloisters and garden:
Mar-Oct daily 11am-5.30pm
Abbey: Mar-Oct Wed-Mon 1pm-5.30pm
Museum (only) open winter w/e's, 11am-4pm
Abbey, museum, cloisters and garden:
£7.40 adult, £3.70 child, £18.90 family (2+3)
M4 J17, take A350, 3 miles S of Chippenham

The Abbey was founded in 1232 as a
nunnery and transformed into a family home
in the 16th century. Children's quiz and
spacious grounds to explore. The Museum

of Photography commemorates the life of
William Henry Fox Talbot who made the
earliest known photographic negative. The
upper gallery has changing exhibitions. The
medieval village with its many lime washed
half-timbered houses has been used as a
location for several period dramas such as
Pride and Prejudice. The Abbey was also used
to film parts of the Harry Potter films. See
photo top left.

Tyntesfield

Wraxall, North Somerset, BS48 1NT
Gardens Mid Mar-Oct
House Mid Apr-Oct Mon, Wed, Sat & Sun:
10am-4pm, Gardens 5.30pm
House, chapel and gardens: £9 adult, £4.50 child,
£22.50 family (2+3)
Gardens only: £4.50 adult, £2.25 child, £11.25 family
7 miles SW of Bristol on B3128
See map on pg 90, ref C3

Spectacular Victorian Gothic-Revival country
house and 500-acre estate, recently acquired
by the National Trust. Situated on a ridge
overlooking the beautiful Yeo Valley, the
mansion bristles with towers and turrets and
contains an unrivalled collection of Victorian
decorative arts. Still in the early stages of
development, facilities on the site are limited.
Timed tickets in operation (no guaranteed
entry on very busy days). There's a private
chapel, quiz trail, formal gardens and a
working walled kitchen garden. If you forget
your picnic, there is a kiosk for hot drinks and
sandwiches.

ROMAN BRITAIN

As well as the Roman Baths, see Bath section, there are several other Roman sites near Bristol worth a visit. Always useful for bringing school studies to life!

Chedworth Roman Villa

Yanworth, Near Cheltenham, Glos, GL54 3LJ
01242 890256
www.nationaltrust.org.uk
Mar-Nov: Tue-Sun & B/Hs 11am-4pm
Summer 10am-5pm
£5.50 adult, £3 child, £14.50 family (2+3)
M5 J11A take A417 east, A436 then right via
Withington, follow signs

P WC ♿ ⛲ ♿

Owned by the National Trust, this is one of the best examples of a Roman Villa in England. The remains of this substantial dwelling indicate that it would have been inhabited by a very wealthy family. There are two well-preserved bathhouses, hypocausts demonstrating how the Roman invention of under-floor heating worked, beautiful mosaics, a latrine, and a museum housing objects from the villa. Entertaining audio guide and holiday activities. If you can, visit on a Living History Day when you can join in with demonstrations of day-to-day Roman life. There are good walks in Chedworth Woods and along the disused railway track.

National Roman Legion Museum

High St, Caerleon, Gwent, NP18 1AE
01633 423134
www.nmgw.ac.uk
Museum: Mon-Sat 10am-5pm, Sun 2pm-5pm
Fortress baths: Mon-Sat 9.30am-5pm
Free admission
Museum, Barracks and Amphitheatre: £2.90 adult,
£2.50 child, £8.30 family (2+3)
M4 J24 follow signs to Caerleon and Museum
See map on pg 90, ref B2

WC ♿ ♿

Nearly 2000 years ago, the Romans established a fortress at Caerleon. In the museum you can discover how the Roman soldiers lived, fought, and worshipped. At weekends and during the holidays, a barrack room can be visited where you can try on replica suits of armour. See the remains of the Fortress Baths, with video, sound and light displays. A short walk from the museum is Britain's best example of a Roman Amphitheatre where gladiators battled to the death. Impressive re-enactments are held here every June (ring 01633 430041).

Caerwent

10 miles from Caerleon on the A48 or from Bristol
M4 then M48 J2
See map on pg 90, ref B2
Having visited the museum at Caerleon, you could stop off at Caerwent where the remains of shops, a courtyard house, temple and forum can be seen. In the 4th century, when the Romans were struggling to retain power, a high wall was built around the town, most of which still stands today.

WILDLIFE

Avon Wildlife Trust

32 Jacobs Well Rd, Bristol, BS8 1DR
0117 917 7270
www.avonwildlifetrust.org.uk

This charity is dedicated to the promoting and protecting of wildlife. It has two centres at Folly Farm in the Chew Valley and Willsbridge Mill in Keynsham. It offers activities, walks and events in the holidays. See Walks, pg 68.

Longleat

Nr Warminster, Wiltshire, BA12 7NW
01985 844 400
www.longleat.co.uk
Safari Park: Apr-Nov daily 10am-4pm
w/e's, B/Hs & summer hols 10am-5pm
House opening/tours phone or check website
Passport ticket: £19 adult, £15 child,
(available for one season, online booking available)
A37 (Wells Road) south to Farrington Gurney, left
onto A362, through Frome and follow brown signs

Longleat comprises a stately home, safari park and other attractions. Drive through the safari park (soft top cars not permitted) and see giraffes, zebras, tigers and lions in their enclosures. The monkey jungle is optional as they will clamber on your car, so it's not recommended for the car proud. For some reason, Mondeo's seem to come off particularly badly! (Safari bus available).

Other attractions include the Butterfly Garden, King Arthur's Mirror Maze, Blue Peter maze, adventure playground and a safari boat trip.

The National Birds of Prey Centre

Newent, Gloucestershire, GL18 1JJ
0870 990 1992
www.nbpc.co.uk
Feb-Oct: daily 10.30am-5.30pm
£8 adult, £5.50 child, £22 family (2+2)
M5 J11a, A40 Ross-on-Wye, B4215 to Newent

One of the most significant collections of birds of prey in the UK. Over 60 species and flying displays three times daily.

Tropiquaria

Washford Cross, Watchet, West Somerset, TA23 0QB
01984 640 688
www.tropiquaria.co.uk
Apr-mid Sep: daily 10am-6pm,
Mid Sep-Oct: 11am-5pm
Nov-Mar: w/e's & sch hols only
£6.95 adult, £5.95 child, £24.95 family (2+2)
M5 J23, take A39 twds Minehead. It's between Williton and Washford

Great aquarium housed in the old BBC transmitting station. Outside there are lemurs, wallabies and chipmunks. Other attractions include: The Shadowstring Puppet Theatre, Wireless in the West Museum (a history of broadcasting) and an adventure playground.

WWT Slimbridge

The Wildfowl and Wetlands Centre, Slimbridge, GL2
0870 334 4000
www.wwt.org.uk
Daily 9.30am-5.30pm, winter 9.30am-5pm
£6.75 adult, £4 child, £18.50 family (2+2)
M5 Jct 13 or 14, follow brown tourist signs
See map on pg 90, ref E1

The chance to get close to and feed, exotic, rare and endangered water birds. You can view from hides and towers. Humming birds can be seen in the Tropical House. The visitor centre includes the Hanson Discovery Centre, a cinema and views over the River Severn.

Cotswold Wildlife Park

See pg 100

Prinknash Bird and Park

See pg 100

FARMS

These are probably of more interest to our younger readers, but if you are into animals, check out these great farms and parks.

Avon Valley Country Park

Pixash Lane, Bath Rd, Keynsham, BS31 1TS
0117 986 4929
See map on pg 90, ref D4

See listing in Out & About in Bristol, pg 70.

Court Farm Country Park

Wolvershill Rd, Banwell, Weston-super-Mare, BS29
01934 822 383
www.courtfarmcountrypark.co.uk
Mar-Nov: daily 10am-5.30pm, winter: 10am-4.30pm
£4.95 adult, £3.75 child, £16 family (2+2),
ATV rides: £2 adult, £1.50 child
Season ticket: £24 adult, £18 child
M5 J21 the follow brown tourist signs
See map on pg 90, ref A4

A working farm with massive outdoor Adventure Land play area with aerial skyway and trampolines. Also a white knuckle ATV ride for the brave at heart! Maize maze from mid July to the end of September.

Noah's Ark Zoo Farm

Failand Rd, Wraxall, Bristol, BS48 1PG
01275 852606
www.noahsarkzoofarm.co.uk
Feb-Oct: Tue-Sat, B/Hs 10.30am-5pm
Open on Mon sch hols
£8 adult, £6 child, £25 family (2+2) or £23 (1+3)
Annual: £40 adult, £30 child, £125 family (2+2) or £115 (1+3)
Bristol to Clevedon road via Failand (B3128).
Or M5 J20. Follow brown tourist signs.
See map on pg 90, ref C3

P WC 🛗 ✗ 🚻 🚗 ♿

There are 80 kinds of animal, from chicks to rhinos. There is indoor and outdoor play equipment and adventure trails. The theme of this farm (Noah's Ark and the creationist view of evolution) is explored in exhibitions. There is an indoor maze; a lookout tower and the longest hedge maze in the world.

Norwood Farm

Bath Rd, Norton St Philip, Bath, BA2 7LP
01373 834356
www.norwoodfarm.co.uk
Apr-Sep: daily 10.30am-5.30am
£5 adult, £3.50 child
Annual: £20 adult, £14 child
B3110 between Bath and Frome.
Hourly bus service (No 267) from Bath
See map on pg 90, ref E5

P WC 🛗 ✗ 🚻 🚗 🚌 ♿

This environmentally-aware working farm is the only Organic Rare Breeds Centre in the region. The farm opens in spring with the lambing of 12 native breeds. There are walks, gardens to picnic in and a new organic veg and plant centre.

Cattle Country Adventure Park

Berkeley Heath Farm, Berkeley, GL13 9EW
01453 810 510
www.cattlecountry.co.uk
Easter-Sep: Sat-Sun 10am-5pm, daily sch hols
Some winter openings, call for details
£5-£6.50 adult/child, prices seasonal
M5 J14 take A38 and follow brown tourist signs.
See map on pg 90, ref D1

P 🛗 ✗ 🚻 🚗 ♿

This is a good family day out for U15s. Lots of indoor and outdoor play equipment where parents can join in too. A farm trail passes a willow maze and a herd of American bison.

SEVERN ADVENTURES

The Severn Estuary has the second highest tidal range in the world — it can be as much as 50 feet. This contributes to the great natural spectacle of the Severn Bore, details below. The estuary itself can be explored by steamships Waverley and Balmoral, see Transport chapter. See also Bay Island Voyage, Cardiff Bay, pg 109.

The isalnds of Flat Holm and Steep Holm are wildlife havens and well worth visiting.

Severn Bridges Visitor Centre

Shaft Rd, Off Green Lane, Severn Beach, BS35 4HW
01454 633511
www.onbridges.com
Easter-Oct: Sat,Sun & B/Hs 11am-4pm, pre-booked group winter visits
£1 adults, 75p child
M5 J17 take B4055 through Pilning. Continue straight on. At mini-r'about follow Green Lane over M49. Right at lights into Shaft Rd.
See map on pg 90, ref C3

P WC ✗ 🚻

Exhibition showing history of the River Severn crossing and the construction of the two road bridges. Although there's no pedestrian access to the new Severn Crossing you can walk or cycle across the old bridge away from the traffic (park at Aust Services off J1 M48).

The Severn Bore

www.severn-bore.co.uk

The Severn Bore is a large surge wave in the estuary of the River Severn which makes a truly spectacular sight at its best. It occurs because of the shape of the estuary — it narrows from 5 miles wide at Avonmouth, to less than 100 yards wide by Minsterworth. As the water is funnelled into an increasingly narrow channel, a large wave is formed. This occurs at least once during most months of the year, but the Bore is largest around equinoxes. Surfing the Bore has become a competitive sport. See website for timetable and viewing points. Get there early, as the Bore can arrive up to half an hour either side of the scheduled time.

Flat Holm Project

The Pier Head, Barry Docks, Barry, CF62 5QS
01446 747661
www.cardiff-info.com/flatholm
Trips run from end Mar-Oct, tide & weather
dependant
£13.75 adult, £6.75 child, £35 family (2+2)

A day trip to this tiny island in the Bristol
Channel gives you three hours on the island
and includes a guided walk. Since the Dark
Ages, the island has been used as a retreat
for monks, then as a sanctuary for Vikings,
Anglo Saxons, smugglers and cholera victims.
Fortified in Victorian times and WW2, it is now
a haven for wildlife. Take a picnic.

Steep Holm Nature Reserve

Knightstone Causeway, Marine Lake, BS22 8EA
01934 632307
Trips run Apr-Sept, tide & weather dependent
£20 adult, £10 child accompanied (5-16)
M5 J21, take A370 to seafront then to Knightstone
See map on pg 90, ref A4

The Kenneth Allsop Memorial Trust organise
visits to Steep Holm from Weston-super-Mare.
There are great views of the Severn Bridges
and as far down the coast as North Devon.
There is a variety of wildlife including muntjac
deer, cormorants and gulls. In summer, you
may see grey seals fishing. Visitors need to be
reasonably fit as there is no landing stage on
the island and the paths are steep. You should
have about six hours on the island. Take a
torch to explore underground ammunition
stores, binoculars, camera and a picnic.

Oldbury Power Station Visitor Centre

Oldbury-on-Severn, South Glos, BS35 1RQ
01454 893500
Mar-Oct: daily 10am-4pm, pre-booked winter visits
Admission free
A38 north, take B4061 through Thornbury, then left
to Oldbury-on-Severn and follow signs
See map on pg 90, ref D2

Find out how a nuclear power station works
with interactive displays and videos.

BOAT TRIPS

Bristol Queen

01934 613 828
www.bristolqueen.com
Apr-Oct
From £8 adult, £4 U14
See map on pg 90, ref A4

Sailings from Knightstone Harbour, Weston-
super-Mare and occasionally from Portishead.
Most popular cruises are 1hr trip from
Weston along the Brean Down peninsula.
Also 2hr cruises around both Holm Islands,
and occasional trips to Cardiff Bay and Steep
Holm. Facilities: snack shop, high weather
viewing deck, toilets and commentary.

Canal Boat Trips on MV Barbara McLellan

Wharf Cottage, 15 Frome Rd, Bradford-on-Avon
01225 868683
www.katrust.org
End Mar-Oct: w/e's & B/Hs & Wed pm
From £4.50 adult, £3.50 child, £13 family
See map on pg 90, ref E4

A relaxing way to see the canal is on this
comfortable narrowboat. Advance bookings
can be made at the Cottage Shop, except in
Aug when tickets can only be bought on the
day. Boat leaves from the cottage on Canal
Wharf, half a mile south of town centre.

Canal Narrow Boat Hire

If you've ever fancied taking a canal boat out
yourself for a day or more contact:

Sally Boats
01225 864923, www.sallyboats.ltd.uk
Operates out of Bradford-on-Avon.

Anglo-Welsh Waterway Holidays
0117 304 1122, www.anglo-welsh.co.uk
Bases in Bath, Bristol and Monkton Combe.

Wessex Narrow Boats
www.wessexboats.co.uk, 01225 765243
Located 3 miles from Bradford-on-Avon, at
Staverton Marina, day hire possible.

Bath Narrow Boats
Bathwick Hill, Bath
01225 447276, www.bath-narrowboats.co.uk

The Bath & Dundas Canal Co.

Brass Knocker Basin, Monkton Combe, Bath
01225 722292
www.bathcanal.com
Daily 8am-dusk, some seasonal variations
Electric boats from £59 per day,
Canadian canoes from £14 for 2hrs
Take A36 south of Bath, at Monkton Combe turn left
at lights on to B3108
See map on pg 90, ref E4

You can hire electric boats, canoes and even narrow boats for holidays or short breaks. There are no locks on the canal between Bradford-on-Avon and Bath.

The Lock Inn

48 Frome Rd, Bradford-on-Avon, Wiltshire, BA15 1LE
01225 868068
www.thelockinn.co.uk
Daily 9am-6pm
Canoe Hire: £20 up to 3 hours, £30 up to 9 hours
See map on pg 90, ref E4

You can hire canoes to paddle along the canal from The Lock Inn. It's easiest to go towards Bath as there are no locks to negotiate (canoes must be carried round) and there are plenty of pubs and tearooms on the way. Pre-booking is advisable. See Cycle Hire, pg 174.

Waverley & Balmoral

0845 130 4647
www.waverleyexcursions.co.uk
May-Sep, from £14 adult, child half price

Sailings from Clevedon Pier, Bristol and Weston-super-Mare (also from Minehead, Ilfracombe, Watchet, Sharpness and Bridgwater). Cruise in "Big Ship" style aboard the Waverley, the last sea-going paddle steamer in the world and the Balmoral, a traditional pleasure cruise ship. Cruises around Holm Islands and the coast of Wales. For details, contact Waverley Excursions or the Weston-super-Mare Tourist Information Centre, see pg 93.

To land on Steep Holm and Flat Holm see Severn adventures pg 116. To land on Lundy island see camping pg 210.

WHEELS & WINGS

Cotswold Motoring Museum and Toy Collection

The Old Mill, Bourton-on-the-Water, Glos, GL54 2BY
01451 821 255
www.cotswold-motor-museum.com
Feb-Oct: daily 10am-6pm
£3.50 adult, £2.45 child, £10.85 family (2+2)

Impressive car collection dating back to the 1920s, and lots of other transport memorabilia including over 800 enamel signs, a toy collection, a 1920s village garage workshop.

Diggerland

Verbeer Manor, Cullompton, Devon, EX15 2PE
08700 344437
www.diggerland.com
Feb-Nov: w/e's, B/Hs & daily sch hols, 10am-5pm
£12.50pp
Online booking available
Buy credits for riding/driving motorised diggers
M5 J27 take A38 east, follow signs for 3 miles

In this large adventure park, kids and adults can ride in, and drive different types of construction machinery including dumper trucks and diggers. There are also pedal power diggers and computer digger games.

Haynes Motor Museum

Sparkford, Nr Yeovil, Somerset, BA22 7LH
01963 440804
www.haynesmotormuseum.co.uk
Daily 9.30am-5.30pm, some seasonal variations
£6.50 adult, £3.50 child, £8.50-£19 family
M5 J25 then A358 & A303 to Sparkford. Or A37
south to A303.

Britain's most extensive car collection on permanent display although it is more look than touch. Hundreds of cars, ranging from the Chevrolet Corvette to the Sinclair C5. There is also a Hall of Motor Sport and a motorbike display.

Steam

Kemble Drive, Swindon, SN2 2TA
01793 466646
www.steam-museum.org.uk
Mon-Sat 10am-5pm, Sun 11am-5pm
£5.95 adult, £3.95 child, £15.20-£18.30 family
M4 J16, follow signs to Outlet Centre

The Museum of the Great Western Railway gives you an idea of what it was like to work on and use the GWR with lots of hands-on exhibits. Reconstructed platforms, a cab simulator, and activities during the school holidays.

The Helicopter Museum

The Heliport, Locking Moor Rd,
Weston-super-Mare, BS24 8PP
01934 635 227
www.helicoptermuseum.co.uk
Wed-Sun, B/Hs 10am-5.30pm, winter variations
Daily Easter and summer hols
£4.95 adult, £2.95 child, £13 family (2+2)
M5 J21, on the A368/A371, follow signs
See map on pg 90, ref A4

The world's largest dedicated helicopter museum housing the world's oldest, fastest and ugliest helicopters! Special events include Helicopter Experience Flights and the annual Heliday (usually the last weekend in July), a static helicopter display on Beach Lawns as well as pleasure flights from the beach.

Fleet Air Arm Museum

RNAS Yeovilton, Ilchester, Somerset, BA22 8HT
01935 840565
www.fleetairarm.com
Apr-Oct: daily 10am-5.30pm
Nov-Mar: Wed-Sun 10am-4.30pm
£10 adult, £7 child, £30 family (2+3)
Take the A37 south of Bristol (50mins)

The largest collection of Naval aircraft in Europe, this museum appeals to all aircraft enthusiasts. Follow the development of British aircraft from wooden bi-planes through to Concorde. You can sit in the cockpit of a jet fighter, experience life on an aircraft carrier or take a simulated helicopter ride.

RNAS Yeovilton Airday

www.yeoviltonairday.co.uk

Impressive flying displays at this annual show.

Royal International Air Tattoo

RAF Fairford, Gloucestershire, GL7 4NA
01285 713 456
www.airtattoo.com
M4 J15, follow signs

This huge aircraft fest takes place annually at RAF Fairford in mid July. Check website for further details.

STEAM RAILWAYS

Avon Valley Railway

Bitton Station, Willsbridge, BS15
0117 932 7296 talking timetable
0117 932 5538 general enquiries
www.avonvalleyrailway.co.uk
Easter-Oct: Sun, B/Hs
Tue-Thu during school holidays
£5 adult, £3.50 child, £13.50 family (2+2)
See map on pg 90, ref D4

Fare allows unlimited travel on day of issue. This line runs along the former Mangotsfield to Bath Green Park branch of the old Midland Railway. The line has been extended to a new platform at the Avon River side with links to boat trips and the Avon Valley Country Park.

Dean Forest Railway

Norchard Railway Centre, Lydney, Gloucestershire
01594 843423 information line
01594 845840 enquiries
www.deanforestrailway.co.uk
Apr-Oct: Sun, B/Hs, some weekdays in the summer
£8 adult, £5 child, £24 family (2+2)
M4, M48 Chepstow, Norchard is on B4234 just north of Lydney (Accessible by train and bus)
See map on pg 90, ref D1

This line runs from Norchard to Lydney Junction, then on to Parkend. Other attractions include riverside walks, boating lake, park, Railway Museum, café in classic restaurant coach open on Steam Days.

East Somerset Railway

Cranmore Railway Station, Shepton Mallet, Somerset, BA4 4QP
01749 880417
www.eastsomersetrailway.com
Apr-Oct: w/e's & some weekdays in the summer
Nov-Easter: Sun only
£6 adult, £4 child, £17 family (2+2)
A37, A361
See map on pg 90, ref D6

A round trip of 35 minutes. Platform tickets include the train shed, signal box and museum. Restaurant and model shop (only open on Steam Days).

Gloucestershire and Warwickshire Railway

The Railway Station, Toddington, Glos, GL54 5DT
01242 621405 (talking timetable when closed)
www.gwsr.com
£9.50 adult, £6 child, £26 family (2+3)
M5 Jct 9, A46, B4077 junction with B4632

Fare allows unlimited travel on day of issue. The railway operates a round trip of 20 miles from Toddington to Cheltenham Race Course station with a brief stop along the way at Winchcombe. The line passses through the beautiful Cotswold hills and you will have views over the Vale of Evesham to the Malvern Hills beyond.

Perrygrove Railway

Coleford, Forest of Dean, Glos, GL16 8QB
01594 834991
www.perrygrove.co.uk
Apr-Sep selected days & Oct half term
£4 adults, £3 child (no credit cards)
½ mile south of Coleford on B4228, nearest mainline railway station Lydney
See map on pg 90, ref C1

Fare allows unlimited travel on day of issue. Narrow gauge railway runs through farm and woodland for a 1½ mile return trip.

West Somerset Railway

The Railway Station, Minehead, Somerset, TA24 5BG
01643 707650 talking timetable
01643 704996 general enquiries
www.west-somerset-railway.co.uk
All year but not daily, phone for full timetable
£3.20-£12.40 depending on journey length, discount for children
M5 Jct 25, follow brown tourist signs to Bishops Lydeard

The train line runs for 20 miles between Bishop's Lydeard and Minehead along the coast and Quantock Hills. Ten restored stations along the line have a variety of signal boxes, museums, displays and steam and diesel engines to visit. Buffet on all regular, timetabled trains. Summer and Christmas special events require booking.

GOING UNDERGROUND

Also see Hopewell Colliery Museum pg 106.

Big Pit National Mining Museum

Blaenafon, Torfaen, north of Newport, NP4 9XP
01495 790311
www.nmgw.ac.uk/bigpit
Mid Feb-Nov: daily 9.30am-5pm, tours 10am-3.30pm
Free admission
J 25a M4 follow brown signs.
See map on pg 90, ref A1

P WC 🚻 ✗ 🛍 ⊞

Walk around this coal mine and find out how men, women and children worked here for over 200 years.

Cheddar Caves & Gorge

Cheddar, Somerset, BS27 3QF
01934 742 343
www.cheddarcaves.co.uk
Daily 10am-5pm, minor seasonal variations
£11.50 adult, £8.50 child, £31.50 family (2+2)
SW of Bristol on the A371, between A38 & A37
See map on pg 90, ref B5

P WC ✗ 🛍 ⊞ 🚌 ♿

Impressive caves located in spectacular gorge. The Cheddar Man museum looks at Stone Age man and cannibalism. During the summer, there are outside demonstrations of stone age survival techniques. Jacobs Ladder offers a 274 step climb to the top of the gorge with fantastic views of the Mendips. There is also caving, climbing and abseiling for 11+yrs.

Wookey Hole

Wookey Hole, Wells, Somerset, BA5 1BB
01749 672 243
www.wookey.co.uk
Daily 10am-5pm, winter 4pm
£10.90 adult, £8.50 child
2 miles north west of Wells, follow brown signs.
See map on pg 90, ref C5

P WC ✗ 🛍 ⊞ 🚌 ♿

A guided tour takes you through this series of caves carved out by the River Axe. Recently opened is a Valley of the Dinosaurs. Other attractions include a Victorian paper mill, a mirror maze and playable Edwardian Penny Arcade machines.

WALKS

You don't have to drive very far out of Bristol to find somewhere to stretch your legs, whether it's a gentle potter or a proper hike. Below, you'll find a few ideas, some requiring basic map reading skills, others just being nice places to wander around.

We do not have the space to write about walking safety, rights of way and countryside law but there are some excellent books out there that do. The Pathfinder series comes recommended, featuring walks of 3-9 miles.

Along with a guide book it is useful to have an Ordnance Survey map of the area. There are two types of OS map:

OS Explorer: the essential map for outdoor activities. These orange-covered maps are ideal for off-road enthusiasts as they show every track including bridleways, selected cycle routes and public rights of way. OS Explorer Maps also show the extent of new "open access" areas – land where people are permitted to walk away from public footpaths.

OS Landranger Map: A pink-covered OS Landranger Map gives you all the information you need to make the most of a day out. Keep one handy if you're looking for visitor attractions, car parks, museums, tourist offices and the best way to get there.

THE MALVERN HILLS

On a clear day, the Malvern Hills can be seen from miles around. This ancient rock formation is eight miles long rising to over 1,000 feet and provides many walking tracks.

A website we found very useful is:

www.countrywalkers.co.uk

Here Steve Dempster, a local writer, has written up some of his favourite walks. There are detailed directions and loads of historical facts. Did you know that Herefordshire Beacon is an Iron Age hill fort with ramparts and ditches where 2,000 people once lived?

THE BRECON BEACONS

Just over an hour's drive from Bristol will take you to the heart of the Brecon Beacons. Over 500 sq miles of dramatic scenery much of it over 1000 feet. It is incredibly beautiful and the views from the top of Pen y Fan and Sugar Loaf are, on a good day, stunning.

There are hundreds of miles of public footpaths, however none of them are waymarked. As this is a mountainous region where the terrain is challenging and the weather can change rapidly, it is essential certain proceedures are followed before you set out. Appropriate clothing, footwear, maps, guide books and safety precautions should be taken. Contact the centres below for advice on all these areas.

Tourist Information

Cattle Market Car Park, Brecon, LD3 9DA
01874 622485
Open daily
www.exploremidwales.com
brectic@powys.gov.uk

National Park Visitor Centre (Mountain Centre)

Libanus, Brecon, Powys, LD3 8ER
01874 623366
www.breconbeacons.org

Here you will find friendly staff and loads of advice on how to plan your walk. They have a large selection of walking guide books and maps. You can choose publications from the website and then purchase them over the phone. Check out the tea room at Libanus.

EXMOOR NATIONAL PARK

A huge sandstone plateau split by wooded valleys. The scenery is stunning and on a clear day you can see for miles. The heather uplands have a variety of grasses, plants and gorse. There are exmoor ponies and wonderful birds, take your binoculars.

The National Trust and Exmoor National Park manage the moor, maintaining waymarked paths. Great walking for the whole family.

National Park Centre Dulverton

7/9 Fore St, Dulverton, Somerset, TA22 9Ex
www.exmoor-nationalpark.gov.uk

There are five park centres in the region at Combe Martin, County Gate, Dunster, Blackmoor Gate and Dulverton. They all provide information, books and maps. They have a great guide called the Rangers Favourite Walks (£4.95). Two of the walks can be downloaded from their website. They also produce an access leaflet for the less abled.

WEST OF BRISTOL

Weston Big Wood

Nr Portishead, North Somerset
0117 917 7270
www.avonwildlifetrust.org.uk
Open all year
From the B3124 Clevedon-Portishead road, turn into Valley Road just north of Weston-in-Gordano. Park in the lay-by 300m on the right, and walk up the hill. Steps lead into the wood from the road
See map on pg 90, ref B3

One of the area's largest ancient woodlands, dating back to the Ice Age, this nature reserve is rich in wildlife, including butterflies, woodpeckers, tawny owls, bats and badger setts. In spring, the ground is covered with wood anemones, violets and bluebells. The old stones, ditches and banks are thought to be medieval boundaries used to divide the wood into sectors. The reserve is criss-crossed with a network of (sometimes muddy) footpaths; keep away from the quarry sides.

NORTH EAST OF BRISTOL

Brackenbury Ditches, Cotswolds

OS Map 162 Gloucester & Forest of Dean.
Access: Parking on roadside 1 mile north of Wotton-under-Edge at 757943 or at 754941
See map on pg 90, ref E2

A fairly level walk of 2-4 miles through mixed woodland, some mature beech areas, plus some great views. Trainers are OK as long as there's been no recent rain. Mind you don't lose your bearings in the woods. Take the track going north west, or the footpath across the fields depending on where you parked. Take your pick of the tracks through the woods, but aim for the fort and Nibley Knoll in a north westerly direction for the better woodland and views.

Coaley Peak

Nr Nympsfield, Stroud, Gloucesteshire
01452 425666/863170
www.gloucestershire.gov.uk
On the B4066 Stroud-Uley Rd, about ½ mile from Nympsfield

Picnic site on the edge of the Cotswold escarpment with panoramic views towards the Forest of Dean – on a clear day, you can see the Black Mountains in Wales. The 12-acre area has been reclaimed as a wildflower meadow (at its best in summer) with picnic tables and open grassland, good for flying kites. It also includes Nympsfield long barrow, a neolithic burial chamber. The Cotswold Way runs the length of the site, and you can stroll through the adjacent Stanley Woods.

Lasborough Park, Cotswolds

OS Map 162 Gloucester & Forest of Dean.
Access: 5 miles east of Wotton-under-Edge. Parking on wide grass verge by Chapel in Newington Bagpath at 815948

A 4-mile circular walk through delightful Cotswold valleys. Enjoy it during crisp frost in winter, lambs, buds and flowers in spring, warm summer afternoons, or autumn colours, grouse and blackberries. Stout footware and compass required, wellies if recent rain. Behind the chapel, pick up footpath west to Bagpath (across the field

towards the transmission mast). At the lane, turn left going south for 300 metres and take the footpath by the drive of Seaton House. Cross the fields and down into the woods, to the stream at the bottom. Turn left (south) and follow the stream for 1km across several fields. Cross to the west bank when convenient as you approach the derelict stone bridge in the trees. Follow the track as it swings right then take a left along the track alongside the woods below Ozleworth Park. Continue into the woods, then after 200 metres take the track on the left, going due east along the stream. After 1km, take the path into the left valley going north east. After the large lake, take the gate into Lasborough Park, walking below the house and through the park to the gate at the top corner, the path rises to the chapel where you started.

Leyhill Arboretum

HMP Leyhill, Tortworth, Wotton-under-Edge, GL12
01454 264345
Daily 9am-4m
½ mile from M5, J14, on B4509 towards Wotton
See map on pg 90, ref D2

An interesting collection of trees and ornamental gardens managed by Leyhill prison (regular exhibitor at Chelsea Flower Show), adjacent to the Tortworth Court Hotel – an impressive Victorian mansion. Several short, circular walks on small paths through the arboretum.

Lower Lodge Woods

Ozleworth, Wotton-under-Edge, Gloucestershire
01452 383333
www.gloucestershirewildlifetrust.co.uk
From Wotton on the Wortley rd turn left in Wortley at the sign to Ozleworth and continue for about 1 ½ miles along this lane. Limited parking is available on the left in front of Newark Park's Lower Lodge
See map on pg 90, ref E2

A nature reserve owned by Gloucestershire Wildlife Trust, this small ancient woodland, especially pretty in spring, is a haven for wildflowers and birds. Walk through the gate, past Lower Lodge, to find the map of a circular walk about a mile long. Half way round in a clockwise direction, you can either take the track to your right, which leads back to where you started, or continue to the left

(a further ½ mile uphill) to Newark Park, the National Trust house visible through the trees.

Lower Woods

Wickwar, Wotton-under-Edge, Gloucestershire
01452 383333
www.gloucestershirewldlifetrust.co.uk
Approach from Wickwar or Hawkesbury Upton via Inglestone Common. Take the track opposite Inglestone Farm, which leads to the car park by Lower Woods Lodge
See map on pg 90, ref E2

A nature reserve owned by Gloucestershire Wildlife Trust, this ancient woodland is one of England's largest oak-ash woods on heavy clay soils. The area has been wooded since prehistoric times and, as a result, is very rich in wildlife, including wildflowers, butterflies, dormice and birds. There are three waymarked trails of different lengths (up to two miles), which take you through the woods along paths, ancient grassy trenches and rides. The trails are clearly signposted, and free maps are available at the car park. Sturdy footwear is advisable all year round.

Minchinhampton Common

Stroud, Gloucestershire
01452 814213
www.nationaltrust.org
South of Stroud, between Minchinhampton and Nailsworth

A large open space on a hill-top plateau of the Cotswolds with dramatic views over the surrounding countryside. Great for picnics, walks and flying kites. The common has a special mix of wildflowers, including cowslips and orchids, as well as a diversity of birds, butterflies and other insects. It's also one of the most important archaeological sites in Britain, with prehistoric field systems, a Neolithic long barrow, medieval roads and military defences from the Second World War.

Splatts Wood, Cotswolds

OS Map 172 Bristol & Bath
Access: 2 miles North of Hawkesbury Upton. Parking on verge between Hawkesbury Upton and Hillesley at 772880. Alternatively, park in Hawkesbury Upton and adjust the route accordingly
See map on pg 90, ref E3

A gentle 2-3 mile walk through peaceful, lush meadows beneath wooded ridges and woodland, including a stretch of the Cotswold Way. Take the right hand of the two tracks going north, which bears right as it goes into the woods. Follow it round to north east, into the meadows below Splatts Wood. Continue for 1.5 km to the lane at the bottom and turn right. Turn right after 100 metres up the track on the right and continue back to the car through woods and fields. Alternatively, continue South East along the lane, fork right and take the footpath on the right 300 metres after the fork. Walk up the valley taking a choice of footpaths towards Hawkesbury Upton. At the lane either turn right 1.5km back to the car, past the Monument or wander through the village to the pub on the crossroads then back to the car.

Westonbirt Arboretum

Nr Tetbury, Gloucestershire, GL8 8QS
01666 880220
www.forestry.gov.uk/england
Daily 10am-5pm (or dusk if earlier)
£7.50 adult (£6 winter), £1 child,
Annual family: £42
M4 J18, take A46 towards Tetbury, follow brown tourist signs.

The Arboretum consists of miles of beautiful, well-marked tree-lined paths. The Old Arboretum is dog free. The area is especially beautiful in the autumn and hence busier. Ring for details of seasonal events such as Christmas lights. Shop with information and plants for sale.

SOUTH EAST OF BRISTOL

Bradford-on-Avon to Avoncliff

Access: Bradford-upon-Avon Station car park.

A canal-side walk between two villages. Take the path at the end of Bradford-on-Avon Station car park that leads into Barton Country Park. Follow the river until it joins the towpath. Walk along this for a mile or so past narrow boats, until you come to Avoncliff. Here you will find the Madhatter café and The Cross Guns Pub.

Brokers Wood Country Park

Brokerswood, Nr. Westbury, Wiltshire, BA13 4EH
01373 822 238
www.brokerswood.co.uk
Daily from 10am, closing times seasonal
£3 adult, £1.50 child. Train 75p.
A36 12 miles south Bath, follow brown tourist signs

Attractive woodland country park, with a lake (fishing possible) and miles of paths to

explore, many pushchair accessible. Narrow gauge railway operates Easter-Oct, w/e and school holidays. There are two outdoor adventure playgrounds. Caravan/camping available in the park.

Willsbridge Mill

Avon Wildlife Trust, Willsbridge Hill, Bristol, BS30 6EX
0117 932 6885
www.avonwildlifetrust.org.uk
Nature Reserve open all year, mill seasonal
Admission free
A431 Bristol to Bath road, turn into Long Beach Road. Car park on left.

This converted mill housing hands-on wildlife and conservation displays is currently only open when schools are visiting, but there is plenty to do outside. The Valley Nature Reserve, which includes a Heritage Sculpture Trail, a Wild Waste Garden and plenty of lovely sculptural seating areas for picnics is open all year. Pond dipping equipment available for hire.

Dundas Aqueduct to Avoncliff

Access: Take A36 from Bath to Monkton Combe, turn left on B3108 and park at Canal Visitor Centre

This walk starts at Brass Knocker Basin, see Bradford-on-Avon, pg 99. It passes through pretty cuttings and embankments. Take the towpath and follow the signs to Avoncliff. Lots of wild flowers and ducks. Fordside Tea Gardens is about ¾ of a mile from the start of the walk, great for cream teas. The walk to Avoncliff Aqueduct is about four miles. There are many other walks that are possible along the Kennet and Avon canal and it's easy for family cycling (novice cyclists watch the edge). In the other direction, it is about 4 miles to Bathampton where The George is a family-friendly pub for lunch.

SOUTH OF BRISTOL

Folly Farm

Nr Bishop Sutton, Bath & NE Somerset
0117 917 7270
www.avonwildlifetrust.org.uk
Open all year
Follow the A368 west from the A37 for about 1.5 miles. Folly Farm is signposted up a track to the left

A large nature reserve owned by Avon Wildlife Trust including wildflower meadows, ancient woodland and 17th-century farm buildings (being restored to provide visitor facilities), with spectacular views over Chew Valley Lake and the Mendips. Visit in spring to see woodland carpets of bluebells and primroses or in summer for butterflies and meadows brimming with flowers such as ox-eye daisies and orchids. An Access for All trail through the woodland is waymarked from the car park. You could bring a picnic or visit the nearby Carpenters Arms at Stanton Wick, see pg 84.

SOUTH WEST OF BRISTOL

Ashton Hill, Failand

OS Map 172 Bristol and Bath
Access: The car-park is on the B3129 at the southern tip of Failand village

A beautiful walk through woodland areas, don't miss it in the autumn. There are several walks of up to a couple of miles, through mature woodland. The terrain is rough and can get very muddy.

Blagdon Lake

Blagdon Visitor Centre, Blagdon Lake
Visitor Centre, May-Aug: Sun 2pm-5pm

Peaceful and pretty woodland walk along the banks of the lake — but beware fishermen casting. Park on bridge abutting lake.

Brockley Wood, Cleeve

OS Map 172 Bristol and Bath
Access: Take A370 towards Congresbury, turning left in Cleeve immediately before the Lord Nelson pub, down Cleeve Hill Road. Continue for approximately 600 yards and turn left into Goblin Coombe car park

Many pretty walks of up to four miles through the woods, beautiful in autumn.

Burrington Coombe, near Churchill

OS Map 172 Bristol and Bath
Access: From A368 (Churchill to Blagdon) take the B3134. Drive up the valley for nearly 2 miles to the plateau and there is a car-park on the left

A great starting point on the Mendips. Fantastic views, wonderful heathland vegetation (wild grassy meadows, heather, bracken, gorse, silver birch) and wildlife. Whether it's a quiet picnic, a gentle stroll or a few miles with the back-pack, there are lots of options. For picnics and short walks, take the path at the back of the car-park (north, towards Bristol) up 10 yards of rocky path and onto grassy meadow. For longer walks, walk up the road 30 yards and take the track on the right (going south) onto Beacon Batch and head right towards the peak. Continue west through Black Down, into Rowberrow Warren, Dolebury Warren to the Ancient Hill

Fort above Churchill then back along the ridge in the direction of the car-park. This is a seven mile circuit but it can be shortened and there are other access points from Churchill and Shipham.

Chew Valley Lake

Chew Valley Lake Information Centre, Chew Stoke, BS40 8TF
01275 333345
www.bristolwater.co.uk
Daily 10.30am-5.30pm, 4.30pm winter
Parking £1.20

This beautiful lake with wonderful views is a haven for birds, insects and animals. There are two lakeside trails. Park at the visitor centre where there are walk details, gift and tea shop. Dogs on leads allowed.

New Manor Farm Shop

North Widcombe, West Harptree, Bristol, BS40 6HW
01761 220067
Nr Chew Valley Lake

Worth checking out if you are passing.

Clevedon Poet's Walk

Access: Pay & Display at Salt House Fields

A wonderful, easy-going, short walk (about 1.5 miles) around the headland with good views across the Severn. Start at the Salt House Fields car park, walk along the Front towards the headland, up the first flight of steps, and along the path. Continue along the undulating, fenced tarmac path on the top of the cliff to St Andrews Church. On the right hand side of the church you will see a sign for the walk, follow the path back towards your starting point.

Dolebury Warren

Nr Churchill, North Somerset
0117 917 7270
www.avonwildlifetrust.org.uk
Open all year
Follow the A38 south from Churchill; take the first left after the traffic lights into Dolebury Bottom, and follow the lane to the small car park

The site of an imposing Iron Age hill fort, this nature reserve owned by the National Trust and managed by Avon Wildlife Trust offers fantastic views across North Somerset and the Mendips. Late May to August is the best time to visit for rare wildflowers and butterflies, but you can enjoy the views and the feeling of wildness all year round. The site includes the remains of the fort's double ramparts and a medieval rabbit warren. Follow the footpaths from the car park to the summit.

Long Wood

Nr Cheddar, Somerset
01823 652400
www.somersetwildlife.org
Open all year
Off the Charterhouse-Shipham road, parking about ½ mile west of Charterhouse

An ancient woodland in a valley just north of Cheddar Gorge owned by Somerset Wildlife Trust. Check the information board at the entrance, and follow the circular nature trail (about 1½ miles and often muddy). If you visit in late spring, you'll see carpets of bluebells, wild garlic and other flowers. Look out for orchids in the grassland near the entrance. A stream runs through the northern end of the reserve, disappearing underground into the cave of Longwood Swallet (access controlled by Charterhouse Caving Company).

Glastonbury Tor

Tor is open 365 days/year.
Access: 15 minute walk from village to bottom of Tor. From Easter-Sept a tour bus costing approx £1 runs every half hour from the carpark by the Abbey and you can just hop off at the Tor.

This steep hill is a striking feature of the local landscape offering stunning views over Somerset, Dorset and Wiltshire. Renovated in 2003, the 15th century tower on top of the Tor is all that remains of a mediaeval church. Up there you get a sense of why this place is a focus for legend and superstition. The Tor is 158m high and a steep climb, but well worth the effort.

BEACHES

Tide times: www.easytide.ukho.gov.uk

If you fancy a change from the mud of the severn estuary, then travel a little further afield for golden sands and blue sea. South Wales is about an 1¼ hr's drive from Bristol, North Devon takes just under two hours. You'll find some beautiful beaches with rock pools and good surf. For a great day out, just pack a picnic and head off! The beaches below are all recommended by the Marine Conservation Society for their clean water see: www.goodbeachguide.co.uk

Crooklets and Summerleaze beaches — Bude

Bude, North Cornwall
M5 J31, take A30, turn off at Okehampton, along the A3079 and then the A3072. Bude is signposted on the A39

Summerleaze is a huge sandy beach, ideal for sandcastles, rock pooling and paddling.

Close to the town and its facilities. There is a seawater pool at low tide. Gets very busy in summer. Crooklets is a safe, sandy beach, surrounded by sand dunes, with rocks to explore. Smaller and quieter than nearby Summerleaze beach, which can also be reached at low tide. Popular with surfers. MCS recommended. Beach lifeguard service end April to end September.

Croyde Bay

nr Saunton, North Devon
Leave M5 at junction 27 and follow A361 to Braunton. From Braunton follow the signs for Croyde. There is a car park next to beach allowing easy access

Pretty, small bay, with a lovely sandy beach, backed by sand dunes. Good rock pools to explore. Popular with surfers. Enjoyable walk with spectacular views, to nearby Baggy Point. MCS recommended. Beach lifeguard service May-September. Very busy in summer.

Ogmore-by-Sea

Bridgend, Vale of Glamorgan, South Wales
M4 J35, follows signs for Porthcawl, Pen y Bont, then
B4524 to Ogmore-by-Sea

P WC ✗ ♿ ⊞

Huge, popular, west facing beach with good surfing and rock pooling. Beach is accessed over pebbles, with large sandy beach at low tide. Toilets and kiosk for snacks, but no other facilities. Lovely walk along cliff top, with extensive grassy areas to sit and enjoy the views. No beach at high tide. Nearby Southerndown beach (approx ½ mile beyond Ogmore) has flat, easy access from the car park, across a road and consequently gets very busy in summer.

Oxwich Bay

The Gower, Nr Swansea
M4 J42 to Swansea, follow signs to the Gower. On the A4118 head for Oxwich village

P WC ✗ ⊞

A long sandy beach nestled in a bay and adjacent to a Nature Reserve. On a hot day you may think you were on the Mediterranean rather than the Atlantic.

There is a boat slip which attracts owners of speed boats and jet skis. There is a pub at one end of the beach which has a large beer garden. The beach has no lifeguards.

Pembrey Beach

Pembrey Country Park, Llanellin, Carmarthen
M4 J48, follow sign posts to the Country Park

P WC ✗ ⊞

A beach to take your breath away. Eight miles of sand edged with dunes. Fly kites, surf, swim, walk, run, build castles, ride bikes, horse ride or just chill. The beach is MCS recommened. There is a professional lifeguard service during summer months, sand bars are present which can cause strong currents, so swimming is advised within the patrolled area. See camping entry on pg 201.

Rest Bay

Porthcawl, Vale of Glamorgan, South Wales
M4 j37, take A4229 to Porthcawl, follow signs to Rest Bay

P WC ✗ ♿ ⊞

About a mile from Porthcawl, this large, sandy beach is backed by low cliffs and rocks that are just begging to be explored! Faces south west, so excellent surfing. Plenty of space, even during summer months – just keep walking along the beach. Very limited beach at low tide. Large grassy area next to car park and café to sit and watch the sun set. Beach lifeguard service May-September.

Woolacombe Beach and Barricane Bay

Woolacombe, North Devon
M5 J27, take the third exit and follow signs for A361 to Barnstaple, then for Ilfracombe and Braunton. Stay on A361 to Mullacott Cross roundabout, take the first exit and follow signs to Woolacombe

P WC ✗ ♿ ⊞

The village beach is a vast expanse of golden sand, backed by sandy hills. Excellent for surfing. Zoned areas for water sports. Woolacombe village at north end of beach. MCS recommended. Professional lifeguard service during summer months. Three large car parks in Woolacombe. Barricane Bay is a lovely sand and shingle beach, smaller and quieter than the village beach. Safe swimming and a great place to find unusual shells. MCS recommended. Car park next to beach. Toilets at village beach.

SHOPPING & SERVICES

Lu Hersey
Rachel Miller

CONTENTS

INTRODUCTION

The new £500 million re-development in Broadmead is already well underway, ahead of its completion in 2008. The shopping centre will boast a Harvey Nichols department store and many more new shops based around a public square, as well as a 13-screen cinema.

In the meantime, there's no shortage of places to shop, whether you prefer the convenience of the larger centres such as the Galleries and the Mall or the independent shops of Park Street, Clifton and Bath.

We've covered everything in this chapter, from clothes shops to music and book stores as well as second hand shopping and specialist outlets. However, we've focused mainly on the independent shops where you can find both good service and merchandise that's a bit different to what's generally available in the high street chain stores.

Happy hunting!

OPENING TIMES

We haven't listed full opening times for all the stores in this chapter, due to space restrictions. The times for the main centres appear below. In every entry, we have highlighted which days the stores are open and mention times only if they are unusual. Those shops that open on Sundays tend to open between 11am and 4-5pm. If in doubt, ring or check the website.

SHOPPING CENTRES & DEPARTMENT STORES

The Galleries

0117 929 0569
www.galleries-shopping.co.uk
Mon-Wed 8.30am-6pm, Thu 8.30am-8pm,
Fri-Sat 8.30am-6pm, Sun 11am-5pm

The Mall at Cribbs Causeway

0117 903 0303
www.mallcribbs.com
Mon-Fri 10am-9pm, Sat 9am-7pm, Sun 11am-5pm
Bank Holidays 10am-6pm
John Lewis opening hours vary.

BHS

The Mall, 0117 950 9493
Broadmead, 0117 929 2261
www.bhs.co.uk

Woolworths

Filton, 0117 969 7303
The Galleries, 0117 922 7778
www.woolworths.co.uk

Boots

The Mall, 0117 950 9744
Broadmead, 0117 929 3631
Avon Meads, 0117 972 8056
www.boots.com

Debenhams

Broadmead, 08445 616161
www.debenhams.com

House of Fraser

Broadmead, 0117 944 5566
www.houseoffraser.co.uk

Ikea

Eastville, 0845 355 2264
www.ikea.co.uk

John Lewis

The Mall, 0117 959 1100
www.johnlewis.com

Marks & Spencer

Broadmead, 0117 927 2000
The Mall, 0117 904 4444
www.marksandspencer.com

CLOTHES

If you want to spend a day shopping for clothes in Bristol, there are no shortage of high street names and we've included some here. But there are also lot of great shops on Park Street, in Clifton village and in Bath.

THE MALL, CRIBBS CAUSEWAY

Free Spirit

The Mall, Cribbs Causeway, BS34
0117 950 2575
Mon-Sun

Surf, snow and skate fashion, plus accessories and equipment. Beach and ski wear in season.

Gap

The Mall, Cribbs Causeway, BS34
0117 950 9667
Mon-Sun

Good quality clothing and shoes (American sizes). It is expensive, but stock changes regularly and there are great sale rails.

H&M

The Mall, Cribbs Causeway, BS34
0117 950 9590
Mon-Sun

Fashionable and inexpensive.

Monsoon

The Mall, Cribbs Causeway, BS34
0117 950 4175
www.monsoon.co.uk
Mon-Sun

Girl's clothes including posh frocks and shoes.

Monsoon Kids' Store

The Mall, Cribbs Causeway, BS34
0117 950 0753
Mon-Sun

This new dedicated children's store caters for girls up to 12yrs.

Next

The Mall, Cribbs Causeway, BS34
0117 950 9033
www.next.co.uk
Mon-Sun

Kids clothes up to 16yrs available to order in store or from the directory.

Republic

The Mall, Bristol, BS34 5GF
0117 959 2380
www.republic.co.uk
Mon-Sun

Describing itself as a "chain of independent stores", Republic started life as a jeans shop and has developed into a hip and trendy urbanwear store with some 85 branches.

River Island

112 The Mall, Cribbs Causeway, Bristol, BS34 5UP
0117 950 9614
www.riverisland.com
Mon-Sun

High fashion at high street prices.

Route One

The Mall, Cribbs Causeway
0117 959 2696
9, Broad St, Bath
Mon-Sun

Small but packed with skate clothes, equipment and accessories.

TK Maxx

Cribbs Causeway
0117 950 8081
Mon-Sun, Thu till 7pm

An amazing array of discounted designer clothes. Brands include French Connection, Calvin Klein, Hooch, Pineapple, Adidas, Peter Worth, Diesel and many more. TK Maxx also sells shoes, accessories, toys and homewares

Top Shop

Unit 25, The Mall, Cribbs Causeway, BS34 5DG
0117 950 1370
www.topshop.co.uk
Mon-Sun

High fashion clothes.

BROADMEAD & THE GALLERIES

Extreme

53 Union St, Bristol, BS1
0117 933 8500
Mon-Sun

Skate clothes for guys and girls as well trucks and decks. Beachwear in season. Accessories include watches, badges, patches, key chains, sunglasses and hats.

Gap

30-32 Broadmead, BS1 3HA
0117 922 0657
Mon-Sun

Good quality, if pricey, clothing and shoes (American sizes).

H&M

Union St, Bristol, BS1
0117 945 1870
Mon-Sun

Fashionable and inexpensive.

Maxed

The Galleries, Bristol, BS1
0117 929 4030
Mon-Sun

Cool surfing, skating and boarding clothes.

Miss Selfridge

81 Broadmead, Bristol, BS1 3DT
0117 930 4402
www.missselfridge.co.uk
Mon-Sun

Up to the minute fashion chain. It also has branches within Debenhams in Broadmead and within Outfit at Avon Meads.

Monsoon

Unit 7, New Broadmead, Union St, BS1 2DL
0117 929 0870
www.monsoon.co.uk
Mon-Sun

Girl's clothes including posh frocks and shoes.

Next

Broadmead (opposite H & M), Bristol, BS1
0117 922 6495
Mon-Sun

Good range of mid-priced clothing and shoes. Clothes up to 16yrs available to order in store or from the directory.

Peacocks

50-60 The Horsefair, Broadmead, BS1 3EY
0117 927 9583
www.peacocks.co.uk
Mon-Sat

Quiksilver Boardriders

Union Gallery, The Galleries, Bristol, BS1
0117 929 2114
Mon-Sun

Surf, snow and skate clothing.

River Island

24-26 Broadmead, Bristol, BS1 3HA
0117 927 7913
www.riverisland.com
Mon-Sun

TK Maxx

The Galleries, Broadmead, Bristol, BS1
0117 930 4404
Mon-Sun, Thu until 7pm

An amazing array of discounted designer clothes. Brands include French Connection, Calvin Klein, Hooch, Pineapple, Adidas and Diesel. It also sells shoes and homewares.

Top Shop

60-62 The Horsefair, Bristol, BS1 3JQ
0117 929 4991
www.topshop.co.uk
Mon-Sun

High fashion clothes.

Warehouse

Unit 8-9 New Broadmead Centre, Bristol, BS1 2DL
0117 927 2471
www.warehousefashion.com
Mon-Sun

There's also a Warehouse in Debenhams in Broadmead and within Outfit at Avon Meads.

PARK STREET & THE TRIANGLE

50:50

16 Park Row, Bristol, BS1
0117 914 7783
www.5050store.com
Mon-Sat until 6pm, Sun 12pm-4pm

A skater's paradise. Everything from clothing and footwear to boards and accessories. A wide selection of specialist Nike trainers including Nike SB.

All Saints Retail

68 Queens Rd, Clifton, Bristol, BS8 1QU
0117 929 4499
www.allsaints.co.uk

A real fashion experience, cool clothes displayed in great surroundings.

BS8

34 Park St, Bristol, BS1
0117 930 4836
Mon-Sat until 6pm

A large funky store boasting several shops under one roof. Everything from street and urbanwear to vintage, retro and eveningwear. The wide range of trousers can be altered at a tailor's across the road (for a small fee). There's also an area devoted to prom dresses with a dressmaker on hand.

Sirens: evening dresses
Apartment: mens, ladies and alternative
Spunky: streetwear
Sobeys: vintage wear
Random: homewares and accessories
Ra-Ra-Ra: jewellery

Chandni Chowk

66 Park St, Bristol, BS1 5JN
0117 930 0059
www.chandnichowk.co.uk

An exciting range of garments for women and men, plus soft furnishings made using natural fibres, cotton/wool/wild tussah and mutka silk. Look out for the hand-spun and hand-woven fabrics and hand-block printing on a range of fabrics.

City Dolls

59 Park St, Bristol, BS1 5NU
0117 927 7307
Mon-Sun

See the latest range of streetwear from Freesalt, Sonneti, Duck and Cover and many more. It also offers a good range of accessories to complete your new look.

Cooshti

57 Park St, Bristol, BS1 5NU
0117 929 0850
Mon-Sun

Keep tabs with the latest fashions here, a haven of cool for the label-conscious. Loads of top brands — pick and mix between See by Chloë, Milla, Diesel, Nolita, G-Star, Maharishi, Stussy or Duffer. Plus they stock Adidas, Fila, Nike and Sergio Tacchini amongst others, so you can find shoes, boots and trainers!

DNA

24 Park St, Bristol, BS1
0117 934 9173
www.donotdisturb.co.uk
Mon-Sat until 6pm, Sun 12pm-5pm

Gorgeous clothes for girls that want to look individual. Quirky retro styles with a modern twist. DNA is also home to the Motel range. Interesting fitting rooms and good sales.

Fat Face

86 Park St, Bristol, BS1
0117 930 4357
www.fatface.com
Also at: The Mall, Cribbs Causeway

A surfer sanctuary and for those that just like the style. Quality clothes and great sales.

Federation

56 Park St, Bristol, BS1
0117 929 9889
Mon-Sat until 6pm, Sun 12pm-5pm

This shop is packed with accessories and clothes. Check out the plastic and metal rings, earrings, necklaces, bracelets and bandannas.

Khoi

40 Park St, Bristol, BS1 5JG
0117 925 8090
Mon-Sun

Funky streetwear with a great range of brands including Lee jeans, Addict, Supreme Being, Hick and Putsch. Khoi aso sells cute baby wear from No Added Sugar.

Jigsaw

80 Park St, Bristol, BS1 5LA
0117 926 5775
Mon-Sat

Well-known high street range of women's casualwear including shoes and accessories.

Kathmandu

11-13 Queens Rd, Bristol, BS8 1QE
0117 927 7814
www.kathmandu.com

This Australian company has been producing quality outdoor clothing and equipment for travel and adventure for over 30 years.

Reiss

84 Park St, Bristol, BS1 5JA
0117 927 6605

Reiss manufactures its own range of quality men's and womenswear. Bridging the gap between the standard high street offerings and cool designer labels, it may be more aspirational than functional.

Rollermania

62 Park Row, Bristol, BS1
0117 927 9981
Mon-Sat

Roller skates, in-line skates, skating clothes and running shoes. The only Bristol stockist of the super-cool Stussy clothing line.

Seven 7

60 Park Row, Bristol, BS1 5LE
0117 929 8898
Mon-Sat

Hidden just off Park Row, this is a great place to search out clothes and shoes. Many of the T-shirts are printed on the premises and they have a great range of clothes made there too.

Shark Bite Surf Shop

68 Park Row, Bristol, BS1
0117 929 9211
Mon-Sun

Surf kit for on and off the beach and great jewellery too. They offer a tailor-made service to build you the skateboard of your dreams!

The Store

53 Park St, Bristol, BS1 5NT
0117 927 7900
Mon-Sun

Owned by West Beach, you can pick up the latest funky clothes for the street or beach. Choose from Split, Spy or Adio shoes and look out for the No Mix winter collection.

Supa 8

54 Park St, Bristol, BS1 5JN
0117 925 6395
www.supa8.com

This skate and snowboarding shop now offers a big selection of knitwear, jeans, jackets and shoes from loads of high-end fashion brands including Volcom, Ezekiel, Element, Zoo York, Insight, I-Path and many more. Also stocks a good range of sunglasses too.

Westworld

35-37 Park St, Bristol, BS1 5NH
0117 925 3843
www.westworldretail.com
Mon-Sun

You can get great hoods, Ts, sweats, jeans, jackets and bags from Carhartt and Eastpak. Downstairs there are dressier things from brands like Hooch, Bench and Million Dollar.

White Stuff

64 Queens Rd, Bristol, BS8
0117 929 0100
www.whitestuff.com
Mon-Sat until 6pm, Sun 11am-5pm

Unisex ski and surf clothing. Well made, hard-wearing, funky and fashionable. Great sales. Mail order also available.

Wired

30 Park St, Bristol, BS1 5JA
0117 903 0942
Mon-Sun

Men's clothes shop for the design-conscious buyer which now includes more mid-priced ranges too.

CLIFTON VILLAGE

Gladrags and Handbags

38b Princess Victoria St, Clifton Village, BS8
0117 973 7687
Mon-Sat

Designer-label clothes, shoes, bags and jewellery at affordable prices as well as a big range of prom and ball dresses. There's a ten per cent student discount on presentation of an NUS card.

Maze Clothing

26 The Mall, Clifton Village, Bristol, BS8 4DS
0117 974 4459
Mon-Sun

Great selection of clothes for men and women ranging from Diesel, French Connection, Great Plains, Joseph and Seven.

GLOUCESTER ROAD

Beast

224 Cheltenham Rd, BS7
0117 942 8200
Mon-Sat
St Nicholas Market (Mon-Sat) & Corn St (Fri & Sat)
0117 927 9535
www.beast-clothing.com

Its mission is to spread Bristolian around the world and Beast is succeeding with its brilliant "Bristle" t-shirts, complete with "Gert lush" and "Cheers drive" emblazoned on them. The full range is available online and the website also has lots of other fun Bristol stuff and some interactive elements too. Beast also sells great bags and other clothing and accessories

Bishopston Trading Company

193 Gloucester Rd, Bishopston, BS7
0117 924 5598
www.bishopstontrading.co.uk
Mon-Sat 9.30am-5.30pm

This fair trade shop was set up by a workers' co-operative to create employment in the South Indian village of KV Kuppam. It specialises in natural fabrics and organic handloom cotton. Also see Mail Order below.

Katze

55 Gloucester Rd, Bristol, Bishopston, BS7
0117 942 5625
Mon-Sat 9.30am-5.30pm

The alternative department store stocking everything from Fair Trade clothes, bags and tights to throws, rugs and mobiles.

Pink Lemons

59 Gloucester Rd, Bishopston, BS7
0117 942 0420
3 Church St, Abbey Green, Bath, BA1 1NL
01225 424310

Clothing and accessories including a large selection of Moroccan-made bags, belts and sandals plus leather boots from Denmark.

Pink Soda

59 Gloucester Rd, Bishopston, Bristol, BS7
0117 942 0420
Mon-Sun

Friendly boutique stocking a lovely range of clothes both day, night and even underwear, plus bath products, bags, shoes and jewellery.

RePsycho

85 Gloucester Rd, Bishopston, Bristol, BS7
0117 983 0007
Mon-Sat 10am-5.30pm

Step back in time to the sixties in this retro Aladdin's cave. In the basement you can buy vinyls, while upstairs hunt for lights and furniture before checking out the clothes on the ground floor. A hire service can be offered on most items of clothes — pay the full price and get half back on return.

FURTHER AFIELD

Next Clearance

Abbeywood Retail Park, Station Rd, Filton, BS34
0117 906 2280
Mon-Fri 9.30am-8pm, Sat 9am-6pm, Sun 11am-5pm

End of season and clearance stock. Prices are up to 50% off original selling price.

Outfit

Avon Meads, St Philips Causeway, Bristol, BS2
0117 971 4821
Mon-Sun, Thu till 7pm

All the Arcadia shops under one roof — Wallis, Principles, Burton, Dorothy Perkins and fashion mecca, Topshop.

BATH

Animal

14-16 The Corridor, Bath, BA1
01225 448934
Mon-Sun

Stocks everything for the fashion-conscious surfer, skater or wannabe — clothing, skate shoes, accessories and sunglasses.

Detour

20 Broad St, Bath, BA1
01225 471998
www.detourskatingstore.co.uk
Mon-Sun

This is the place for exclusive streetwear, footwear and accessories, catering for the fashion-conscious and the skateboarder. Brands include Addict, Darkotics, New Era and WESC. Skateboard hardware from Third Foot, Blueprint and Landscape. You can also shop online with free delivery on orders over £50.

Fat Face

4-5 Green St, Bath, BA1
01225 780332
www.fatface.com
Mon-Sun

A surfer sanctuary and for those that just like the look. Quality clothes and great sales.

Free Spirit

5-6 The Corridor, Bath, BA1
01225 425644
Mon-Sun

Clothes and accessories for the surf, skate, snow and bike enthusiast.

Jolly's

13 Milsom St, Bath, BA1
0870 160 7224
Mon-Sun

This lovely old department store sells cosmetics, accessories and clothing.

Laura Ashley

8/9 New Bond St, Bath, BA1 1BE
0871 223 1327
www.lauraashley.com
Mon-Sat 9.30am-5.30pm, Sun 11am-4pm

Lovely clothes for girly girls.

Mask

10 The Mall, Bath, BA1
01225 330126
Mon-Sun

An eclectic mix of clothes, everything from club and street wear to posh frocks.

Mee

9a Bartlett St, Bath, BA1
01225 442250
Mon-Sun

Lovely shop, which prides itself on selling gorgeous things you can't find elsewhere, including lingerie, shoes, jewellery, handbags and beauty products. There's something for everyone, whether you want to spend a couple of quid on funky hair accessories or more on a posh pair of knickers! Mee has its own lingerie line and a website, coming soon, for online shopping.

The Yellow Shop

74 Walcot St, Bath, BA1
01225 404001
Mon-Sat from 10.30am; Sun 12pm-4pm

A few cool labels plus lots of lovely retro gear, including jeans, cords and leather jackets.

PROM DRESSES

Amelia Classics

3 The Causeway, Chippenham, SN15 3BT
01249 445050
www.ameliaclassics.co.uk
Mon-Sat 9.30am-5pm

Huge range of dresses and they promise never to let the same style and colour of dress go to the same prom!

BS8

34 Park St, Bristol, BS1
0117 930 4836
Mon-Sat until 6pm

This large funky store has an area devoted to prom dresses with a dressmaker on hand to assist and alter the dress of your dreams.

Carriages at Three

3 The Woolmarket, Cirencester, Gloucs, GL7 2PR
01285 651760
www.carriagesatthree.co.uk
Mon-Sat 9.30am-5pm

With some 1,500 different posh frocks, in all shapes and sizes, there is something for everyone here and customers come from far and wide, many from Bristol. The shop notes who has bought what to avoid two girls wearing exactly the same dress.

Drop Dead Gorgeous

179 Whitelandies Rd, Bristol, BS8 2RY
0117 973 1867
Mon-Sat 10am-6pm
and at: Seven Dials, Saw Close, Bath, BA1 1EN
01225 444232
Mon-Sat 9.30am-5.30pm
www.dropdeadgorgeousbath.com

Masses of lovely dresses, in all sizes. Look out for the shop's promotional leaflets that offer 10% off, they are distributed around the local schools in the run-up to the prom season.

Elite Fashions

6 Station Hill, Chippenham, SN15 1EG
01249 660775
www.elitefashions.biz
Tue-Fri 10am-5pm, Sat 9.30am-5pm

Cocktail dresses, ball gowns and prom dresses in all sizes.

Gladrags & Handbags

38b Princess Victoria St, Clifton Village, Bristol, BS8
0117 973 7687
Mon-Sat

Designer-label clothes, shoes, bags and jewellery at affordable prices as well as a big range of prom and ball dresses. There's a 10% student discount with an NUS card.

Lady Chique

80 Filton Rd, Horfield, Bristol, BS7 0PP
0117 979 0500
www.ladychique.co.uk
Tue-Sat 9.30am-5pm

Wide range of special occasion wear including prom dresses.

SHOES

The Boot Room

22 Park St, Bristol, BS1 5JA
0117 922 5455
Mon-Sun

Shoe-aholics will find an amazing selection of brands here including Buffalo, Converse, Dunlop, Gola, Road Hog, London Rebel and Ugg, plus a selection of Cowboy Boots. Children's sizes available in Converse and Buffalo. It also offers accessories, including belts, bags, mirror and sunglasses.

Clarks Shoes

The Mall, Cribbs Causeway, 0117 959 2290
35 Broadmead, BS1 8EU, 0117 929 0992
Mon-Sun

You know you can get good quality school shoes here. However, over the past few years their fashion range have become quite funky.

Jade Shoes

82 Park St, Bristol, BS1 5LA
0117 925 1174
www.jadeshoes.co.uk

A great shop to find the perfect shoes to match any occasion, be it a trainer, a pump or a boot! Choose from top brands like D&G, Miss Sixty, Diesel, Timberland, Camper, Birkenstock or Scholl.

John Lewis

The Mall, Cribbs Causeway, 0117 959 1100
Mon-Sun

Shoe department on the first floor selling many different brands including trainers.

KBK Shoes

203 Cheltenham Rd, Cotham, Bristol, BS6 5QX
0117 924 3707
Mon-Fri 9.30am-6pm, Sat 9am-6pm

Sells Dr Martens and Birkenstock sandals.

Clinks

At Charles Clinkard, The Mall, Cribbs Causeway
0117 959 2484

A good selection of brands.

The Handmade Shoe Company

64 Colston St, BS1 5AZ
0117 921 4247
Opening hours vary, please call for details.

Handmade shoes, available in standard sizes and made to measure.

Mastershoe

52 Park St, Bristol, BS1 5JM
0117 929 2020
www.mastershoe-sportshoe.co.uk
Mon-Sun

Huge range of shoes from practical boots to trainers. Choose from Dr Martens, Birkenstocks, Caterpillar, Timberland, Art or Kickers, to name but a few! Sizes start from size 4 for women and either a 6 or 7 for men. Other branches in Broadmead on Bond Street, in Bath and at Trowbridge.

Sportshoe

61 Park St, Bristol, BS1 5NU
0117 922 5516
www.mastershoe-sportshoe.co.uk

A large collection of shoes for all sports including Merrell walking boots, football boots, squash or running shoes. All members of staff are trained to analyse your running gait to make sure you have the right shoes for you!

Thomas Ford

The Clarks Shop, Kingschase Shopping Centre, Kingswood, BS15 2LP
0117 961 3807
Mon-Sat 9am-5.30pm
&
12 St Mary's Way, Thornbury, BS35 2BH
01454 419142
Mon-Sat 9am-5.30pm
&
17 Old Church Rd, Clevedon, BS21 6LU
01275 879512

Full range of Clarks' shoes, including trainers.

FACTORY OUTLETS

Factory outlet centres are great because you always feel like you're saving money — even if you're not! The three listed have a diverse range of shops in their complexes, selling high street and designer labels at a fraction of their original cost.

Clarks Village

Farm Rd, Street, Somerset, BA16 0BB
01458 840064
www.clarksvillage.co.uk
Apr-Oct: Mon-Sat 9am-6pm, Nov-Mar: until 5.30pm,
Thu 8pm, Sun 10am-5pm
Jct 23 M5 or A37, excellent sign-posting

There are now over 80 well known high street stores selling discontinued lines, last season's stock and factory seconds. Street centre also has several discount shoe shops. See Out & About in the West Country, pg 94.

Bridgend Designer Outlet

The Derwen, Bridgend, South Wales, CF32 9SU
01656 665 700
www.bridgenddesigneroutlet.com
Mon-Fri 10am-8pm, Sat 10am-7pm, Sun 10am-5pm
Jct 36, M4.

Offers end of season and excess stock at discounts of up to 50%. There are more than 80 stores at Bridgend and an on-site cinema.

Swindon Designer Outlet

Kemble Drive, Swindon, SN2 2DY
01793 507600
www.swindondesigneroutlet.com
Mon, Tue, Wed & Fri 10am-6pm, Thu 10am-8pm, Sat 9am-7pm, Sun 10am-5pm
Jct 16, M4 follow brown signs.

Offers end of season and excess stock at discounts of up to 50%. It has over 100 shops including fashion, toys, homewares & sport. It is situated in a restored grade II building that once housed the Great Western Railway works and is next door to the Museum of the Great Western Railway. See Steam in Out & About in the West Country pg 120.

MARKETS

Bath Flea Market

Walcot St, Bath, BA1
Sat

Great market every Saturday where you can pick up a bargain, on a fascinating street full of diverse and diverting shops.

Car boot sales

0117 922 4011
www.bristol-city.gov.uk

Car boot sales can be addictive, as a place to find bargains and for flogging unwanted stuff. There are several sales in Bristol. Some are held regularly, others on an ad hoc basis and are advertised in the local press. Bristol City Council markets department has the details.

Craft Market

Corn St, Bristol, BS1 1LJ
Fri 10am-5pm, Sat 10am-4pm

Lots of crafts including glass and jewellery.

Eastville Market

Eastgate Shopping Centre, Eastgate Rd, BS5 6XY
0117 935 4913 / 0117 934 9870
Fri and Sun until 2.30pm

Varied range of inexpensive goods, with an emphasis on clothes and fabrics. Great for fancy dress and costume fabrics.

Slow Food Market

Corn St, Bristol, BS1 1JQ
1st Sun of the month

Slow food is about good food production. This market is a monthly treat for everyone who loves real food.

Southmead Hospital Market

Southmead Rd, Southmead, BS10
07050 236 682
Sat 9am-4pm

Good for general bargain hunting. Food, clothing, homewares.

St Nicholas Market

St Nicholas St/Corn St, BS1 1LJ
0117 922 4017
Mon-Sat 9.30am-5pm

This is an indoor and outdoor market, situated in the Glass Arcade and the Corn Exchange, selling a wide variety of goods.

The Farmers Market

Corn St, Bristol, BS1
Wed 9.30am-2.30pm

Local farm produce including dairy, meat, fruit and veg, as well as wines and preserves.

The Sunday Market

Alberts Crescent, St Philips Marsh, Bristol
01608 652556
Sun 9am-3pm

In the grounds of the Wholesale Fruit and Veg Market, selling almost everything including inexpensive clothes, with some brand names.

VINTAGE & SECOND HAND

Vintage clothes are both affordable and stylish and Bristol is full of treasure troves, where you can pick up designer cast-offs and retro gems. There are also hundreds of charity shops that are worth checking out.

Clifton Arcade

Boyces Ave, Clifton, Bristol, BS8
Mon-Sun 10am-5.30pm, B/Hs closed

This beautiful shopping arcade is home to several independent retailers selling everything from costume jewellery to kitsch accessories, antique furniture and old books.

Clifton Hill Antique Costume and Textiles

5 Lower Clifton Hill, Bristol, BS8 1BT
0117 929 0644
Mon-Fri 12pm-5pm, Sat 10am-5pm

Since 1975, this fascinating and unique vintage clothes shop has long been a haunt for those searching for more unusual attire!

La Freak Boutique

Picton St, Montpelier, Bristol, BS6
Tue-Sat

This is a real treasure trove, with masses of second-hand clothes, bags, shoes and accessories plus antique furniture. If you are looking for period items, from the thirties to the eighties, then this is the place for you!

Naff Clothing Shop

13 Cotham Hill, Cotham, Bristol, BS6 6LD
0117 973 7458
Mon-Sat from 10.30am

An Aladdin's cave of clothes and accessories from vintage to the bizarre, including fancy dress clothes for hire. Costumes can be reserved in advance, call for further details.

Uncle Sams

54a Park St, Bristol, BS1 5JN
0117 929 8404
Mon-Sun

Vintage clothes sourced from the States. Browse though jeans, leather jackets, combats, basketball tops, minis and belts.

CHARITY SHOPS

Bristol has a wealth of charity shops, too many to list here, however, many are concentrated on Cotham Hill, along the Gloucester Road and Whiteladies Road.

St Peters Hospice

www.stpetershospics.org

This is Bristol's only adult hospice caring for local people with incurable illnesses, as well as supporting their families and children. There's a full list of branches on the website.

Save the Children

24 Regent St, Clifton, Bristol, BS8 4HG
0117 973 4057

Oxfam

11 Regent St, Clifton, Bristol, BS8 4HW
0117 973 9684
61-63 Cotham Hill, Bristol, BS6 6JR
0117 973 5200

SPECIALIST SHOPS

ARTS AND CRAFTS

Art@Bristol

44 Gloucester Rd, Bishopston, BS7
0117 923 2259
www.artatbristol.co.uk
Mon-Fri 9.30am-4.30pm, Sat 10am-4pm

This well stocked shop sells a wide range of art materials as well as materials and accessories for model-makers, graphic designers and photographers.

B Delicious

2 Triangle South, Clifton, Bristol, BS8
0117 929 1789
Mon 1pm-6pm, Tue-Sat 10am-6pm

Creative fun with beads and feathers, ready made, made to order or even made by you!

Bijoux Beads

2 Abbey St, off Abbey Green, Bath, BA1
01225 482024
www.bijouxbeads.co.uk
Mon-Sat

Beautiful beads of all shapes, sizes and colours as well as the "findings" to go with them — that's the clasps, chains and threads to you and me! And they run workshops if you want to find out more.

Children's Scrapstore

The Proving House, Sevier St, St Werburghs BS2 9LB
0117 908 5644
www.childrensscrapstore.co.uk
Mon-Wed 10am-5pm, Thu 10am-8pm,
Sat 10am-5pm

Registered charity that re-uses safe, clean waste for play purposes. There is a members-only warehouse and an art and craft shop, Artrageous, which is open to all (members receive 20% discount). Membership is open to any group working in creative play in an educational or therapeutic setting. U11s are not allowed in the warehouse.

Craft Works

355-357 Gloucester Rd, Horfield, BS7 8TG
0117 942 1644
Mon-Fri 9am-6pm, Sat 9am-5pm

Everything for the craft lover including fine art, needle craft and creative craft.

Creativity

7/9 Worrall Rd, off Whiteladies Rd, BS8 2UF
0117 973 1710
Mon-Sat 9am-5.30pm

Everything creative. It sells decorative mirrors, paints, tapestries, beads, glass and silk paints, candle making kits, ribbons and a lot more.

Evangeline's

58-61 St Nicholas Market, Bristol, BS1 1LJ
0117 925 7170
www.evangelines.co.uk
Mon-Sat 9.30am-5pm

Small shop stocking all kinds of arts and crafts — glass paints, acetate sheets, beads, embroidery material, origami paper and more.

Harold Hockey

170-174 Whiteladies Rd, Clifton, Bristol, BS8
0117 973 5988
Mon-Sat 8.45am-5.30pm

Packed with all things artistic, from easels to sketchpads, pens, cards and picture frames. Also a good selection of puzzles and games.

Hobbycraft

Centaurus Rd, Cribbs Causeway, BS34 5TS
0117 959 7100
www.hobbycraft.co.uk
Mon-Fri 9am-8pm, Sat 9am-6pm, Sun 10am-4pm

Superstore packed with craft and art materials plus occasional in-store demonstrations.

Rajani's Superstore Ltd

Fishponds Trading Estate, Maggs Lane, BS5 7EW
0117 958 5801
Mon-Fri 9am-6pm, Thu 8pm, Sat 9am-5.30pm,
Sun 10am-4pm

Here you will find artists' materials at very reasonable prices: paints, canvasses, brushes and frames. You will also be amazed at the other household bargains in this huge store.

BAGS AND BLING

Accessorize

The Mall, Cribbs Causeway, Bristol, BS34 5UR
0117 950 7728
72 Broadmead, Bristol, BS1 3DR
0117 929 9097
www.accessorize.co.uk
Mon-Sun

Colour-coordinated bags, scarves and jewellery.

Claire's Accessories

The Mall, Cribbs Causeway
0117 959 4779
Broadmead Gallery, Broadmead
0117 922 6657
Mon-Sun

A great selection of beauty and hair accessories. Branches in Yate and Weston-super-Mare.

Federation

56 Park St, Bristol, BS1
0117 929 9889
Mon-Sat until 6pm, Sun 12pm-5pm

This shop is packed with accessories and clothes. Check out the plastic and metal rings, earrings, necklaces, bracelets and bandannas.

Gladrags & Handbags

38b Princess Victoria St, Clifton Village, BS8
0117 973 7687
Mon-Sat

Designer-label clothes, shoes, bags and jewellery at affordable prices. There's a ten per cent student discount on presentation of an NUS card.

Iota

83 Gloucester Rd, Bishopston, Bristol, BS7
0117 924 4911
Mon-Sat 9.30am-5.30pm

Funky shop that sells jewellery as well as interesting retro homewares

Katze

55 Gloucester Rd, Bishopston, BS7 8AD
0117 942 5625
Mon-Sat 10.00am-5.30pm

Sells giftware and jewellery.

Mee

9a Bartlett St, Bath, BA1
01225 442250
Mon-Sun

Lovely shop, which prides itself on selling
gorgeous things you can't find elsewhere,
including jewellery, handbags, fragrance
and beauty products. There's something
for everyone, whether you want to spend a
couple of quid on funky hair accessories or
more on a posh pair of knickers! Its best-
sellers are gorgeous butterfly garlands for
decorating your room.

BIKES

Bike

Queens Avenue, Clifton, Bristol, BS8 1SB
0117 929 3500
www.bike-uk.co.uk
Mon-Sun

Bike heaven, with cross country, road and
freeride bikes, as well as kids' bikes for all
ages plus servicing and customisation.

Bristol Bike Workshop

84 Colston St, BS1 5BB
0117 926 8961
www.bikeworkshop.co.uk
Mon-Sat

Everything for the cyclist, from mountain and
road bikes to second hand bikes plus a full
servicing and repairs workshop.

Fred Baker Cycles

144 Cheltenham Rd, Bristol, BS6
0117 924 9610
Mon-Sat
292 Lodge Causeway, BS16
0117 965 5510
www.fredbakercycles.co.uk
Mon-Sat, closed Wed

These guys are all active cyclists and they

really know their stuff whether you are
shopping for a bike, accessories or need some
repairs done. The Lodge Causeway shop also
sells mopeds and electric bicycles.

Mud Dock Cycleworks

40 The Grove, Harbourside, Bristol, BS1
0117 929 2151
www.mud-dock.co.uk
Mon-Sun

Mud Dock stocks all types of bikes for all
ages — mountain, road and hybrids —
including the Trek brand. It also has a wide
range of shoes, clothing and accessories and
does repairs. In addition, it runs the Bike-
shed, a place where for £2.50 a day you can
leave your bike in a secure indoor bike park
and use the lockers and showers. There are
special deals for those using the Bike-shed on
a regular basis. Great café upstairs, see
Eating Out on pg 78.

BOOKS

Arnolfini

16 Narrow Quay, Harbourside, Bristol, BS1
0117 917 2300
Mon-Sun, 10am-8pm

Fabulous bookshop stocking architecture, art, visual culture, design, fashion, film and music books plus contemporary fiction, a wide selection of magazines and posters and cards.

Bookbarn

Central Trading Estate, Bath Rd, Totterdown
0117 300 5400
www.bookbarn.co.uk
Mon-Sat

Bookbarn has hundreds of thousands of books so you've an excellent chance of finding what you want. You can check online before visiting if you want to be certain of locating that hard to find tome! Bookbarn also trades through Amazon (www.amazon.co.uk) and Abe Books (www.abebooks.co.uk). It buys used books.

Blackwell's

89 Park St, Clifton, BS1 5PW
0117 927 6602
www.blackwell.co.uk
Mon-Sat 9.30am-7pm, Sun 11.30am-5.30pm

Friendly, expert staff. The array of books, CDs and academic publications is impressive. Within the shop is the popular Cafe Nero where you can have coffee while you browse. There is a separate section for young adults.

Book Cupboard

361-363 Gloucester Rd, Horfield, Bristol, BS7 8TG
0117 942 8878
www.bookcupboard.co.uk
Mon-Sat 9am-5.30pm

An excellent range of books including a substantial reference section and a separate section for teenage books. Free 24-hour book ordering service.

Books for Amnesty

103 Gloucester Rd, Bishopston, Bristol, BS7
0117 942 2969
www.booksforamnestybristol.org.uk
Mon-Fri 10am-4pm, Sat 11am-5pm

Excellent secondhand bookshop, with lots of fiction and non-fiction, CDs and DVDs as well as first editions and antiquarian books.

Borders

Clifton Promenade, 48-56 Queens Rd, BS8 1RE
0117 922 6959
Mon-Sat 9am-10pm, Sun 12am-6pm

A huge book shop catering for all ages and tastes. This store is very popular with teenagers with its Starbucks Coffee Shop, so you can browse while drinking coffee! See advertisement inside cover.

The Clifton Bookshop

84 Whiteladies Rd, Clifton, BS8 2QP
0117 983 8989
Mon-Sat 9am-5.30pm

A large selection of fiction, non-fiction and books of local interest. Ordering service.

Durdham Down Bookshop

39 North View, Westbury Park, Bristol, BS6 7PY
0117 973 9095
Mon-Sat 9am-6pm

For a small bookshop, it has a large section of books for all ages. 24 hour ordering service.

Family Books

3 Temple Court, Keynsham, BS31
0117 986 8747
Mon-Sat 9am-5pm

Children's books and Christian titles. Ordering service available.

Ottakas

Sovereign Centre, High St, Weston-s-Mare, BS23
01934 642588
www.ottakas.co.uk
Mon-Sun

Books to suit all ages including educational and those for young adults.

Oxfam Charity Bookshop

1 Queens Rd, Clifton, Bristol, BS8 1QE
0117 929 4890

Stanfords

29 Corn St, Bristol, BS1 1HT
0117 929 9966
www.stanfords.co.uk
Mon-Sat

This is a great shop for young explorers. Stanfords specialise in maps, but also stocks a wide range of travel and guide books. There are guide books for the young traveller and those taking gap years abroad. Online ordering is available.

Watershed

Watershed, Canons Rd, BS1
0117 927 6444
www.watershed.co.uk
Mon-Sun

There's a small shop at the entrance to the Watershed that sells film-related stuff that you can't easily find anywhere else, including books, cult DVDs, cards and posters.

Waterstones

College Green, Bristol, BS1 5TB
0117 925 0511
www.waterstones.co.uk
The Mall, Cribbs Causeway
0117 950 9813
The Galleries, Broadmead, BS1 3XF
0117 925 2274
Mon-Sun

Full range of books available for children, teenagers and parents. Ordering service.

WH Smith

The Galleries, Broadmead, BS1 3XB
0117 925 2152
www.whsmith.co.uk
The Mall, Cribbs Causeway, BS34
0117 950 9525
Mon-Sun

Range of books to suit all ages. Also stocks stationery, CDs and toys. An ordering service is available.

CDs, DVDs & VINYL

Chemical Records

Unit C2, St Vincents Trading Estate, Feeder Rd, Bristol, BS2
0117 971 4924
www.chemical-records.co.uk.
Mon-Sat 11am-7pm, Sun 11am-5pm

This successful online outfit also has a shop so you can come and browse through thousands of vinyl titles, with the emphasis on drum & bass, trance, house, techno, UK garage and hip hop. There's also DJ equipment for sale.

Fopp

43 Park St, Bristol, BS1, 0117 945 06858
The Corridor, Bath, BA1, 01225 481949
Mon-Sun

Fantastic offers on CDs and DVDs that cover a wide range of tastes. Upstairs at the Park Street branch is given over to rock, pop, books and DVDs, while the selection downstairs includes jazz, hip hop, R&B and drum and base. It also sells vinyl.

HMV

Broadmead, Bristol, BS1, 0117 929 7467
The Mall, Cribbs Causeway, BS34, 0117 950 6581
13-15 Stall St, Bath, BA1, 01225 466681
Mon-Sun

CDs, games and DVDs for all tastes.

Plastic Wax

222 Cheltenham Rd, Bristol, BS7
0117 942 7368
www.plasticwaxrecords.com
Mon-Fri 9.30am-7pm, Sat 9am-6.30pm

Over 190,000 items are in stock, all second-hand, including vinyl LPs, singles and 12-inches plus CDs, videos and DVDs.

Prime Cuts

85 Gloucester Rd, BS7
0117 983 0007
Mon-Sat

To be found below Repsycho Clothing, Prime Cuts stocks a large range of vinyl, representing every type of music genre, as well as videos, CDs and a few DVDs.

Replay Records

73 Park St, Bristol, BS1
0117 904 1134
Mon-Sun
134a East St, Bedminster, Bristol
0117 330 6393
Mon-Sat

CDs, vinyl and DJ gear. Also buys old CDs.

Rooted Records

9 Gloucester Rd, Bishopston, Bristol, BS7
0117 907 4372
www.rootedrecords.co.uk
Mon-Sat

Rooted specialises in drum and bass, dub step and grime, hip hop, reggae, funk, soul, break core and techno. As well as its huge selection of vinyl, it has a clothing line and some CDs.

Virgin Megastore

Broadmead, BS1, 0117 929 7798
The Mall, Cribbs Causeway, BS34, 0117 950 9600
Mon-Sun

CDs, DVDs, videos, t-shirts, games consoles and games.

COMICS, GAMES & HOBBIES

Al's Hobbies

438-440 Gloucester Rd, BS7 8TX
0117 944 1144
Tue-Sat 9.30am-5pm

For all hobby and modelling enthusiasts. Large stacks of balsa wood, building materials, paints, clay, brushes and model kits.

Antics

8 Fairfax St, Bristol, BS1 3DB
0117 927 3744
www.anticsonline.co.uk
Mon-Sat

Packed full of boys' toys, this shop sells model kits, remote-controlled cars, train sets, Scaletrix and much more.

Area 51

230 Gloucester Rd, Bishopston
0117 924 4655
www.area51online.co.uk
Mon-Sat

Comics, graphic novels, Games Workshop, books, Manga, DVDs, toys and games.

Bath Model Centre (The Modellers Den)

2 Lower Borough Walls, Bath, BA1 1QR
01225 460115
www.bathmodelcentre.com
Mon-Fri 9.30am-5.30pm, Sat 9am-5.30pm

Crammed from floor to ceiling with models, including Hornby, Scalextric and cars.

Enkla

21 Broad St, Bath, BA1 5LN
01225 339789
www.enkla.co.uk
Mon-Sat 10am-5.30pm, Sun 11am-4pm

Toys and games related to craft and science for kids up to 13yrs.

The Entertainer

The Galleries, Broadmead, BS1
0117 934 9522
www.theentertainer.com
Mon-Sat

Branches in Keynsham, Yate and Midsomer Norton. Mail or internet ordering available. Call 01494 737002 for a catalogue.

Eric Snooks, The Golden Cot

2 Abbeygate St, Bath, BA1 1NP
01225 463739
www.snooksonline.co.uk
Mon-Sat 9am-5.30pm

Wide range of toys on ground floor, including hobby toys, skateboards and rollerblades.

Forbidden Planet

Units 3-4 Clifton Heights, Clifton Triangle West, BS8
0117 929 8692
www.forbiddenplanet.com
Mon-Sat 10am-7pm; Sun 11am-5pm

Pure heaven for lovers of sci fi and cult stuff, with comics, magazines, games, DVDs, model kits and memorabilia.

Games Workshop

87 The Horsefair, Bristol, BS1 3JR
0117 925 1533
www.games-workshop.com
Mon-Sun

This is the place to come if you are into miniature war games, such as War Hammer. Games Workshop has a wide range of games and all the paints and modelling tools to go with them and it also holds events and offers free painting lessons.

Modelmania

13 Clouds Hill Rd, St George, BS5 7LD
0117 955 9819
Tue-Sat 9.30am-6pm

Stocks die cast models, scalextric and plastic model kits. Also new and second hand model railways.

Model Masters

International House, Clifton Rd, Weston-s-Mare BS23
01934 629 717
www.modelmasters.co.uk
Mon-Sat 9am-5pm

This shop sells model trains and railways sourced mainly from Germany, Switzerland and Austria. To the rear of the shop there is a model railway layout for customers to see the products in operation (closed between Christmas and Easter).

Travelling Man

8 Park St, Bristol, BS1 5NF
0117 925 8833
www.travellingman.com
Mon-Sun

At the bottom of Park Street, this is a good place to buy comics — new and old, action figurines, DVDs, board games and more! Every Tuesday, from 6pm-9.30pm, they hold a games night, turn up and play with your own board game or cards, or join in with others. For those into comics, you can join a fortnightly forum to discuss your favourite comic and share your artwork and stories.

COMPUTER GAMES

Eplay Ltd
22 Merchant St, Bristol, 0117 927 6060
3 Lower Borough Walls, Bath, 01225 444101
Mon-Sun

Game
30-32 Merchant St, Bristol, 0117 929 8626
Debenhams, Broadmead, 0117 921 1661
The Galleries, Broadmead, 0117 925 8180
The Mall, Cribbs Causeway, 0117 950 9292
Stall St, Bath, 01225 46345285
High St, Weston-s-Mare, 01934 416345

Pink Planet DVD & Games Xchange
3 Broad Walk, Knowle, 0117 977 0007
115 Gloucester Rd, 0117 942 0555
41a East St, Bedminster, 0117 953 1776

Three great shops in Bristol where you can
sell your old games or part-exchange them for
new or used ones.

COSMETICS & SMELLIES

The Body Shop
3 New Broadmead, Bristol, BS1 3HF
0117 923 0508
Queens Rd, Bristol, BS8 1QE
0117 926 0164
28 The Mall, Cribbs Causeway, Bristol, BS34 5GF
0117 950 9899
Mon-Sun

Lovely cosmetics and bath stuff.

Culpeper
28 Milsom St, Bath BA1
01225 425875
90 Park St, Bristol, BS1
0117 945 0698
www.napiers.net
Mon-Sun

Aromatherapy and herbal products, including
essential oils, natural and organic food and
drink and books and accessories.

Lush
73 Broadmead, Bristol
0117 925 7582
12 Union St, Bath, BA1 1RR
01225 428271
Mon-Sun

Lovely soaps and bath bombs.

Neal's Yard Remedies
126 Whiteladies Rd, BS8 2RP
0117 946 6034
Treatment clinic 0117 946 6035
www.nealsyardremedies.com
Mon-Sun

Knowledgeable staff can advise on their wide
range of aromatherapy, herbs, homeopathy
and flower remedies. Some 25 different
treatments are available at the clinic
upstairs (including massage, sports therapy,
aromatherapy and acupuncture) which is open
every day until 9pm.

Superdrug
www.superdrug.com
Mon-Sun
Branches at: Broadmead, Bedminster, Knowle,
Fishponds, Kingswood, Cribbs, Nailsea, Yate & Bath.

Massive selection of make-up and smellies, all
at great prices.

DANCEWEAR

Cavalier Dancewear

45 Deanery Rd, Warmley, BS15 9JB
0117 940 5677
Mon-Fri 10.30-5pm, Closed Wed, Sat 10am-4pm

Good range of clothing and shoes for ballet, tap and jazz. Also stocks fancy dress and party wear.

Dance World

52 Bedminster Parade, Bedminster, BS3 4HS
0117 953 7941
www.danceworld.ltd.uk
Mon-Sat 9am-5.30pm

Extensive range of dancewear and dance shoes for ballet, tap and salsa.

Dancewell

60 Cotham Hill, Bristol, BS6 6JX
0117 973 0120
www.dancewell.com
Mon-Sat 9am-5pm

Supplying Bristol's dancers for 40 years. Dancewear and shoes for all types of dance.

Holbrooks

1-2 Boyce's Ave, Clifton, BS8
0117 973 8350
Mon-Sat 9am-5.30pm

Dance shoes available for ballroom, latin, ballet, tap and jazz.

Kathy's Dancewear

Alexandra Park, Fishponds, BS16 2BG
0117 965 5660
www.dancestation.org.uk
Mon-Fri 9am-12.30pm,
1.30pm-6pm term time, 5pm sch holidays

Good range of ballet, tap, modern & jazz dance wear, plus shoes & leotards.

Weston Dancewear

32a-34 Orchard St, Weston-s-Mare, BS23 1RQ
01934 419818
Mon-Sat 9am-5pm

Large range of dancewear, gym leotards and shoes for ballet, tap,modern and jazz.

ECO SHOPS

Seven Generations

10-12 Picton St, Montpelier, BS6
0117 942 0165
www.sevengenerations.co.uk
Mon-Sat

New eco-emporium with everything from environmentally-friendly cleaning products to green paints and a big range of books.

FANCY DRESS

Christmas Steps Joke Shop

47 Colston St, Bristol, BS1 5AX
0117 926 4703
Tue-Sat 10am-5pm (4.30pm costume hire)

Jokes, wigs, magic tricks and lots of costumes and accessories as well as costume hire.

Dauphine's of Bristol

7 Cleeve Rd, Downend, Bristol, BS16 6AD
0117 955 1700
Mon-Sat 9am-5pm

Sells wigs, face painting and theatre make-up. There are make-up courses for children.

Starlite Costumes

275-277 Lodge Causeway, Fishponds, BS16 3RA
0117 958 4668
www.starlitecostumes.co.uk
Mon-Sat 9.30am-5.30pm, Wed closed

Quality fancy dress hire, theatrical costumes and wigs. Face paints and novelties.

GIFTS AND GOODIES

About Face

22 Princess Victoria St, Clifton Village, BS8 4BU
0117 923 7405
Mon-Sun

If you are stuck on what to buy a friend or relative, this is the shop for you. Beautiful contemporary jewellery, photo frames, bags, candles along with intriguing gimmicks, gadgets and decorations.

Bristol Guild of Applied Art

68-70 Park St, BS1 5JY
0117 926 5548
www.bristolguild.co.uk
Mon and Sat 9.30am-5.30pm, Tue-Fri 9am-5.30pm

Large store selling gifts, household goods and furniture as well as toy and games.

Katze

55 Gloucester Rd, Bishopston, BS7 8AD
0117 942 5625
Mon-Sat 10.00am-5.30pm

Sells giftware and jewellery popular with teenagers. There is a craft department upstairs selling things llike beads and fabric.

Iota

83 Gloucester Rd, Bishopston, Bristol, BS7
0117 924 4911
Mon-Sat 9.30am-5.30pm

Funky shop that sells bits and bobs to make your home look like a palace, plus jewellery.

Pod

24 The Mall, Clifton, BS8
Mon-Sun

A tempting array of lovely stuff that caters for everyone. There's baby and kiddie stuff, gadgets for men, homewares, candles, coffee table books, leather luggage, Kath Kidston goodies, clocks, picture frames and more.

Ripe

6 Perry Rd, BS1
0117 909 4415
www.ripeshop.co.uk
Mon-Sat

Colourful shop full of kitsch and design-led items, including jewellery, novelty items, clocks, lighting, postcards, stickers, key rings, cards and wrap.

Shrinking Violet

20 Park St, Bristol, BS1 5JA
0117 929 4566
www.shrinkingviolet.com

A quirky gift shop selling everything from cards, to lights and bags.

Soukous

1a Pitville Place, Cotham Hill
0117 923 9854
www.soukous.co.uk
Mon-Sat

This independent giftware company is an Aladdin's cave of lovely stuff including Indian throws, cushions, cards, curtains, jewellery, fairy lights, candles, bead curtains and bedding.

Village

2a Boyces Ave, Clifton, BS8
0117 908 0007
Mon-Sun

Lots of lovely stuff to tempt you or to give as gifts, from groovy mugs and laundry bags to bead curtains, cushions, picture frames and jewellery. Kids clothes and accessories as well as grown-up fashion downstairs.

KITES

Bristol Kite Store

39A Cotham Hill, Redland, BS6 6JY
0117 974 5010
www.kitestore.co.uk
Mon-Fri 10am-6pm, Sat 9.30am-5.30pm

Kites and kite surfing equipment, DIY kites and spare parts. Also frisbees, yo-yos, juggling and circus equipment.

UFO Power Kites

41 Alexandra Parade, Weston-s-Mare, BS23 1QZ
01934 644 988
Mon-Sat 10am-5.30pm

Kites, kite surfing equipment, spare parts, skateboards, inline skates, frisbees, yo-yos, juggling equipment and clothing.

MAIL ORDER

American Apparel

www.americanapparel.co.uk

Ethical US company that makes top quality sweatshirts, sweaters and t-shirts in a myriad of colours.

Badges

www.funkybadges.com

Badges of every type to suit all types of personalities! From smiley faces to delicate flowers with everything else in between including a great range of skull designs.

Bishopston Trading Company

193 Gloucester Rd, Bristol, BS7 8BG
0117 924 5598
www.bishopstontrading.co.uk

Co-operative selling clothes made from organic handloom cloth, creating employment in the South Indian village of KV Kuppam.

Howies

www.howies.co.uk

Ultra cool, environmentally conscious casual clothes for cyclists, skaters and surfers.

I want one of those

www.iwantoneofthose.com

Loads of unusual toys, gifts and gadgets.

Joe Browns

www.joebrowns.co.uk

Casual clothes for adventurous people.

Oxfam

www.oxfam.org.uk

For more unusual gifts or donations.

Nitty Gritty

1 Oakwood Court, Kensington, London, W14 8JU
0207 460 0166
www.nittygritty.co.uk

This company, created and run by three mums, offers a chemical-free Head Lice Solution and Repellent Spray that comes with loads of recommendations. Their award-winning NitFree Comb effectively removes head lice, nits and eggs. See advertisement on inside cover.

Raindrops

01730 810031
www.raindrops.co.uk

Raindrops sells good quality Scandinavian outdoor clothing. Products include dungarees and jackets, camouflage trousers, wellie boots, ski kit, thermals and swim wear. Sizes up to 13yrs.

MUSIC & INSTRUMENTS

Bristol Music Shop/Hobgoblin

30 College Green, Bristol, BS1
0117 929 0390
Mon-Sat 9.30am-5.30pm

A wide range of musical instruments,
accessories and sheet music.

Clevedon Music Shop

19 Alexandra Rd, Clevedon, BS21 7QH
01275 342 090
Mon-Sat 9.30am-5.30pm
Road is opposite pier, café Scarlett's on corner.

Great selection of instruments and
accessories, particularly guitars. Walls lined
with sheet music. Ordering system.

Drumbank Music Drum Centre

203 Gloucester Rd, Bristol, BS7
0117 975 5366
www.drumbankmusic.co.uk
Mon-Fri 10am-7pm
Sat 10am-6pm

Drums and percussion. Tuition available,
nearby practice rooms.

Drumbank Music Guitar centre

235 Gloucester Rd, Bristol, BS7
0117 924 7222
www.drumbankmusic.co.uk
Mon-Fri 10am-7pm
Sat 10am-6pm

Guitars, accessories, keyboards and PAs.
Tuition available, nearby practice rooms.

The Drum Store

125 St George's Rd, Hotwells
0117 929 8540
www.bristoldrumstore.co.uk
Tue-Sat 10.30am-5pm

This shop has been around for some 30

years and it offers all the kit as well as repairs and advice.

Mickleburgh

1-9 Stokes Croft, Bristol, BS1 3PL
0117 924 1151
www.mickleburgh.co.uk
Mon-Sat 9am-5.30pm

Large selection of new and second hand upright and grand pianos. Also guitars, drums, violins, amplifiers, brass and woodwind instruments. Sheet music and accessories.

Music Room

30 College Green, Bristol, BS1 5TB
0117 929 0390
Mon-Sat 9.30am-5.30pm

A large range of printed sheet music. Also sells basic school recorders, percussion instruments, flutes, saxophones, clarinets, trumpets and keyboards. There is an instrument hire scheme and mail order.

Oasis Sound and Lighting

19 Windmill Farm Business Centre, Bartley St, Bedminster
0117 966 3663
www.oasis-online.co.uk
Mon-Sat

The place for PA, disco and karaoke kit.

Rikaxxe Music

8-10 Bond St, Bristol, BS1
0117 929 8481
Mon-Sat 10am-5.30pm

Every type of guitar under the sun plus accessories and parts. Music tuition available.

Saunders Recorders

205 Whiteladies Rd, Bristol, BS8 2XT
0117 973 5149
www.saundrecs.co.uk
Mon-Sat 9.30am-1.15pm & 2.30pm-5.30pm, early closing, Wed from 11.30am & Sat from 1.15pm

International supplier of recorders. The walls are lined with a vast selection of recorders. Large range of sheet music for recorders.

Sound Control

5 Rupert St, Bristol
0117 934 9955
www.soundcontrol.co.uk
Mon-Fri 10am-6pm, Sat 9am-5.30pm

Guitars, drums, PA kit, music technology, computer recording systems and software.

Treble Rock Music

149 St Michael's Hill, Bristol, BS1
0117 974 2675
Mon-Fri 10.30am-6.30pm, Sat 10am-6pm

Large range of new and second-hand guitars plus second-hand amplification and on-site set-up and repair.

ORGANIC & SPECIALIST FOOD

Soil Association

Bristol House, 40-56 Victoria St, Bristol, BS1 6BY
0117 314 5000
www.soilassociation.org

The Soil Association has a wealth of information on organic food and healthy living. It sells the Organic Directory, listing all organic outlets, which is also on their consumer website: www.whyorganic.org

Earthbound

8 Abbotsford Rd, Cotham, BS6 6HB
0117 904 2260
Mon-Sat 9am-6pm

Friendly store specialising in locally produced organic foods. Sells a wide range of fresh fruit and veg, basic and luxury organic groceries, wholefoods and fair trade products.

Fresh & Wild

85 Queen's Rd, Clifton, Bristol, BS8 1QS
0117 910 5930
www.freshandwild.com
Mon-Fri 8am-9pm, Sat 9am-8pm, Sun 11am-5pm

This natural food store has a vast range of fresh produce and dry goods. There is a salad bar for eating in or take-away.

Harvest Natural Foods

11 Gloucester Rd, Bishopston, BS7 8AA
0117 942 5997
www.harvest-bristol.coop
Mon-Sat 9am-6pm

This workers' co-operative sells a wide range of organic products including bread, fresh fruit and veg suitable for vegans. They also stock a wide range of gluten-free products and have a delicatessen.

Southville Deli

262 North St, Bedminster, BS3 1JA
0117 966 4507
www.southvilledeli.com
Mon-Sat 9am-5.30pm

Organic whole foods, ground coffee, herbal teas, preserves and goats milk.

Stoneground Health Foods

5 The Mall, Clifton Village, BS8 4DP
0117 974 1260
Mon-Fri 9am-5pm, Sat 9am-3pm

Combination of organic, GM-free and natural products, 100% vegetarian. Sells fruit, veg, dairy products and dry goods. Take-away sandwiches, home-made soup, jacket potatoes, smoothies and fresh juice.

The Bay Tree

176 Henleaze Rd, Henleaze, BS9
0117 962 1115
Mon-Sat 9am-5pm

Stocks a wide variety of natural, organic and gluten-free foods as well as supplements, natural toiletries, Bach Flower and other homeopathic remedies.

Viva Oliva

30 Oxford St, Totterdown, BS3 4RJ
0117 940 7419, 07980 634926
Mon-Sat 10am-6pm

Friendly delicatessen that stocks a variety of Mediterranean delights including breads, olives, sundried tomatoes, homemade sauces and pestos, preserves, cheeses and meats. The stuffed vine leaves are highly recommended.

PETS

The recommended independent pet shops listed below stock smaller animals. It is not possible to buy puppies and kittens from pet shops — contact your vet or rescue centre.

Bath Cats and Dogs Home (RSPCA)

The Avenue, Claverton Down, Bath BA2 7AZ
01225 466129
www.bathcatsanddogshome.org.uk

Bristol Dogs and Cats Home (RSPCA)

50 Albert Rd, St Philips, Bristol BS2 0XW
0117 977 6043
www.bristoldogsandcatshome.org.uk

Mar-Pet

25 Highridge Rd, Bishopsworth, BS13 8HJ
0117 964 3416
Mon-Sat 9am-1pm & 2pm-5.30pm, closed Wed

Specialises in birds, cold water fish and small animals. Sells cages, hutches and accessories.

Pet & Poultry Stores

5 Worrall Rd, Clifton, BS8 2UF
0117 973 8617
Mon-Sat 9am-5.30pm, Wed until 3.30pm

Friendly shop with a range of small animals, birds, animal feed and accessories. Specialises in garden bird food and feeders. Free delivery.

Roxfords

155 Gloucester Rd, Bishopston, BS7 8BA
0117 924 8397
Mon-Sat 9am-5.30pm

Large range of small animals, rodents and fish. Pet toys, leads (can engrave discs) and cages. Lodges small animals for the holidays.

SKATEBOARDS

50/50 Skateboard Supplies

16 Park Row, BS1 5LJ
0117 914 7783
www.5050store.com
Mon-Sat 9am-6pm

Skateboard specialists stocking hardware, footwear, clothing, accessories, videos. Mail order available, see website. "Skateboarder owned and operated."

Extreme

53 Union St, Bristol, BS1
0117 933 8500
Mon-Sun

Skate clothes for guys and girls as well trucks and decks. Beachwear in season. Accessories include watches, badges, patches, key chains, sunglasses and hats.

Routeone

9 Broad St, Bath, BA1 5LJ
01225 446710
www.routeone.co.uk
Mon-Sat 9.30am-6pm, Sun 11am-5pm

Skateboards and hardware, roller blades, inline skates, power kiting, frisbees and BMX. They also have clothing.

Shark Bite Surf Shop

68 Park Row, Bristol, BS1
0117 929 9211
Mon-Sun

It offers a tailor-made service to build you the skateboard of your dreams!

UFO Power Kites

41 Alexandra Parade, Weston-s-Mare, BS23 1QZ
01934 644 988
Mon-Sat 10am-5.30pm

Large shop selling kites, kite surfing equipment, spare parts, skate boards, inline skates, frisbees, yo-yos, juggling equipment and clothing.

SPORT & OUTDOOR PURSUITS

Beach Shack

16 Kellaway Avenue, Bristol, BS6 7XR
0117 923 2255
www.beachshack.co.uk
Mon-Sat

Surf, beachwear and water sports specialists. Wetsuits, surfboards and accessories.

Bristol Angling Centre

12-16 Doncaster Rd, Southmead, Bristol
0117 950 8723
Mon-Sat

Everything for the fishing enthusiast.

Easy Runner

6 Horfield Rd, Off St Michael's Hill
0117 929 7787
Mon-Fri 10am-6pm, Wed until 7pm,
Sat 9.30am-5.30pm

If it's running shoes you're after, then make sure you check out this shop.

Geronimo

171 North St, Ashton, Bristol, BS3 1JD
0117 953 3400
www.geronimosports.co.uk
Mon/Tue/Sat 9am-5pm, Wed 9am-4pm,
Thu/Fri 9am-6pm. Later opening by appointment

Everything for the adventurous, including rock climbing and snowboarding equipment.

Gilesports

The Mall, Cribbs Causeway
0117 950 9445
Mon-Sun

Sports clothing, equipment, footwear and swimwear.

Gyles Bros Ltd

188 Whiteladies Rd, Clifton, BS8 2XU
0117 973 3143
Mon-Sat 9am-5.30pm

This is a family-run business, selling quality equipment for most major sports. They offer a racquet restringing service (next day) and on the spot grip replacement.

Ikon (UK) Ltd

190 Henleaze Rd, Bristol, BS9 4NE
0117 962 0011
www.ikon-uk.com
Mon-Fri 9am-5pm, Sat 10am-5pm

Recently opened and keen to help with any sporting equipment/clothing or uniforms you may need.

Kathmandu

11-13 Queens Rd, Bristol, BS8 1QE
0117 927 7814
www.kathmandu.com

This Australian company has been producing quality outdoor clothing and equipment for travel and adventure for over 30 years.

Marcruss Stores

177-181 Hotwells Rd, Hotwells, BS8 4RY
0117 929 7427
Mon-Sat 9am-5.30pm

Large range of camping equipment and accessories. Family ski and outdoor wear.

Millets The Outdoor Shop

9-10 Transom House, Victoria St, BS1 6AH
0117 926 4892
10 Broadmead, Bristol BS1 3HH
0117 922 1167
Mon-Sat 9am-5.30pm, Sun 10am-4pm

Well-known chain selling a wide selection of tents, outdoor equipment and clothes.

Skate and Ski

104 High St, Staple Hill, Bristol
0117 970 1356
Mon-Sat

Sells everything connected with skiing, skateboarding and skating. Leisure clothing and accessories. Also hires out ski gear.

Outdoor Pursuits

If you are looking for adventure:

Snow & Rock Superstore

Shield Retail Centre, Filton, BS34 7BQ
0117 914 3000
www.snowandrock.com
Mon-Fri 10am-7pm, Thu until 8pm, Sat 9am-6pm, Sun 11am-5pm

Packed full of stylish outdoor clothing for all ages, Snow & Rock stocks a huge selection of ski and rock climbing equipment.

Taunton Leisure

38-42 Bedminster Parade, Bedminster, BS3 4HS
0117 963 7640
www.tauntonleisure.com
Mon-Sat 9am-5.30pm, Thu until 7pm

Taunton Leisure stocks a broad range of outdoor clothing and camping equipment as well as climbing, cycling and walking gear. It also sells guidebooks, maps and rucksacks.

Wet & Windy Company

5 Ashton Drive, Bristol, BS3 2PN
0117 966 9582
www.wet-windy.co.uk
Mon-Sat 10am-6pm, Thu until 7pm

The place to buy everything to do with water sports, from kayaks and dinghies to wetsuits and surfboards, including the NSP range of boards which are very light and strong — perfect for novice surfers.

STATIONERY

Harold Hockey

170-174 Whiteladies Rd, Clifton, Bristol
0117 973 5988
Mon-Sat 8.45am-5.30pm

Packed with all things artistic, from easels to sketchpads, pens, cards and picture frames. Also a good selection of puzzles and games.

Paperchase

Borders, Queens Rd, 0117 922 6959
House of Fraser, Broadmead, 0117 929 1021
31 Milsom St, Bath, 01225 446824

Large selection of brightly coloured notebooks and matching pens. Also birthday cards and art supplies.

Stationery World

63 Park St, Bristol, BS1 5NU
0117 929 8099
www.stationeryworldonline.co.uk
Mon-Sun

This independent retailer can offer you anything and everything for your stationery and art supply needs.

WH Smith

The Galleries, Broadmead, BS1 3XB
0117 925 2152
The Mall, Cribbs Causeway, BS34
0117 950 9525
www.whsmith.co.uk
Mon-Sun

Books, stationery and CDs. An ordering service is available.

TRAVEL

Nomad Travel Stores

38 Park St, Bristol, BS1 5JG
0117 922 6567
www.nomadtravel.co.uk
Mon-Sun

This welcome addition to Park Street can help you with all aspects of your travel planning, from clothes, books, compasses and sunglasses to protection from the sun or even nasty bugs! The store has its own travel clinic, closed on Sundays, offering on-the-spot vaccinations for protection from Yellow Fever, Diphtheria, etc. There's no need to be registered, simply ring for an appointment and you can get vaccinated that day, if necessary.

UNIFORMS

Most department stores and supermarkets sell school uniforms and offer good value ranges. Below are specialist stockists.

National School Wear Centres

22 Gloucester Rd Nth, Filton Park, BS7 0SF
0117 969 8551
www.n-sc.co.uk
Mon-Fri 9am-5pm, Sat 10am-4pm

Sells generic and some North Bristol state school uniforms. Also clothing for Scouts, Guides, ballet, bowling and sportswear.

School Togs Nailsea Ltd

110 High St, Nailsea, BS48 1AH
01275 857 491
Mon-Fri 9am-5.30pm, Sat 9am-5pm

Comprehensive range of uniforms for local schools, along with school sports, Scouts, Guides & dance clothing, up to 16yrs.

Ikon (UK) Ltd

190 Henleaze Rd, Bristol, BS9 4NE
0117 962 0011
Mon-Fri 9am-5pm, Sat 10am-5pm

Recently opened and keen to help with any sporting equipment/clothing or Scout/school uniforms you may need.

SERVICES

HAIRDRESSERS

AKA

23 Zetland Rd, Redland, BS6 7AH
0117 904 2244
Under 16yrs 20% off all cuts, prices charged
according to length of hair; women's cuts start from
£25, men from £18
Mon & Tue: 9am-6pm, Wed & Thurs: 9am-8pm,
Fri: 9am-7pm, Sat: 8am-6pm

A great salon offering a friendly and
professional service in a contemporary setting.

Bonomini

22 Alma Vale Rd, Clifton, BS8
0117 923 9169
£16 5-9yrs, £25 10-14yrs

This sophisticated salon welcomes children
and young people of all ages. An appointment
is not always needed.

Bristol Barber Company

17 The Mall, Clifton, BS8 4DS
0117 970 6466
Mon-Thu 8.30am-6pm, Fri 8.30am-6.30pm,
Sat 8.30am-6pm
Gents cut from £8, Students £6
£17 face massage & cut throat shave

An authentic barbers offering cut throat
shaving, short back 'n' sides, plus a range of
treatments including manicures just for men.

The Business Hair Studio

69 Islington Rd, Southville, BS3
0117 966 6618
Mon & Wed 9am-5pm, Tue closed,
Thu/Fri 9am-8pm, Sat 8.30am-4.30pm

A friendly Southville salon.

Central Studio

Monarch House, Queen Charlotte St, BS1 4EX
0117 929 0120
Tue-Sat late night Fri & Wed
last appointment at 7.15pm
8-12yrs old cuts cost £21
Over 12yrs cost varies

Newer second location for Central Studio
where they can offer a full hair, colour and
nail service to complete the new you! While
you are waiting enjoy one of their juices from
their juice bar.

Grades

44 Broad St, Bristol, BS1
0117 926 8332
49a West Park Rd, off Whiteladies Rd, BS9
0117 973 1866

A modern barbershop with cuts for students
from £7.50. Show your NUS card.

Hanski

107 St. George's Rd, Hotwells, BS1 5UW
0117 927 9262
Tues-Sat 10-5.30pm, (late closing Thur 6.30pm)
Men £16, Women from £27.50
20% Student discount

Cool salon, conveniently located by the
college with experienced father and son team
offering great-looking styles at excellent rates.

Hobbs

50 Park Row, BS1 5LH
0117 929 1635
Tue/Wed/Fri 10am-6.30am, Thurs 10am-8pm,
Sat 9am-5pm
Under 14yrs (provided parents have hair cut there)
cuts cost £5 plus your age i.e. £17 for a 12 year old
Over 14yrs old 15% off a cut; men from £19.50,
women from £28
Plus 15% student discount.

Style abounds in this trendy salon, complete
with its own landscaped gardens, underfloor
fish tank and cappuccino bar. Choice of
several stylists cutting upstairs with a separate
colour room downstairs.

Jon Hurst Hairdressing

18 Cotham Hill, Cotham, Bristol, BS6 6LF
0117 373 0044
Mon-Fri 10am-7pm, Sat 9am-5pm

Full range of hairdressing services available to children, teenagers and adults.

Mack Daddy's

8 Perry Rd, BS1 5BQ
0117 929 3866
Tue-Sat: 10am-6pm
Wet cut from £35, under 14yrs £25

Mack Daddy's is a unisex hairdressers that offers a cut and dry service and also specialises in a range of colouring techniques including highlights, lowlights and tints. Student discounts (with proof of ID) are provided.

Maximum FX

3 St Augustines Place, BS1 4UD
0117 923 0231
Tue-Sat, Tue/Thu until 7.30pm
£18 up to 16yrs old for girls
£15 for boys up to 16yrs

Seriously stylish city centre hair salon, serving up fantastic cuts and colour.

Paul Stein

16 Park St, BS1 5HR
0117 926 4400
Mon-Wed 9am-6pm, Thurs 9am-9pm, Fri 9am-7pm, Sat 8.30am-5pm
Men £17, Women £24
10% student discount

Glitzy salon with nationally acclaimed stylists – the perfect pick me up for a new you

Pride Hair and Beauty Salon

236 Stapleton Rd, Easton, BS5 0NT
0117 951 9518
Tue/Wed 9am-5.30pm, Thu 10am-6pm,
Fri 11.30am-8pm, Sat 8.30am-4.30pm
£11.50 girls, £7 infants & boys under 12yrs

Cuts all types of hair but specialises in Afro hair. An appointment is required.

Reflections

Branches: Clifton, Bedminster, Broadmead, Fishponds, Kingswood, Knowle, Keynsham, Nailsea, Thornbury and Yate
£13 boys 6-16yrs, £15.40 girls 6-16yrs
Trim priced at discretion of management

A recommended chain of salons with branches acoss Bristol.

Supercuts

The Mall, Cribbs Causeway
0117 959 2597
Mon-Fri 10am-9pm, Sat 9am-7pm, Sun 11am-5pm
And: In store at Asda Walmart, Cribbs Causeway
0117 923 6180
Mon-Fri 9am-6pm, Sat 8.30am-4.30pm
And: 7 Union Gallery, Broadmead
0117 929 2184
£11.95 over 8s

A national chain of salons. Opening times vary between stores. You do not need an appointment.

Toni & Guy

1-2 St. Augustines Parade, BS1 4XJ
0117 930 0077
Mon-Fri 9am-8pm, Sat 8.30am-6pm
Up to 12 years old 50% off prices starting from; men £24, women £32 (discount not available on Sat or after 5pm)

One of the most well-known names in hairdressing. The price of cuts varies according to the experience of the stylist and there is a price range to suit all budgets. For those over 16 years there is an opportunity for a reduced price cut and/or colour at the Training Academy open Mon-Thurs from 11.30am-2pm. You must have an assessment and then return for your cut. Expect to pay £5-10 for a cut and £15-20 for colour.

Urban Halo

Kaarina Neate
07951 357982
kaarina@urbanhalo.co.uk
Wash, cut and blow dry costs from £18
Re-style from £22

Professional hairdresser and colour technician offering a complete hair and make up service in your home. Group discounts for four or more, perfect for a girls' (or lads') night in!

PAMPERING

There's no shortage of places to get pampered in Bristol. If you're really strapped for cash, contact Filton College where student health and beauty practitioners often give free treatments.

Filton College Health & Beauty Department
0117 909 2319

Atkinson's

5 Waterloo St, Clifton, BS9
0117 974 1394,
www.atkinsonsspabeauty.com

Purely for pampering this place, and popular to boot. Now an appointed Guinot salon, specialising in hydrodermy, it also offers body relaxation with aromamud and fresh spa treatments and products including the delicious-sounding cinnamon and chocolate wraps alongside the usual facial and body treatments — manicures, pedicures, facials and detoxes and a good range of beauty products.

Avalon Beauty

91b Whiteladies Rd, Bristol, BS9
0117 923 7630

For all your beauty needs, Avalon offer facials, electrolysis, waxing, bronzing, massage and much more.

Beauty Basics

Katie Wilkins
07890 774 891
0117 962 9527
£5 call out charge, treatment costs vary

Qualified beautician based in Westbury-on-Trym, able to bring a range of treatments to your home from waxing and facials to massages and pedicures. Katie will also do a Beauty Party lasting two hours, offering girls the chance to learn more about how to apply make up and care for their skin.

Bliss

9 Waterloo St, Clifton, Bristol, BS9
0117 974 1066

Treat a friend to an hour or two of pure pampering pleasure. Try the "tea for two" choose between facials, manicures, pedicures, massages and many more treatments, while having a bonding session with your best buddy. They'll also take care of your beauty parties. Products by OPI, Jessica and Creative.

Bo Jo Brownz

10 Park Row, Bristol, BS1
0117 922 7744
www.bojobrownzhairandtanning.co.uk
Beds start from £3.50
Spray tans from £25.00

Providing you are over 16yrs old, you can pop in to Bo Jo Brownz for an instant tan. Whether it is a quick session on one of their beds or a spray tan with a therapist, it's best to call in first to see what would suit your skin.

The Massage Centre at Kingsdown Sports Centre

Portland St, Kingsdown, BS2 8HL
0117 942 6582
www.bristol-city.gov.uk/sport

Neal's Yard Remedies

126 Whiteladies Rd, BS8 2RP
0117 946 6034
Mon-Sun
Treatment clinic: 0117 946 6035
www.nealsyardremedies.com

Knowledgeable staff can advise on their wide range of aromatherapy, herbs, homeopathy and flower remedies. Some 25 different treatments are available at the clinic upstairs (including massage, sports therapy, aromatherapy and acupuncture) which is open every day until 9pm.

Relaxation Centre

9 All Saints Rd, Clifton, BS8 2JG
0117 970 6616
www.relaxationcentre.co.uk
Mon-Thu 11am-10pm, Fri-Sun 9am-10pm

Offers holistic treatments, spa facilities and gift vouchers; no membership required.

The Treatment Rooms

14 Park Row, BS1
0117 922 7711
www.tr-bristol.co.uk
Mon-Sat, Wed/Thu/Fri until 8pm

Beautifully-decorated salon offering a full range of beauty, holistic and alternative therapies from spray tanning to Hopi ear candles and Indian head massages. The Brazilian waxes, though a tad expensive, are the best around.

Wish Beauty

24 Gloucester Rd, Bishopston, BS7
0117 907 7446

Regular treatments such as waxing, manicures and massage at pretty good prices. Even better when you take along your NUS card durng the week to receive a 15% discount.

LATE NIGHT PHARMACIES

Pharmacies have a rota for opening outside normal retail hours. Details can be found in the Bristol Evening Post or by calling NHS Direct. The pharmacies listed below are open after 5.30pm and on Sundays.

NHS Direct

0845 606 46 47

Gives out of hours pharmacies in your area.

Asda Walmart

Highwood Lane, Cribbs Causeway
0117 979 0426
Mon-Fri 9am-10pm, Sat 8.30am-10pm,
Sun 10am-4pm

Boots The Chemists

19 St Augustines Parade, (near to Hippodrome)
0117 927 6311
Mon-Fri 8am-7pm, Sat 8.30am-5.30pm
&
59 Broadmead, Bristol City Centre
0117 929 3631
Mon, Wed, Fri 8.45am-5.30pm, Tue 9am-5.30pm,
Thu 8.45am-7pm, Sat 8.45am-6pm, Sun 11am-5pm
&
Upper Mall, Cribbs Causeway
0117 950 9744
Mon-Fri 10am-9pm, Sat 9am-7pm, Sun 11am-5pm
B/Hs 10am-6pm

Morrisons

688-718 Fishponds Rd, Fishponds
0117 965 3014
Mon-Sat 8.30am-8.00pm, Sun 10am-4pm

Sainsbury's

Sainsbury's, Winterstoke Rd, Ashton
0117 953 7273
Mon-Fri 8am-10pm, Sat 7.30am-10pm,
Sun 10am-4pm
&
Fox Den Rd, Stoke Gifford, S Glos
0117 923 6459
Mon-Sat 8am-8pm, Sun 10am-4pm

Tesco

Callington Rd, Brislington
0117 991 7400
Mon-Sat 8.30am-8pm, Sun 10am-4pm
&
Eastgate Centre, Eastville
0117 951 1156
Mon-Sat 8am-8pm, Sun 10am-4pm

PARTY PLACES

Arty Party Ceramics

Wells Emporium, 18 Priory Rd, Wells, BA5 1SY
01749 671509
www.artypartyceramics.co.uk
artypartyceramics@yahoo.co.uk

Paint your own pottery at this café in Wells or
at a venue of your choice (in the south west)
for a birthday party. Suitable for all ages.

Avon Sports Academy

0117 904 6686
www.avonsportsacademy.co.uk
info@avonsportsacademy.co.uk
£40

Football parties with one hour of qualified
football instruction at a venue of your choice,
20 children max. Includes balls, bibs, cones
and goals. Enquiries are dealt with by email.

Bristol Climbing Centre

St Werburgh's Church, Mina Rd, St Werburgh's, BS2
0117 908 3491
www.undercover-rock.com

Climbing parties are very popular at this
dedicated indoor climbing centre, which
features over 150 climbs up to 10 metres
high, catering for all abilities. Groups of up to
nine climbers for a flat rate of £90, including
invitations and a t-shirt. The session lasts
90mins. There is a café serving drinks and
snacks. You can bring your own food and eat
in the large gallery area. It's necessary to
book well in advance.

Bristol Ice Rink

Frogmore St, Bristol, BS1 5NA
0117 929 2148
www.jnll.co.uk
£9.50 per child

Ice skating parties from £9.75 per person.
Price includes ½ hr private tuition, skating
on public session, skate hire, two adult free
skating tickets, meal in party area and gift
for birthday child. Disco skating sessions also
available. Ice karting from 18 years.

Castle Combe Kart Track

Castle Combe Circuit, Chippenham, SN14
01249 783010
www.castlecombecircuit.co.uk

Junior kart racing for 10-15yrs (with a min.
height of 4'8" on 1st and 3rd Sunday of every
month. Pre-booking essential.

Coombe Dingle Tennis Centre

Coombe Dingle Sports Complex, Coombe Lane,
Stoke Bishop
0117 962 6718
www.peterbendall.org.uk

Tennis parties with games and prizes.

Damian Forder Cricket Academy

07771 560338
www.dfca.co.uk

Parties for budding cricketers including some
tuition and fun games plus food can be
provided. Usually held at the County Cricket
Ground but can be at a venue of your choice.

Hollywood Bowl

Avonmeads Retail Park, St Philips Marsh, BS2 0SP
0117 977 1777
www.hollywoodbowl.co.uk
hollywoodbowl.bristol@MBPLC.com

Bowling parties for all ages.

Hollywood Bowl at Cribbs Causeway

The Venue, Cribbs Causeway, Bristol, BS10 7TT
0117 959 2100
www.hollywoodbowl.co.uk

Bowling parties for all ages.

Laserquest Bristol

The Old Firestation, Silver St, Bristol, BS1 2PY
0117 949 6688
www.laserquest.co.uk
Mon-Fri 12pm-10pm; Sat 10am-10pm,
Sun 10am-8pm
£7.95 pp

Laserquest parties offer two interactive laser games, each lasting 20 minutes plus free drinks, party bags and a gift for the birthday child and vouchers. Minimum of six in a group up to max of 20. No food, but you can get 20% off your bill at the nearby Deep Pan Pizza if you eat there after a party at Laserquest.

Megabowl

Brunel Way, Ashton Gate, Bristol, BS7
0117 953 8538
www.megabowl.co.uk

Bowling parties for groups of six or more.

Play Centre — Electric Car Racing

Pier St, Burnham on Sea
01278 784693

The Play Centre offers electric car racing parties with a 70-foot long car race track. Group size and age restrictions apply, call for further details. Six cars can race at once and races last 15 minutes at a time.

The Action Centre

Lyncombe Drive, Churchill, N Somerset, BS25 5PQ
01934 852335
www.highaction.co.uk

Parties can be held at this floodlit dry ski slope, based on a range of activities. Food and drink available. Phone for more information.

West Country Karting

The Lake, Trench Lane, Winterbourne, BS36 1RY
01454 202666
www.westcountrykarting.com

Karting and quad bike parties. Age and height restrictions apply.

PARTY PEOPLE

A1 Entertainments

36 Lanaway Rd, Oldbury Court, Fishponds BS16 2NN
0117 939 6619
www.a1entertainments.pwp.blueyonder.co.uk

Disco and karaoke equipment, karaoke hosts, DJs, PA systems lighting and live bands.

Amanda Frost Designs

Mandy: 01225 720383

If you like beautiful jewellery, you could host a party where your friends can buy lovely earrings and necklaces and you get 20% of the sales made, off what you buy. If you want to raise money for a good cause, then Mandy offers 15% of sales made as a cash sum.

Aqua Turtle

Trevor: 0117 967 6190
www.aquaturtle.co.uk

Scuba diving parties for up to ten at a time, held at Kingswood Leisure Centre.

Bristol Bouncy Castles

34 Green Dragon Rd, Winterbourne, BS36 1HF
07796 775522
From £45

Hires out bouncy castles, gladiators etc for indoor and outdoor parties. Delivery (within 25 miles of Bristol) and set up are free.

Cakes by Alison

01454 315742
www.cakesbyalison.co.uk
From £25

Personalised cakes for all occasions, delivered free within 20 miles of Bristol.

Hotshots

0117 939 6966
wwww.hotshotskd.co.uk

This firm offers DJs with mobile discos and karaoke systems.

Oasis Sound and Lighting

19 Windmill Farm Business Centre, Bartley St, Bedminster
0117 966 3663
www.oasis-online.co.uk

The place for PA, disco and karaoke kit.

Parties2do

7 Thomas Avenue, Emersons Green, BS16 7TB
0117 957 3448
www.parties2do.co.uk

Party organiser offering The Model Experience for teenage girls — outfits, make-up and photo shoot.

Pizzazz

Top Floor Flat, 6 Charlotte St, Bath, BA1 2NE
01225 333093
Mobile: 07721 831263
From: £90

Entertainment for all ages: circus skills, giant games, sumo suits, space hoppers, retro arcade games, caricatures and silhouettes.

Wastenot Workshops

0117 941 4447
from £70 within Bristol area

All ages can create their own masterpieces from recycled materials — from puppets to costumes and masks.

PHOTOGRAPHERS

James Nicholas Photography

27 Pool Rd, Kingswood
0117 985 9520
www.jamesnicholasphotography.co.uk
From £14.95 for 7"x5" print.

Free studio fee, or £25 for a venue anywhere in Bristol.

Mark Simmons

The Fire Station, 82-84 York Rd, Bedminster, BS3
0117 914 0999
www.marksimmonsphotography.co.uk
Appointment only
Studio Fee is £85, prints start at £8 for a 7"x5" print

Mark is an established Bristol portrait photographer with a warm, spacious and comfortable studio. He is friendly, relaxed and favours an informal style of portraiture.

Michael Rich Studios

3 Prospect Lane, Frampton Cotterell, BS36 2DR
01454 778816
www.richphotos.com
£25 for 8"x 6", studio fee £25

Family portraits in colour or black and white.

James Owens Studios

Charlton Studio, 18 Charlton Rd, Keynsham
0117 986 5114
www.jamesowens.co.uk
£15 1 hr studio session, there is no minimum order, prints start at £25

A family-run photographic studio with 25 years experience. Examples of previous work are shown on the website.

Paul Burns Photography

72 Shirehampton Rd, BS9 2DU
0117 968 6300
www.paulburns.co.uk
From £25, includes studio fee and one 8x6 print

Photographs for all occasions. Friendly family-run business. Contemporary style portraits from a photographer with a royal warrant!

RECYCLING

We know you're committed to the environment. To help you do your bit, we've checked out where you can recycle some of your stuff such as computers, mobile phones and even your smelly old trainers. For information on all aspects of recycling in Bristol: www.bristol-city.gov.uk

ActionAid Recycling

Kingsland Trading Estate, St Philips Rd, BS2 0JZ
0117 304 2390
www.actionaidrecycling.org.uk

Takes printer cartridges and mobile phones

Bristol Computer Recycling

07900 903902

It re-uses or recycles all types of IT kit. Free collections in the Bristol area but it charges £10 per monitor.

Byte Back Computer Recycling

The Lamp, Lampton Avenue, Hartcliffe BS13 0PU
0117 370 6456/0791 959 5612
www.btyeback.org.uk

Provides refurbished computers and components to three charities that supply schools in Africa. They charges £2 per computer and £5 per monitor to take them off your hands, which helps to cover their costs.

Reuse-A-Shoe

www.nike.com

Don't just chuck your old trainers in the bin. You can drop them off at any Salvation Army Collection Bank, based in many supermarket car parks. They will reuse those in good condition. The rest are dispatched to Nike, whose Reuse-A-Shoe project is turning thousands of old trainers into new running tracks, basketball courts and athletic fields.

TRANSPORT

Diana Beavon
Lindsey Potter

CONTENTS

INTRODUCTION

This chapter is all about getting from A to B. We give you a directory of contacts for buses and trains. There's information on cycling, to get you where you want to go and also for fun days out. We also tell you everything you need to know about learning to drive.

If you are looking for more unusual modes of transport, we have created a directory so you can easily find the listings that cover such things as steam trains, boat trips, canoeing, sailing and even recreational flying!

Travel Information
www.travelbristol.org

This website, designed by Bristol City Council, provides a range of travel and transport information. It includes a trip planner whether you are on foot, public transport or bike, and real time information for selected bus services, as well as links to other travel information websites.

Bus Passes

www.firstgroup.com

Using buses regularly for school or work can can be costly, however if you are eligible for a bus pass you will find fares can be a lot cheaper.

Free bus passes

If you are 15 or under, you're still eligible for a child's fare on the buses, but it's advised that you get a Child Photocard so that you can prove your age. The photocard is free, and all you need is to complete an application form and provide a passport-sized photo. Download an application form or pick one up from your local bus station, travel shop or participating school or college.

Student bus passes

If you are in full-time education after your 16th birthday, you will be eligible for student fares. You will need to go through the process above but it will cost you £10 per year.

Travel Bristol Centre

11 Colston Ave, Bristol, BS1 4UB
Mon-Fri 10.30am-5.30pm, Sat 10am-1pm

Self-serve terminal, booking hotline, leaflets and brochures.

Transport Direct

www.transportdirect.info

This useful website allows you to choose your destination and check out the most convenient form of transport to get to where you are going.

Traveline — public transport information

0870 608 2608
www.traveline.org.uk

AIRPORT

Bristol International Airport

Lulsgate, BS19 3DY
0870 121 2747
www.bristolairport.co.uk

See Holidays & Weekends Away, pg 216.

BUS & COACH

First Buses

0845 602 0156
www.firstgroup.com

Operating 38 services throughout the Bristol area, with ticket offers for all day use:

- FirstFamily ticket: unlimited travel all day on First buses in Bristol, after 9am Mon-Fri and at any time on weekends and bank holidays. £6.50 for a family of up to five, but no more than two adults.

- FirstDay South West ticket gives you unlimited travel all day on FirstGroup services in the West of England (some restrictions apply). £7 adult before 9am, £6 after, £5 child, £15 Family (2+2).

- FirstAttraction tickets are also available, combining your fare with your attraction ticket, including Zoo Safari, Bus Skate Special, First Film Odeon and At-Bristol.

Tickets can be purchased at the Travel Bristol Centre (Colston St), Bristol Bus Station booking office and at your local bus shop.

South Gloucestershire Bus Co.

Timetable 0117 979 3311

Bristol Bus Station

Marlborough St, BS1 3NU
0117 926 8843

A major redevelopment of the bus station is now complete, facilities include toilets, shops, café and ticket offices.

Bristol International Flyer

Daily 5.30am-10.30pm
Return fares: £7 adult, £6 child, £16 family (2+2)

Non-stop 30-minute bus service from Bristol Bus & Coach Station or Bristol Temple Meads direct to the airport. No prebooking necessary. Plans to increase frequency and add a new stop on Whiteladies Road now in place.

National Express

Enquiries & reservations 08705 808080
8am-10pm
www.nationalexpress.com

Many economy fares available but some need to be booked in advance. Economy tickets exclude travel on Fridays and many Saturdays. Tickets can be bought online or at Bristol Bus Station, some Bus Shops, travel agents and Tourist Information Centres. A Family Coachcard allows children to travel for free, at £8 (1+1) or £16 (2+2). Coaches depart from Bristol Bus Station.

Bristol City Sightseeing Tour

0870 4440654 information hotline
www.bristolvisitor.co.uk, www.city-sightseeing.com
Easter-Sep: 10am-5pm
Call for prices, one child free per adult passenger

Tickets available on the bus or from Bristol Tourist Information Centre and the Travel Bristol Information Centre. This open-top, live guide sightseeing bus takes in all the major attractions including At-Bristol, Bristol Zoo, ss Great Britain, Clifton Village and the British Empire and Commonwealth Museum. Discount available on entry to a number of attractions on presentation of your bus ticket. You can hop on and off the bus at any of the 20 stops en route. See advertisement, pg 190.

RAIL

National rail enquiries
08457 48 49 50
www.nationalrail.co.uk

First Great Western
www.firstgreatwestern.co.uk
Information & customer service 0845 7000 125
Mobility impaired 08457 413775

Wessex Trains
Has now merged with First Great Western.

Train Tracker
0871 200 4950
Voice-automated information about direct trains for that day.

Young Persons Railcard

You are eligible for discounted rail fares if: you're aged between 16-25 or a mature student, over 26 in full-time education.

This entitles you to 34% off standard fares, with the exception of travelling at peak times (before 10am Sep-Jun, Mon-Fri). This ruling does not apply to Virgin trains.

If you travel regularly before 10am, then a weekly or monthly season ticket may be more appropriate.

To get the card, you will need to pay £20 and provide a passport size photograph along with proof of your age, such as your passport or birth certificate.

Bristol Parkway

Stoke Gifford, Bristol, BS12 6TU
Ticket office Mon-Sat 5am-7pm, Sun 8am-7pm
Parking £4.50/day on weekdays, £2/day at weekends

This station has a number of facilities including lifts to platforms, disabled access, bicycle storage, self-service ticket machines, a shop and café on the first floor and a regular bus service into Bristol city centre.

Temple Meads

Booking office open Mon-Sat 5.30am-9.30pm, Sun 6.45am-9.30pm
Short-term parking on station forecourt (up to 20 mins free) longer-term parking £6.50/24hrs, £9/24hrs undercover

Beautiful historic station. Lifts down to subway then up to platforms. Main toilets in subway. Refreshment outlets to be found on platforms 3 and 10, as well as in the subway. WH Smith in main entrance. Shuttle bus operates to the airport, as well as regular bus services into and around Bristol.

Bristol Severn Beach Line

www.wessextrains.co.uk
0870 900 2320
Day returns from only £2.30
Pay on the train

The Bristol to Severn Beach railway line runs from Temple Meads to the Avonmouth, from here there is a bus service that connects you to Severn Beach.

Friends of Suburban Bristol Railway (FOSBR)

www.fosbr.org.uk

A campaign group whose aim is to keep, promote and improve the services and facilities on the Severn Beach line.

PARK & RIDE

0870 608 2608 (Traveline)

Brislington Park and Ride

Located: off A4, Bristol-Bath Road
Mon-Fri 6.45am-7pm, every 10 mins, Sat 7.40am-7pm, Thu last bus leaves the centre at 8.03pm

The journey time is approximately 15 mins. It operates a circular route stopping at: Temple Gate, Old Market, Temple Way, Haymarket and Broad Quay.

Long Ashton Park and Ride

0117 966 0399
Located: A370 towards the SW of the City
Mon-Fri 7am-7pm every 10-12 mins, Sat 8am-6pm, Thu last bus leaves the city centre at 8pm

The journey time is 10-15 mins. It operates a circular route stopping at: Harbourside, Augustine's Parade, Baldwin St, Victoria St and the Haymarket. Saturday service stops at: St Augustine's and St James Barton, outside House of Fraser. Up to three children travel free with a paying adult.

Portway Park and Ride

Located: A4 Portway, Shirehampton
Mon-Fri 6.50am-7pm, every 15 mins, Sat 7.30am-7pm

The journey time into central Bristol is approximately 30mins. Up to three children travel free with a paying adult.

FERRY TRIPS

Bristol ferries can get you around the centre of the Bristol, for example from Temple Meads station to the Watershed or from there to Hotwells. For further information, see the Dockside pg 53 and Boat Trips pg 118.

CYCLING ORGANISATIONS

Bristol Cycling Campaign

Box No. 60, Booty, 82 Colston St, BS1 5BB
www.bristolcyclingcampaign.org.uk
Membership £5, concessions available

Regular Sunday rides organised, some quite short and suitable for families. BCC members also campaign to improve accessibility and safety for cyclists. For further information, either obtain a leaflet (distributed in cycle shops) or visit the website.

CTC (Cyclist Touring Club)

Cotterell House, 69 Meadrow, Godalming, Surrey
01483 417217
www.ctc.org.uk

Campaigns for the rights of cyclists. Membership provides you with 3rd party insurance, legal aid, route information and a bi-monthly magazine.

Cycling in Bristol

www.bristol-city.gov.uk

Bristol City Council offers a range of services to cyclists:

Free cycle route maps

To obtain maps covering the Greater Bristol and Avon Cycleway, call 0117 903 6701.

Bristol's Biggest Bike Ride

Annual event attracting thousands of cyclists.

Car Free Day

Held every September.

The Bristol Bike Shed

The Grove, Queen Sq, BS1 4RB
www.mud-dock.co.uk

Provides secure bike parking, showers, lockers and access to maintainence facilities as well as cheap coffee at Mud Dock!

Life Cycle UK

86 Colston St, Bristol, BS1 5BB
0117 929 0440
www.lifecycleuk.org.uk

Provides information and advice on family cycling. Group cycling courses for 8-11yrs at venues in Bristol. Also courses for 11-18yrs with one instructor to two teenagers, cycling on and off road, teaching road safety and providing free maps. Life Cycle also runs one-to-one parent training lessons costing £25, plus monthly bike maintenance workshops.

Sustrans

2 Cathedral Square,, College Green, Bristol, BS1 5DD
Information line 0845 113 0065
Head office 0117 926 8893
www.sustrans.org.uk

This sustainable transport charity works on practical projects to encourage people to walk, cycle and use public transport in order to reduce motor traffic and its adverse effects. Its main project is the National Cycle Network which currently provides more than 10,000 miles of cycling and walking routes throughout the UK. Maps and free leaflets are available. Sustrans is also involved in the Safe Routes to School project, encouraging children to cycle and walk to school. Call for a free information pack.

for those with special needs. Routes, maps, information, books, parts, accessories and repairs available. The café next door is open winter w/e's and daily in summer — delicious chips! Facilities include showers, toilets, bike wash and parking.

Lock Inn Cottage

48 Frome Rd, Bradford-on-Avon, Wiltshire, BA15
01225 868068
www.thelockinn.co.uk
Daily 9am-6pm
From £7 adults, £5 child for 3hrs

Here you will find an extensive bike/hire shop and canalside café, ideally situated on the Kennet and Avon canal towpath. You can hire (or buy!) all family biking equipment, helmets, seats and trailers. Canoes and boats are also for hire, see pg 119.

The Bath and Dundas Canal Co.

Brass Knocker Basin, Monkton Combe, Bath
01225 722292
www.bathcanal.com
Open daily, but ring first between Nov-Mar
£14 adult, £7 child per day, hourly rates available, pre-booking recommended

Offers a range of family bikes and accessories to hire. They also offer canoes and boats for hire, see pg 118.

Buying a bike or need repairs?

Check out Bike Shops listed in the Shopping & Services chapter, pg 146.

CYCLE HIRE COMPANIES

Bristol Bicycle Hire

Smeaton Rd, adj to Bonded Warehouse,
Cycle Route 41, Hotwells
0117 965 5192, 0780 3651945 (mobile)
Easter-Oct: £10-£12 per day, £7-£9 half day, additional days half price

Pre-booked bike hire with a selection of bikes for all the family. Parking nearby.

Forest of Dean Cycle Hire

Pedalabikeaway Cycle Centre, Colliery Offices,
Cannop Valley, near Coleford
01594 860065
www.pedalabikeaway.com
Daily: Jul, Aug & school holidays
Apr-Oct: Tue-Sun 9am-6pm, Nov-Mar: Tue-Sun 9am-5pm
From £7 adult 2hrs, £4 child 2hrs

This friendly shop is situated on the 10-mile circular family cycle trail, hiring out bikes and trailers, for all ages. Helmets are free. A family rate discount is available. Their motto is "bikes for everyone", particularly

CYCLE ROUTES

Ashton Court

After passing through the entrance to Ashton Court by the suspension bridge, take the second track on the right (after the road for the golf course). There are numerous trails through the woods but it is very hilly and quite rough.

Ashton to Pill cycle way

This pretty route starts from the Create Centre on Cumberland Road, or from Leigh Woods if you take the first right after the Clifton suspension bridge and follow the road for ¾ mile; it is signposted from there. Refreshments can be bought in Pill.

Bristol and Bath cycle way

This is a 13-mile route which you can start either from Bristol Bridge or from St Phillips Road, Old Market. Bitton is an interesting place to stop, where there is a steam railway (or start your ride from here, as the route crosses the road). Pubs along the way include the Bird in Hand and the Jolly Sailor on the river at Saltford.

Forest of Dean cycle trail

This is a beautiful area for cycling. There is a popular circular 10-mile family cycle route, with several access points (one being near the Forest of Dean Cycle hire, see above).

Kennet and Avon canal towpath

This path goes east out of Bath, starting behind Bath Spa railway station. Three easy access points are: Bradford-on-Avon (station car park); Hilperton Marina (car parking and toilets); and the visitor centre at Devizes Wharf (pay and display). A cycle route with plenty to look at on the canal and several places to stop for food and drink. Besides the aquaducts at Avoncliff and Dundas, the other amazing feat of engineering is the flight locks at Caen, West of Devizes. Canal cycle tracks can be narrow in places, so they are not suitable for inexperienced cyclists but the plus side is they are flat!

LEARNING TO DRIVE

Learning to drive can provide a welcome increase in independence, provided your parents are willing to let you borrow their car or if you can afford wheels of your own.

FINDING AN INSTRUCTOR

If you're 17 or over, you can learn to drive. You need an application for a provisional driving licence, from the Post Office, costing £38. This enables you to drive with a licensed driver in the passenger seat. It can take up to three weeks for your licence to arrive.

The next step is to select a driving instructor, making sure they are fully licensed and qualified (licences are displayed in the car).

The bigger companies tend to have a good track record, but can be more expensive than independent instructors, who sometimes give discounts. Prices range from £16 to £24 per hour. There are often discounts for block bookings and for NUS cardholders.

DRIVING SCHOOLS

BSM
08457 276 276
www.bsm.co.uk

AA Driving School
0800 294 1218
www.theaa.com/drivingschool

Gemini School of Motoring
0117 904 1033
www.smartdriving.co.uk/gemini

A female instructor working around Hanham, Warmley, Kingswood and St George.

Keith's School of Motoring
0117 942 2599
www.keiths.co.uk

A good independent driving school.

Field School of Motoring
0117 959 0654
www.fieldschoolofmotoring.co.uk

In Westbury-on-Trym, the first hour is free.

TAKING YOUR THEORY TEST

You have to take, and pass, your theory test before you can book your driving test. Your instructor will advise you when you are ready to take it, but there is usually a two or three week waiting list when you book. There are two sections to the theory test, the whole thing lasts around 45mins, and it's taken in a large room with computer booths. The first part is multiple choice and you have a limited amount of time. The second part is called Hazard Perception, and it involves watching videos from a driver's perspective, and clicking the mouse when you see a potential hazard.

There are many resources to aid you with your theory test, such as a Theory Test practice book, the Highway Code, and a PC-based Hazard Perception practice programme. The test costs £21, and the theory test centre is just off the St James Barton roundabout towards Gloucester Road.

To book a theory test, go to:

www.DSA.gov.uk or call 0870 010 1372

THE DRIVING TEST

Once you've passed your theory test, and your instructor is happy with your driving (they usually know best!), you can book your practical test. The test costs £45.50 on weekdays, or £55 for evenings and Saturdays. There can be a wait of up to ten weeks.

During your test, you will be asked to do two manoeuvres out of a possible three, and one in three tests include the emergency stop. You are allowed up to 15 minor errors, any major is a fail. Three or more of the same minor error is also a fail.

You have to take several documents to the test: your test booking letter, both your paper and photocard licences and your theory test pass certificate. You cannot take the test without these, and you'll have to re-book the test and pay again. To book a test, visit: www.DSA.gov.uk, or call 0870 010 1372.

PASS PLUS

Once you have passed, you may not feel confident driving at night, on wet roads or on motorways. Pass Plus lessons are provided by most instructors, and can give you extra confidence. If you do Pass Plus, you may also get discounts on car insurance.

Taking the scenic route

This book is packed with ideas for more unusual ways of getting around, from canoeing to flying. Here's a handy guide to finding out more.

REFERENCE SECTION

Maps
courtesy of Destination Bristol

Festivals & events

Sport & leisure centres

Icon	meaning		Icon	meaning
P	parking		♿	disabled facilities
WC	toilets		🎠	outdoor play area
🛗	lift		⛱	picnic area

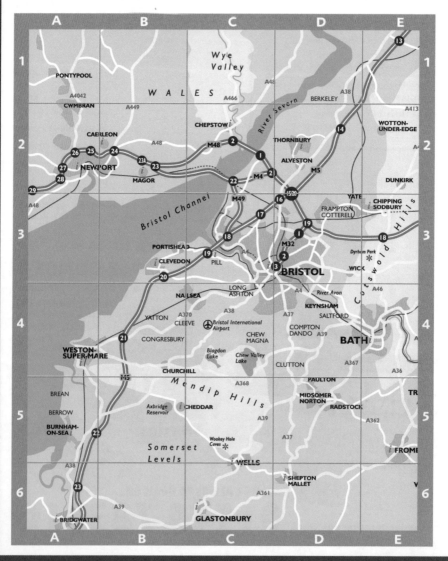

Icon	meaning
🚌	nearby public transport
🍴	café
🧺	shop

ICON KEY
& MAPS

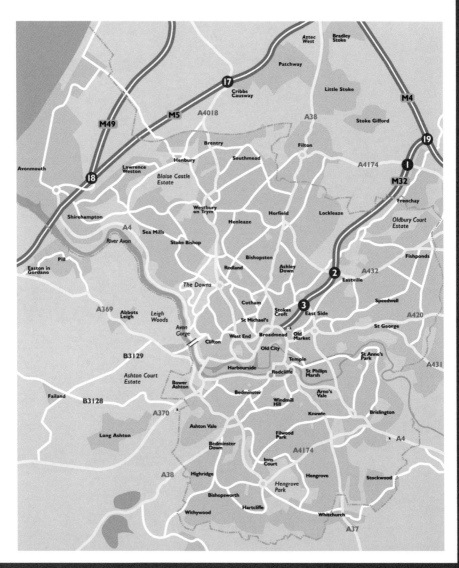

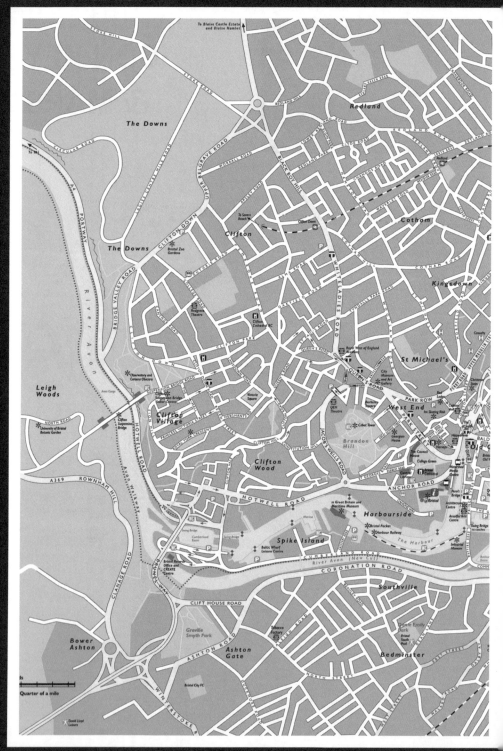

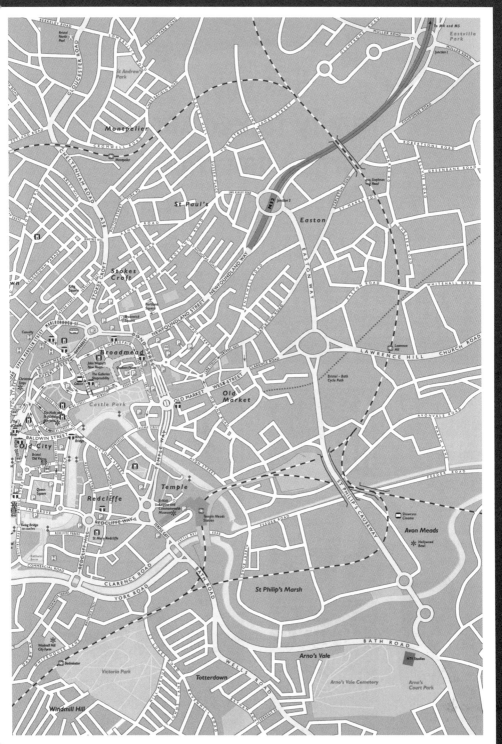

MORE GREAT SOURCES OF INFORMATION

Bristol Tourist Information
www.visitbristol.co.uk

Venue Magazine
www.venue.co.uk
The what's-on guide covering Bristol and Bath, for sale at newsagents throughout the region.

www.freedomguide.co.uk
See our website for seasonal events, new or changed listings.

I.C.E.

In case of emergencies. This is an excellent safety precaution for mobile phone users.

Put I.C.E. into your mobile phonebook with an emergency contact number.

The Spark Magazine
Quarterly, looking at environmental and social issues in the West plus lots more. Available free at libraries, bookshops and cafés.

The Bristol Magazine
Free at libraries and through your door if you live in the right postcode.

Local papers and radio stations

Bristol Evening Post
www.thisisbristol.co.uk

Bath Evening Chronicle
www.thisisbath.co.uk

GWR Radio
www.gwrfmbristol.co.uk

Star Radio
www.starbristol.co.uk

Radio Bristol
www.bbc.co.uk/bristol

ANNUAL
EVENTS &
FESTIVALS

The lowdown on festivals & events

There are a huge number of annual events across the West, many of which are free. Below is a taster of some of the favourites but for an overview of the year check out the next couple of pages.

Ashton Court Festival

www.ashtoncourtfestival.com

This festival usually goes off with a bang. The 2005 festival was rocking, with an estimated 150,000 people attending each day. The evenings are filled with live music from top bands on the two main stages and in the music big-tops. The days can be for relaxing in the sunshine, funfair rides or shopping round the many stalls. Ashton Court is a non-profit festival, and at only £5 entry, with proceeds going to charity, it's unmissable.

Easily accessible by buses from the centre and Whiteladies Rd.

Balloon Fiesta

www.bristolfiesta.co.uk

Held annually at Ashton Court, the balloon fiesta is a coming together of 150 hot air balloons, along with live bands, funfair rides and stalls. The famous Night-Glow is the highlight, where the balloons burn, flicker and flash to music for a spectacular show. This festival is great no matter what your age, and if you're daring enough, there is usually a bungy-jump on site!

Clotheshow Live

www.clotheshowlive.com

There are designers and catwalk shows galore, it's a fabulous place to celeb-spot, you can shop till you drop and you might even end up being talent-spotted as a potential model. This event usually takes place at the NEC in Birmingham in December, check the website for details.

NASS (National Adventure Sports Show)

NEC, Birmingham
www.nass2006.com

This summer event has moved from Shepton Mallet to Birmingham, reflecting its popularity. Kids are welcome and there are special family passes for those with U14s. The KAOS (Kids Activity's OutSide) area has everything from quad bike racing, power trampoline, inflatable slides, gladiator duel, inflatable obstacle course and sumo-suit wrestling. There is also a public access kid's street course, so bring your bikes and boards and experience riding a pro course first hand.

Reading & Glastonbury Festivals

www.readingfestival.com
www.glastonburyfestivals.co.uk

Both these events are held in the summer, and whether you get sunshine or rain, you'll have a fantastic time. With live music to suit all tastes playing throughout the weekend at Glastonbury, or more alternative bands playing at Reading, tickets sell out pretty quickly, so you have to get in there quick. The "real" selling price is around £100-£120 (for a weekend), if you're too late to get tickets, there's a chance you can catch some on E-Bay, but beware, the cost gets high! Unfortunately, Glastonbury is not being held in 2006 – every four years they give the grass a chance to recover!

MAY

Bath International Music Festival
www.bathmusicfest.org.uk

JUNE

Bristol Harbour Fun Run
www.thisisbristol.co.uk
For all ages, in aid of British Heart Foundation.

Bristol's Biggest Bike Ride
www.bristol-city.gov.uk/biggestbikeride
Five different routes from nine to 40 miles.
Fun, traffic-free cycling. Event concludes at
Brunel Picnic Park.

Bristol Bike Fest
www.bristolbikefest.com
Serious cyclists take part in serious races.
See all the latest bike kit. Live music. All at
Ashton Court Estate.

Bristol Festival of Nature
www.thisisbristol.co.uk
Films, animal encounters, walks and more.

Bristol Motor and Classic Car Show
www.thisisbristol.co.uk

Cheltenham Festival of Science
www.cheltenhamfestivals.co.uk
Fun event for budding scientists.

Glastonbury Festival
www.glastonburyfestivals.co.uk
The biggest and best and it's on our doorstep
but you will have to wait until 2007.

St Werburghs Art Trail
www.stwerburghs.org.uk

View artists work in their houses and studios.

Westonbirt Festival of Gardens
www.forestry.gov.uk/westonbirt

Royal Bath & West Show
www.bathandwest.co.uk
Animal action at Shepton Mallet Showground.

JULY

Ashton Court Festival
www.ashtoncourtfestival.com
The best music, theatre and arts from Bristol.
See The Lowdown on events, pg 186.

NASS (National Adventure Sports Show)
www.nass2006.com
Held at the Birmingham NEC. Bike and board heaven for urban adventurers! See The Lowdown on events, pg 186.

St Paul's Carnival
www.netgates.co.uk
Spectacular carnival, music and great food.

The Cotswold Show & Country Fair
www.cotswoldshow.co.uk

Old fashioned country fair with some modern additions — quad bikes, helicopter rides and off-road racing. Held at Cirencester Park.

Truckfest
www.truckfest.co.uk
Trucking heaven at Shepton Mallet.

AUGUST

Bristol Children's Festival
www.childrensworldcharity.org
Fun activities for under 12s at Bristol Downs.

Bristol Harbour Festival
www.bristol-city.gov.uk/harbourfestival
The city's most spectacular waterside event.

Bristol International Balloon Fiesta
www.bristolfiesta.co.uk
150 hot air balloons go up at 6am and 6pm.
See The Lowdown on events, pg 186.

Reading Festival
www.readingfestival.com
This hugely popular event is held over the bank holiday weekend. See The Lowdown on events, pg 186.

The Big Chill
www.bigchill.net

Music and arts festival set in Eastnor Castle Deer Park, Malvern Hills.

SEPTEMBER

Bristol International Kite Festival
www.kite-festival.org
Colourful kites at Ashton Court Estate.

Bristol Half Marathon
www.bristolhalfmarathon.co.uk

Doors Open Day
www.bristoldoorsopenday.org
Peek inside Bristol's most interesting buildings.

Organic Food Festival
www.organicfoodfairs.co.uk
Harbourside event with tempting treats!

OCTOBER

The Ski and Snowboard Show
www.dailymailskishow.com
Huge London exhibition held at Olympia.
Dedicated to all things snowy, from equipment
to clothing.

DECEMBER

Clotheshow Live
www.clotheshowlive.com
See and be seen at this mecca for fashion
fans. Held at the NEC Birmingham. See The
Lowdown, pg 186.

NOVEMBER

Encounters
www.encounters-festival.org.uk
Short film festival including animation.

Firework Fiesta
www.visitbristol.co.uk
Bonfire and fireworks at Bristol Downs.

Somerset Carnivals
www.somersetcarnivals.co.uk
Impressive illuminated processions.

Totterdown Art Trail
www.frontroom.org.uk

North Bristol Art Trail
www.northbristolartists.co.uk

Professional and amateur artists display their
work on these two popular art trails.

BEST OF THE WEST

You've probably realised by now that this book is absolutely packed with amazing things to do and places to go. Here, we pick some of the most inspirational entries and those that our panel of teenage experts rate most highly.

2442 Squadron ATC, pg 47
The chance to go flying and gliding. Chocks away!

50:50, pg 158
Skateboarding mecca.

Animation & cartoons, pg 34
Let UWE Bristol School of Art show you how to be the next Nick Park.

Ashton Court Festival, pg 186
Music, stalls and fun in the sun (hopefully).

Bay Island Voyages, pg 109
High speed boat trips for thrill-seekers in the Bristol Channel and Severn estuary.

Beast, pg 137
Get your Gert Lush t-shirts here!

Bizarre Bath Comedy Walk, pg 96
Stroll around Bath and enjoy comedy, street theatre and improvisation.

Boston Tea Party, pg 72
Garden, sofas upstairs and stonkingly good coffee and food.

Bristol Biggest Bike Ride, pg 32 & 187
Cycling fun for all, five different routes.

Bristol Orienteering Klub, pg 27
Race around the countryside in a competitive manner.

Bristol Surfing Club, pg 31
Surfing tuition as well as trips to the coast every weekend.

Bristol Water Ski Club, pg 28
Water ski in the harbour but keep your mouth tight shut if you fall in!

BS8, pg 135
Lots of shops under one roof, one of Park Street's finest.

DJ Academy, pg 38
Beat mixing and scratching for all budding DJs.

Down's Football League, pg 9
Join 700 players on a Saturday afternoon.

ITV West Television Workshops, pg 41
Looking for fame? Past students have been in Harry Potter and Casualty.

Megamaze, pg 102
Get lost in a maize maze, with two miles of paths.

New World Karaoke Restaurant, pg 79
Gorgeous Chinese buffet and karaoke too, heaven for divas.

Portishead Open Air Pool, pg 15
Sunbathing terraces, heated pool, what more do you want on a British summer's day?

Quartier Vert, pg 36
Learn to cook decent grub and impress you friends.

Rocotillos, pg 75
Best burgers in town in this fab Fifties-style diner.

Shaken Stephens, pg 75
123 flavoured shakes. How will you choose?

St Nicholas Market, pg 143
Lovely setting selling everything under the sun.

Thermae Bath Spa, pg 97
Long-awaited spa offering open air swims overlooking the city.

The Works, pg 62
Monthly nights for 13-17yr olds, featuring bands, fruit cocktails and, occasionally, foam.

**LEISURE
CENTRES
& POOLS**

Reference Section

BRISTOL SWIMMING POOLS

For more details see: www.bristol-city.gov.uk/sport except Filton Sports and Leisure see: www.filton-town-council.co.uk

Leisure Centres
Open daily
♿ P ♿ apply to all centres

Address	Pool Size	Aquafit Classes	Lessons	Swimming Club	Learner Pool	Off Poolside Changing Rooms	Spa Facilities	Disabled Facilities	Parking	Public Transport	Sub-aqua	Water Slide	Parties, floats & inflatables	Other Swimming Activities
Bishopworth 0117 964 0258 — Whitchurch Lane, Bishopworth	25m	✓	✓	✓		✓		✓	✓	✓	✓		✓	
Bristol South 0117 966 3131 — Dean Lane, Bedminster	30m	✓	✓	✓						✓	✓		✓	water polo, canoeing
Easton Leisure Centre 0117 955 8840 — Thrissell St, Easton	25m	✓	✓	✓	✓	✓		✓	✓	✓		✓	✓	
Filton Sports and Leisure Centre 01454 866686 — Elm Park, Filton	25m	✓	✓	✓	✓	✓	✓	✓	✓	✓			✓	
Henbury 0117 353 2555 — Avonmouth Way, Henbury	25m	✓	✓	✓	✓	✓		✓	✓	✓	✓			
Horfield Sports Centre 0117 903 1643 — Dorian Rd, Horfield	25m	✓	✓	✓	✓	✓		✓	✓	✓			✓	
Jubilee 0117 977 7900 — Jubilee Rd, Knowle	25m	✓	✓	✓				✓		✓			✓	

BRISTOL LEISURE CENTRES

For more details see: www.bristol-city.gov.uk/sport or www.filton-town-council.co.uk — centres may not necessarily provide courses or instruction in each sport listed

Leisure Centres
Open daily
♿ P 🚌 apply to all centres

Leisure Centre	Address	Aerobics	Badminton	Basketball	Boxercise	Cricket Nets	Dance Classes	Football	Gymnastics	Gymnasium	Holiday Timetable	Martial Arts	Netball	Outdoor Facilities	Parties	Squash courts	Swimming	Tennis	Trampolining	Volley Ball	Yoga
Ashton Park Sports Centre 0117 377 3300	Ashton Park School, Blackmoor's Lane, Bower Ashton	✓	✓			✓	✓			✓	✓	✓	✓	✓	✓			✓	✓		✓
Easton Leisure Centre 0117 955 8840	Thrissell Street, Easton	✓	✓	✓				✓		✓	✓	✓			✓		✓				✓
Filton Sports & Leisure Centre 01454 866686	Elm Park, Filton		✓						✓		✓	✓			✓	✓	✓	✓			
Henbury Leisure Centre 0117 353 2555	Avonmouth Way, Henbury	✓	✓				✓		✓	✓	✓	✓	✓	✓	✓	✓	✓				✓
Horfield Sports Centre 0117 903 1643	Dorian Road, Horfield	✓	✓			✓	✓	✓	✓	✓	✓	✓	✓	✓	✓	✓	✓	✓	✓	✓	✓
Kingsdown Sports Centre 0117 942 6582	Portland St, Kingsdown	✓	✓	✓	✓		✓	✓	✓		✓				✓	✓	✓		✓	✓	
St Paul's Community Sports Academy 0117 377 3405	Newfoundland Road, St Paul's	✓	✓				✓	✓	✓	✓	✓		✓	✓	✓		✓	✓			✓
Whitchurch Sports Centre 01275 833911	Bamfield, Whitchurch	✓	✓						✓	✓	✓		✓	✓	✓		✓	✓	✓	✓	✓
Withywood Sport Centre 0117 377 22294	Withywood Community School, Molesworth Drive	✓	✓				✓	✓			✓			✓	✓				✓		

SOUTH GLOUCESTERSHIRE LEISURE CENTRES

For more details see: www.southglos.gov.uk — centres may not necessarily provide courses or instruction in each sport listed

Leisure Centres
Open daily
♿ P ♨ apply to all centres

Leisure Centre	Address	Aerobics	Badminton	Basketball	Boxercise	Cricket Nets	Dance Classes	Football	Gymnastics	Gymnasium	Holiday Timetable	Martial Arts	Netball	Outdoor Facilities	Parties	Squash Courts	Swimming	Tennis	Trampolining	Volley Ball	Yoga
Bradley Stoke Leisure Centre 01454 867050	Fiddlers Wood Lane, Bradley Stoke	✓	✓	✓			✓	✓	✓	✓	✓	✓	✓		✓	✓	✓		✓	✓	✓
Downend Sports Centre 01454 862221	Garnett Place, Downend		✓	✓		✓		✓			✓	✓	✓	✓	✓					✓	
Kingswood Leisure Centre 01454 865700	Church Rd, Staple Hill	✓	✓	✓				✓		✓	✓	✓	✓	✓	✓	✓	✓		✓		✓
Patchway Sports Centre 01454 865890	Patchway Community College, Hempton Lane, Almondsbury		✓	✓	✓	✓		✓		✓	✓	✓	✓	✓	✓	✓	✓	✓	✓	✓	
Thornbury Leisure Centre 01454 865777	Alveston Hill, Thornbury	✓	✓	✓	✓	✓	✓	✓	✓	✓	✓	✓			✓	✓	✓	✓	✓	✓	✓
Yate Leisure Centre 01454 865800	Kennedy Way, Yate	✓	✓	✓		✓	✓	✓	✓	✓	✓	✓	✓		✓	✓	✓		✓	✓	✓
Yate Outdoor Sports Complex 01454 865820	Behind Brinsham Green School, Yate							✓			✓		✓	✓	✓			✓			

NORTH SOMERSET LEISURE CENTRES

For more details see: www.n-somerset.gov.uk — centres may not necessarily provide courses or instruction in each sport listed

Leisure Centres Open daily	Address	Aerobics	Badminton	Basketball	Boxercise	Cricket Nets	Dance Classes	Football	Gymnastics	Gymnasium	Holiday Timetable	Martial Arts	Netball	Outdoor Facilities	Parties	Squash Courts	Swimming	Tennis	Trampolining	Volley Ball	Yoga
Backwell Leisure Centre 01275 463726 ⬦ P ♿	Farleigh Rd, Backwell	✓													✓		✓				
Churchill Sports Centre 01934 852303 ⬦ P	Churchill Green, Weston-super-Mare	✓	✓												✓	✓	✓	✓	✓		
Gordano Sports Centre * 01275 843942 P ♿	Gordano School, St Mary's Rd, Portishead	✓	✓	✓			✓		✓							✓		✓	✓		
Hutton Moor Leisure Centre 01934 425900 ⬦ P ♿	Hutton Moor Rd, Weston-super-Mare	✓	✓				✓	✓		✓	✓	✓	✓	✓	✓	✓	✓	✓	✓	✓	✓
Parish Wharf Leisure Centre 01275 848494 ⬦ P ♿	Harbour Road, Portishead	✓	✓		✓	✓		✓		✓	✓	✓	✓	✓	✓	✓	✓			✓	✓
Scotch Horn Leisure Centre 01275 856965 ⬦ P ♿	Brockway, Nailsea	✓	✓		✓						✓					✓					✓
Strode Leisure Centre 01275 879242 ⬦ P ♿	Strode Way, Clevedon	✓	✓	✓		✓	✓	✓		✓	✓	✓	✓	✓	✓		✓				✓
Swiss Valley Sport Centre * 01275 877 182 P ♿	Clevedon School, Clevedon		✓			✓	✓			✓	✓		✓	✓	✓	✓		✓	✓		
Wyvern Sports Centre * 01934 642426 ⬦ P	Marchfields Way, Weston-super-Mare		✓				✓	✓			✓		✓	✓				✓	✓	✓	

*Leisure centre attached to a school so restricted opening times during school hours

BATH AND NORTH EAST SOMERSET LEISURE CENTRES

For more details see: www.aquaterra.org — centres may not necessarily provide courses or instruction in each sport listed

Leisure Centres
Open daily
♿ P 🏊 apply to all centres

Leisure Centres / Address	Aerobics	Badminton	Basketball	Boxercise	Cricket Nets	Dance Classes	Football	Gymnastics	Gymnasium	Holiday Timetable	Martial Arts	Netball	Outdoor Facilities	Parties	Squash Courts	Swimming	Tennis	Trampolining	Volley Ball	Yoga
Bath Sports and Leisure Centre, North Parade Road, Bath, 01225 462565	✓	✓	✓	✓		✓	✓	✓	✓	✓	✓	✓	✓	✓	✓	✓	✓	✓	✓	✓
Chew Valley Leisure Centre *, Chew Lane, Chew Magna, www.cvleisure.com, 01275 333375	✓	✓	✓		✓			✓	✓	✓	✓	✓	✓	✓	✓		✓		✓	✓
Culverhay Sports Centre *, Rush Hill, Bath, 01225 486902 Mon-Fri, 01225 480882 Eve/WE's	✓	✓	✓		✓		✓					✓	✓	✓		✓			✓	
Keynsham Leisure Centre, Temple St, Keynsham, 01225 395161	✓	✓	✓			✓		✓	✓	✓	✓			✓	✓	✓			✓	✓
South Wansdyke Sports Centre, Rackvernal Rd, Midsomer Norton, 01761 4015522	✓	✓								✓	✓		✓	✓	✓	✓	✓	✓	✓	✓
Writhlington Sports Centre, Radstock, Knobsbury Lane, www.writhlingtonsportscentre.co.uk, 01761 438559	✓	✓	✓	✓	✓	✓	✓	✓		✓	✓	✓	✓	✓			✓	✓	✓	✓

*Leisure centre attached to a school so restricted opening times during school hours

HOLIDAYS & WEEKENDS AWAY

Lucy Saunders
Lindsey Potter

CONTENTS

INTRODUCTION

This chapter tries to take some of the stress out of planning your holiday by catering for a wide range of budgets and types of holidays. These range from campsites and YHAs to self-catering cottages and luxury family hotels. Bristol is well-placed as a starting point for a wide variety of holiday destinations within a 2-3 hour car journey.

We've found plenty of inspirational ideas, whether your family like to be active on holiday, hang out on a beach or chill in a spa. What's even better is that many of the places offer all of the above, so every member of the family can enjoy themselves in their own way!

We've divided up this chapter into regions and according to types of accommodation, so you can find something to suit your preferences and budget. And you can book in confidence, knowing that all our listings have been highly recommended by families.

ACTIVITY HOLIDAYS

There are many opportunities for adventurous and independent young people to go away with or without their parents. What's great about these activity holidays is that the kids get to make friends as well as trying a huge range of sports and challenges.

British Activity Holiday Association
www.baha.org.uk

Offers a consumer guide for anyone seeking an activity holiday in the UK or abroad. It is also the trade association for private sector activity holidays companies in the UK. Member centres must abide by the BAHA Code of Practice and are committed to high standards of safety, value for money and service.

PGL
Alton Court, Penyard Lane, Ross-on-Wye, Herefordshire, HR9 5GL
www.pgl.co.uk
08700 507507

For nearly 50 years, PGL has been offering young people activity holidays. It has centres in the UK, France and Austria. There are two types of holiday:

PGL Activity Holidays for 7-17yr olds. Kids go on their own or with siblings/friends, whatever their situation there are loads of new friends to make and no time to be bored. There is a huge range of sports and activities including canoeing, quad biking, abseiling, raft building and archery to name but a few. With locations in Devon, Herefordshire, the Brecons and Dorset they needn't travel far for adventure.

PGL Family Active holidays give parents a chance to be the first down the zip wire! There are weekends, mini-breaks and full weeks to choose from in 11 locations in the UK and France. Check out their website — if you're game!

Acorn Family Adventure
Acorn House, Prospect Rd, Halesowen, B62 8DU
www.acornadventure.co.uk/families
0800 074 9791
From £259pp pw

Offering active family holidays in some stunning locations. It has six centres across Europe where families stay in comfortable tents with a village community atmosphere. There is an action-packed programme of activities included in the price. The UK locations are Derwentwater and the Brecon Beacons where activities include kayaking, high ropes, archery, sailing, hill walking and something called mission impossible! See the website for inspirational pictures.

ACCOMMODATION

Family Holiday Association

16 Mortimer St, London, W1T 3JL
020 7436 3304
www.fhaonline.org.uk

The Family Holiday Association helps provide holidays for families in need. Applications are accepted from referring agencies (social workers, health visitors) on behalf of families. Families have to be on a low income, have at least one child over 3 years old and have not had a holiday in the past four years.

HOTELS

Staying in hotels, though it may not come cheap, has never been better for parents and children. The choice, from basic to luxury, is increasing, the facilities for children improving, and the possibility to rest and relax inviting.

All the hotels we feature in this guide have many facilities that make your stay, not to mention your packing, easier but they are also truly welcoming of children and there will be lots for your children to do once you are there. As with all types of accommodation, however, if you need something specific for your stay, make sure that you confirm it is available prior to booking.

SELF-CATERING

Self-catering in this country ranges from cottages in remote locations to chalets and lodges in holiday parks. Self-catering is arguably the most home-from-home situation that you will get with a holiday, which may be a blessing or a curse depending on your situation. If you self-cater, you can cook for different diets and keep to a budget. There are also often washing facilities and usually there's more privacy than other options.

Many of the places that we mention allow you to have the flexibility of self-catering with the convenience of onsite restaurants and facilities.

Helpful Holidays

01647 433593
www.helpfulholidays.co.uk

Over 500 self-catering holiday cottages across the South West from Dorset to Cornwall. Established in 1982, this company comes well recommended. Quality accommodation.

NCT Houseswap

01626 360689
www.bristolnct.co.uk
Annual: £25.85

The houseswap register is a list of over 257 families who are willing to swap houses with each other in order to have free accommodation. The Register is a list by county of members' homes, so you can match up with someone whose home is suitable for your age of children. At least one child must be under 13yrs.

B&Bs

Unlike hotels, B&Bs generally do not offer evening meals. However they often offer a more personal and affordable service.

Alistair Sawday's Special Places to Stay: British Bed & Breakfast

01275 464891
www.specialplacestostay.com
Guides from £12.99

This is one of the many guides produced by this local publisher. The B&B guide is specially recommended although the guide on British hotels, inns and other places is also excellent. There is a clear key in all guides indicating whether children are welcome.

For those of you venturing to France, take a look at their French B&B guide, this too has been recommended as family friendly.

YOUTH HOSTEL ASSOCIATION

0870 770 8868
www.yha.org.uk

One of the leading budget accommodation providers in the UK. Its name suggests it is only for the young, free and single traveller but this is no longer the case. It attracts travellers of all ages and hostels welcome families. There are more than 200 YHAs all over the UK in some stunning locations. There are a further 4000 in 90 overseas destinations. It is no longer necessary to be a member of the YHA, however annual family membership is £25, which is good value. **All prices listed in this chapter apply to YHA members. Add on a per night supplement of £3 per adult, £1.50 per child if you are a non-member.**

CAMPING

Camping with children of all ages can be enormous fun and an affordable way to get away from it all. Camping no longer needs to equate to roughing it either as many campsites have excellent facilities — should you want them! The many benefits include lots of freedom for children to run around and you can cook your own food.

Possible disadvantages include the noise of the other campers and of course ... the rain!

SOUTH WALES

Stunning countryside from the mountains near Brecon to the unspoilt and sweeping beaches of the Gower and Pembrokeshire.

B&Bs

Four Seasons Guest House

62 Gwscwm Rd, Pembrey, Carmarthenshire, SA16
01554 833367
Open all year
£25pp 2 sharing, £6 child sharing the room

P WC ⚠ ⌂

A small, friendly guest house set very close to Pembrey country park and Burry Port Harbour. It makes an excellent touring base to visit the Gower Peninsula, Pembrokeshire and the magnificient beach at Pembrey.

YHAs

Brecon YHA

Groesffordd, Brecon, Powys, LD3 7SW
0870 7705718
www.yha.org.uk
Feb-Nov Open daily
Nov-Feb w/e's only
£30.90 2-bed, £54.50 4-bed, £59.50 5-bed,
£5 for ensuite

P ⚠ ✂ ⌂ 🛏

Two miles from Brecon, this Victorian family house, built 175 years ago, stands in ample grounds. Facilities include, a washing machine, games room and TV. The surrounding countryside is fantastic for hill walking families.

Broad Haven YHA

Haverford West, Pembrokeshire, SA62 3JH
0870 770 5728
www.yha.org.uk
Mar-Oct
Group bookings in winter
£27 2-bed, £48 4-bed

P ⚠ ✂ ♿

Single storey hostel overlooking St Brides Bay, close to the beach just 100yrds away. All rooms are ensuite with shower. Games room, TV, washing facilities and garden. Restaurant for breakfast and evening meals.

Penycwm YHA & YMCA

Whitehouse, Penycwn, Haverfordwest, Pembrokeshire, SA62 6LA
0870 770 5988
www.yha.org.uk
Open all year
£45.50 3-bed, £54.50 4-bed, £74.95 6-bed

P ⚠ ✂ ⌂

This 5 star hostel has all ensuite bedrooms with TVs. There are large grounds, games room, washing facilities and towel hire. At the time of going to press, the hostel is changing to a YMCA hostel but will be run on the same lines.

Poppit Sands YHA

Seaview, Poppit, Pembrokeshire, SA43 3LP
0870 7705996
www.yha.org.uk
Open all year, closed Sun/Mon except Jul & Aug
£31.95 2-bed, £49.50 4-bed, £69.95 6-bed

A charming hostel, YHA Poppit Sands sits in five acres of grounds that reach down to the sea and overlook a blue flag sandy beach.

Port Eynon YHA

Old lifeboat house, Port Eynon, Swansea, SA3 1NN
0870 770 5998
www.yha.org
Easter-Nov open daily
Winter group bookings only
£26 2-bed, £45 4-bed,

Port Eynon YHA was once a lifeboat station and is right on the beach on the beautiful Gower Peninsula. The hostel is ideal for water sports enthusiasts, bird watchers, walkers or beach-lovers. (See photo above.)

CAMPSITES

Llanmadoc Caravan & Campsite

Llagadranta Farm, Gower, Swansea, SA3 1DE
01792 386202
www.caravancampingsites.co.uk (link from here)
Apr-Oct

Great campsite on one of the Gower's best beaches. The site is basic but peaceful. Plenty of walking and stunning views.

Pembrey

Pembrey Country Park, Pembrey, Carmarthan, SA16
01554 833913
www.sirgaer.com (link from this site)
Mar-Oct
Caravans £5-10, tents £1.60-£2.50 pp
Only takes groups of 6 units or more

A very basic campsite, no showers, but it's a short walk to a world-class beach, sandy with surf. Within this forested park, facilities include a dry ski slope, horse riding, cycling, playground, pitch and putt and crazy golf.

Pencelli Caravan and Camping

Pencelli, Brecon, Powys, Wales, LD3 7LX
01874 665451
www.pencelli-castle.co.uk
Closed Nov-Dec
Caravan £16 2 adults, tents £8 adult, £4.50 child

Pencelli Castle campsite is highly recommended as having the "cleanest and best equipped campsite toilet block". It won the national tourism award for Wales 2003, "best place to stay".

Porthclais Farm

St Davids, Pembrokeshire, Wales, SA62 6RR
01437 720 256
www.porthclais-campsite.co.uk
Easter-Oct open daily
£5 adult, £2 child pppn

Set within the Pembrokeshire National Park, Porthclais Farm is a small, family-run campsite, with acres of space. The site has basic but adequate facilities and is located on the sea front. Caerfai, Porthsele and Whitesands beaches are nearby, as is St David's, the smallest city in the UK.

GLOUCESTERSHIRE

A very pretty county which includes the Cotswolds, with beautiful stone villages.

HOTELS

Calcot Manor Hotel

Nr Tetbury, Gloucestershire, GL8 8YJ
01666 890391
www.calcotmanor.co.uk
Open all year
£235-£370 family room, B&B, plus child supplement

A charming Cotswold farmhouse, converted into a stylish hotel with a luxury spa. There's an indoor pool and a Mez area with games, PlayStation and cinema. "So geared up for children you don't notice they are there!"

SELF-CATERING

Hoburne Cotswold Water Park

Broadway Lane, South Cerney, Cirencester, Glos
01285 860 216
www.hoburne.com
Please contact the park for pricing

Accommodation includes caravans, lodges, chalets and touring pitches surrounding four lakes teeming with wildlife. There is a huge range of facilities in and around the Lakeside Club. There are indoor and outdoor pools, family restaurants and bars, 10-pin mini bowling, adventure playground, pool, table tennis, tennis, canoes and an amusement arcade.

YHAs

Slimbridge YHA

Shepherds Patch, Slimbridge, Glos, GL2 7BP
0870 7706036
www.yha.org.uk
Feb-Oct daily during sch hols, w/e's only term time
£25.50 2-bed - £62.50 6-bed

A large brick-built building close to the famous WWT Wildfowl and Wetlands centre, not far from Bristol. Visitors can watch birds on the duck pond in the observation lounge. There are grounds to explore and a games room.

Stow-on-the-Wold YHA

The Square, Stow-on-the-Wold, Glos, GL54 1AF
0870 7706050
www.yha.org.uk
Feb-Oct daily
Nov-Jan w/e's only
£50 4-bed, £65 6-bed, £5 supp for ensuite

A listed 16th century townhouse right in the main square of this charming Cotswold market town. It has been comfortably refurbished but has managed to retain its original exposed beams and 17th century staircase. There are laundry facilities and a restaurant serving breakfast and supper.

Welsh Bicknor YHA

Welsh Bicknor YHA, Nr Goodrich, Ross-on-Wye, HR9
0870 7706086
www.yha.org.uk
Easter-Oct open
Oct-Easter open w/e's only
From £31.95-£69.95, 2-6-bed

P ⚒ ⊞ ▦

This is a charming YHA in a pretty former
Victorian rectory set in the Wye Valley with a
river running through the grounds. It enjoys
beautiful views of the Forest of Dean and
Symonds Yat rock. Facilities include a games
room, TV, washing machine and a restaurant
serving breakfast and evening meals.

The Cotswolds

Make the most of your holiday
in the Cotswolds — there some
beautiful walks, stately homes
and wildlife parks to visit, see
pgs 99 & 124.

CAMPSITES

Christchurch Caravaning and Camping Site

Bracelands Drive, Christchurch, Coleford, GL16 7NN
0131 314 6505
www.forestholidays.co.uk
End Mar-early Nov
£6.90-£16.20 per pitch per night

P ⌂ ♿

Excellent for families, this site is on a gentle
slope high above the beautiful Wye Valley,
with waymarked walking routes down to the
river through the surrounding woodland.
Nearby are the Clearwell Caves ancient
iron mines.

Croft Farm Leisure & Waterpark

Bredons Hardwick, Tewkesbury, Glos, GL20 7EE
01684 772 321
www.croftfarmleisure.co.uk
1st Mar-31st Oct
Please call for more information.

Lakeside camping and caravan park with sailing, windsurfing and canoeing — tuition and equipment hire.

Hoburne Cotswold Water Park

Broadway Lane, South Cerney, Cirencester, Glos, GL7 5UQ
01285 860 216
www.hoburne.com
Caravans: from £225-£550 per week. Chalets and lodges: from £246 per week. (Dependent on season)

For full description, see Self-Catering.

WILTSHIRE

A great touring base to see some World Heritage tourist sites and other attractions: Stonehenge, Avebury, Bath and Longleat.

SELF-CATERING

Center Parcs

Longleat Forest, Warminster, Wiltshire, BA12 7PU
08705 200 300
www.centerparcs.co.uk
Open all year.

With nature on your doorstep and over 100 activities to choose from, it's the perfect place to take a short break. You can choose to do as much or as little as you like. The only mode of transport is on foot or by bike. There is a covered swimming pool with outdoor heated rapids, slides and wave machine. There are a wide range of activities and sports for kids of all ages. At busy times these may need to be pre-booked at the start of your stay or before you arrive, most incur an additional charge.

CAMPSITES

Brokerswood Country Park

Brokerswood, Westbury, Wiltshire, BA13 4EH
01373 822 238
www.brokerswood.co.uk
£8-£23 per pitch per night depending on season and type

A Gold Conservation Award winning site, Brokerswood is well located for visiting Bath, Salisbury, Stonehenge, Longleat and beyond. The site offers generous size pitches on a flat, open field. There is a centrally-heated shower block ensuring a comfortable stay all year round. There is no additional charge for awnings or showers, and pitch prices, which include access into the Country Park, are based on two adults and up to two children.

DORSET & HAMPSHIRE

The coastline offers lovely coves and a variety of pebble and sandy family beaches, keep your eyes open for fossils!

HOTELS

Moonfleet Manor

Fleet, Nr Weymouth, Dorset, DT3 4ED
01305 786948
www.luxuryfamilyhotels.com
Open all year
£160-£200 double, B&B

Moonfleet Manor is beautifully set lying at the end of a winding two mile lane. It overlooks Chesil Beach and the Fleet lagoon. The manor is Georgian and has a colonial feel with planters chairs and parquet floors. There is an outdoor play area, tennis and squash courts and indoor swimming pool (in need of some refurbishment). For rainy days there is a huge indoor area with table tennis, pool tables, giant Jenga and bowling alley.

The Sandbanks Hotel

Sandbanks, Poole, BH13 7PS
01202 707377
www.sandbankshotel.co.uk
Open all year.
From £83.50 B&B pppn, £88.50 DB&B, £35 8-12yrs,
£19 3-8yrs, £10 2-3yrs

P ⌂ ☆ ✗

Located on a Blue Flag award beach. Most
bedrooms have a sea or harbour view and
a balcony. Its beach-side brasserie has an
AA red rosette. There are many leisure
facilities including a recently opened spa with
treatment rooms. Many activities are laid on
for children and teenagers, there are holiday
clubs, games, discos and karaoke. The indoor
pool has a flume.

SELF-CATERING

Sandy Balls Holiday Centre

Godshill, Fordingbridge, Hampshire, SP6 2JY
01425 653042
www.sandy-balls.co.uk

For full description, see Camping, pg 206.

YHAs

Swanage YHA

Swanage, Dorset
0870 7706058
www.yha.org.uk
Open Feb-Nov, w/e's only during term-time
Closed Dec-Jan
£34.50 2-bed, £55 3-bed, £69 4-bed,

P ✗ ⌂ ⌂ ⌂

This is a large Victorian manor house close
to the centre of Swanage and its safe, sandy
beaches. TV and games room. Closed on
weekdays in term-time due to school groups.

CAMPSITES

Sandy Balls Holiday Centre

Godshill, Fordingbridge, Hampshire, SP6 2JY
01425 653042
www.sandy-balls.co.uk
Open all year
Accommodation per week from £93-£1113, many variations. Touring/camping from £14 pn

Sandy Balls is situated in the New Forest, bordered by the river Avon and set in 120 acres of woods and parklands. The holiday centre consists of forest lodges, luxurious holiday homes, camping and touring site. There are first class facilities including a swimming pool, riding stables, children's acitivities, bar and restaurant.

Tom's Field Camping

Tom's Field Rd, Langton Matravers, Swanage
01929427110
www.tomsfieldcamping.co.uk
Open March-Oct
£3.75 pp per night, family tent £9.50
Walkers barn £8.50 per night

Tom's Field is a lovely, peaceful campsite. It is right in the middle of the beautiful Dorset coastline, ideal for walking, climbing and family holidays. It is near Swanage with its good sandy beach and 20 minutes' walk from the Dorset coastal footpath. Tom's Field also has a walkers barn, available all year with three bunk rooms, bathroom and kitchenette.

SOMERSET

Beautiful and varied scenery from the tranquil countryside around Bath and Wells to the rugged landscape of Exmoor National Park.

HOTELS

Woolley Grange

Woolley Green, Bradford-on-Avon, BA15 1TX
01225 864705
www.woolleygrange.com
From £135 per room pn

Jacobean Manor House set in open countryside on the outskirts of Bradford-on-Avon, eight miles from Bath. Family facilities include croquet, bikes, football, PlayStations and an outdoor heated swimming pool.

SELF-CATERING

Butlins

Minehead, Somerset, TA24 5SH
0870 242 1999 general, 01643 703331 Minehead
www.butlinsonline.co.uk
Open all year
Costs vary

Good quality self-catering and half-board accommodation. Apartments are airy with four different grades dependent on position and equipment. Indoor and outdoor activities from high rope courses and horse riding to fairground rides and a water park.

Pitcot Farm Cottages

Pitcot Lane, Stratton on Fosse, Bath, BA3 4SX
01761 233108
www.pitcotfarm.co.uk
Open all year
From £300-£630 pw high season

The newly converted cottages in a single storey barn are well equipped with log burners and TV/video. Indoor tennis court.

Westermill Farm Cottages

Exford, Exmoor, Somerset, TA24 7NJ
01643 831238
www.westermill.com
From £160-£490 pw

Share the beautiful 500 acre sheep and beef farm. Delightful Scandinavian-style accommodation set in beautiful, grassy paddocks. Seven cottages sleeping 2-8 people. Stabling for horses available.

YHAs

Minehead YHA

Alcombe Combe, Minehead, Somerset, TA24 6EW
0870 770 5968
www.yha.org.uk
Daily Jul-Aug
Flexible winter openings
£41 3-bed, £44 4-bed, £63 6-bed

Attractive country house high on Exmoor hills just two miles from beaches. Plenty of easy walking routes from the back door. Exciting trails for mountain bikes. There are laundry facilities and a meal service for breakfast and dinner. Please note there is limited parking. See photo above left.

CAMPSITES

Newton Mill Camping

Newton Rd, Bath, BA2 9JF
01225 333909
www.campinginbath.co.uk
Open all year.
Tent & car: £13 caravans/motorhomes: £15,
£2.50 3-16yrs family rate, £2.50 hook-up

Newton Mill Camping is located in a hidden valley close to the centre of Bath. There is free fishing, nearby café, bar and restaurant. There is also the level, traffic-free Bath-Bristol cycle path and frequent bus services.

DEVON

A family favourite with our readers. It has a wonderful coastline and dramatic scenery across the Dartmoor National Park.

HOTELS & B&Bs

Cheriton Guest House

Vicarage Rd, Sidmouth, Devon, EX10 8UQ
01395 513810
Open all year
£27 pp B&B, children over 3yrs half price

A large town house backing onto the river Sid with parkland beyond. Half mile walk to sea front. All bedrooms are ensuite with TV. Large rear garden. Evening meals and packed lunches available on request.

Dodbrooke Farm

Michelcombe, Holne, Devon, TQ13 7SP
01364 631461
www.dodbrookefarm.com
£27 pp B&B

Judy runs this beautiful 17th century longhouse. Lovely family atmosphere. Fabulous garden, cobbled yard with goats and hens. There is also a converted barn available for self catering.

Fingals Hotel

Dittisham, Dartmouth, TQ6 0JA
01803 722 398
www.fingals.co.uk

This is a fabulous, individual, quirky hotel run with much energy and imagination by Richard and Sheila. Richard has restored the farmhouse into an informal yet stylish hotel. This is particularly suitable for teenagers, with activities including swimming, snooker and tennis and even a mini-cinema.The hotel also has a self-catering family barn available for hire which is perfect for a family of four.

Saunton Sands Hotel

Braunton, Devon, EX33 1LQ
01271 890 212
www.sauntonsands.co.uk
From £77 pn, please call for rates and special offers

Saunton Sands has a range of hotel rooms and self-catering apartments to suit the particular needs of your family. Facilities include an indoor and outoor heated swimming pool, games room, junior putting green, adventure area, holiday activities, table tennis, pool tables, tennis, squash, gym, sauna, solarium, and beauty treatments.

The Cottage Hotel

Hope Cove, Kingsbridge, South Devon, TQ7 3HJ
01548 561555
www.hopecove.com
From £48 pppn DB&B low season, includes children sharing parents room, £16.50 9-12yrs

A traditional family hotel, set in 2½ acres leading via sloping footpaths to two beautiful beaches and the pretty village of Hope Cove. There is a relaxed atmosphere making this a place for a classic seaside holiday.

Thurlestone Hotel

Thurlestone, Nr Kingsbridge, Devon, TQ7 3NN
01548 560382
www.thurlestone.co.uk
From £79 pppn DB&B for a min of 2 nights (low season)

A lovely family-friendly hotel set very close to the beautiful Blue Flag Thurlestone Sands beach. Activities for the family include indoor and outdoor pools, sailing, riding, tennis, squash, badminton, snooker, table tennis and a 9-hole golf course. There is also a spa and sauna for parents to escape.

Woolacombe Bay Hotel

Woolacombe, Devon, EX34 7BN
01271 870388
www.woolacombe-bay-hotel.co.uk
Feb-Dec
Low season/peak season £150/£250 double per person, £10/£50 child sharing, Prices vary throughout the year, phone for more details

This grand Victorian hotel overlooking the stunning beach of Woolacombe is well-equipped, with indoor and outdoor pools and adventure playground. There is a beach club with organised activities from quad biking to surf lessons.

SELF-CATERING

Gabriel's Loft

2 Dartmouth Rd, East Allington, Nr Totnes, Devon
01548 853089
www.toadhallcottages.com
May-Sept
From £260-£671

Lovely little cottage, 4½ miles from the beach, 200yrds from the pub. Sleeps 4-6 people. Enclosed rear garden. Virtual tour of the house on the website.

Hall House

Cornworthy, Nr Totnes, Devon
01548 853089
www.toadhallcottages.com
Open all year
£427-£1099

Stunning house with beautiful decorations throughout, in the pretty village of Cornworthy, near the river Dart. Sleeps 8. Beach 7 miles, pub opposite, shops 2 miles. Take a virtual tour of the house on the website. Dogs allowed by arrangement.

Lundy Island

Bristol Channel, North Devon, EX39 2LY
01271 863636
www.lundyisland.co.uk
Contact Lundy Island Shore Office for prices.

Lundy offers visitors a wide range of buildings in which to stay, including a castle, lighthouse and gentleman's villa. There are 23 self-catering properties. For more details on Lundy itself, see entry under Camping.

Ruda Holiday Park

Croyde Bay, North Devon, EX33 1NY
0870 220 4600
www.parkdeanholiday.com
Mar-Nov
Please phone for accommodation prices

Ruda Holiday Park is a short walk from a Blue Flag beach. Activities include surf lessons, mountain boarding, tennis courts, fishing, horse riding, cascades tropical adventure pool and children's clubs. There is an entertainment lounge, bar, café and take away, supermarket and gift shop.

Salcombe Holiday Homes

Orchard Court, Island St, Salcombe, TQ8 8QE
01548 843485
www.salcombe.com
Rents vary

Set in this idyllic Devon seaside town. There are a wide range of holiday homes available, sleeping 2-18 people. Excellent website with virtual tours. Friendly staff to help you find the right property to meet your family's needs. See photo of estuary above.

Saunton Sands Hotel

Braunton, Devon, EX33 1LQ
01271 890 212
www.sauntonsands.com

Fully equipped 2-4 bed apartments. Extensive range of hotel facilities included.

YHAs

Beer YHA

Towns End, Bovey Combe, Beer, EX12 3LL
0870 7705690
www.yha.org.uk
Mar-Oct open daily
Oct-Mar closed Tue-Wed, occasionally rented out as a complete hostel, phone for availability
£49.50 4-bed, £59.50 5-bed, £69.95 6-bed

This is a lovely YHA on the edge of Beer, set in a light and airy country house. It has a large lawned garden great for games. Breakfast and evening meals available.

Okehampton YHA

Klondyke Rd, Oakhampton, Dartmoor, EX20 1EW
0870 770 5978
www.yha.org.uk
Open Jan-Nov, but phone to check availability
Closed Dec-Jan
£34.95-£77.50, 2-6-bed

This hostel is fantastic for family-based activity holidays, set in 3 acres of grounds. It offers multi-activity breaks with a variety of activities, from kayaking to rock climbing for 5+yrs. On the edge of Dartmoor National Park, YHA Okehampton is based in a uniquely preserved Victorian railway goods shed offering modern two to six bed family rooms. It has a TV and games room.

CAMPSITES

Lundy Island Camp Site

Bristol Channel, North Devon, EX39 2LY
01271 863636
www.lundyisland.co.uk
From £6 pppn
2hr boat crossing from Bideford or Ilfracombe or winter helicopter service from Hartland Point

For a get away from it all holiday or a weekend break, a trip to Lundy Island is a must. After a short boat trip from Ilfracombe on the MS Oldenburg, visitors can camp or stay in one of the many Landmark Trust properties on the island: www.landmarktrust.org.uk.

Booking in advance is essential. Campsite facilities include washroom facilities and showers. It's a haven for birdwatchers, climbers, canoeists and divers, Lundy is a favourite for people with a love of the great outdoors. Described as a child's 1000-acre playground, there is something for everyone.

Ruda Holiday Park

Croyde Bay, North Devon, EX33 1NY
01271 890477
www.ruda.co.uk
From £7 per pitch per night.

For full details, see self-catering pg 209.

Stoke Barton Farm

Stoke, Hartland, Bideford, Devon, EX39 6DU
01237 441 238
Open Easter until October
£4.50 adult, £2 child pppn, £2 hook-up

Stoke Farm is a beautiful spot on the North Devon Coast. There is ample space for camping and for children to run around safely, dogs are allowed. There are basic but adequate facilities, the campsite commands wonderful views down to Hartland Quay. The tea rooms have variable opening times. "Stoke Barton farm is quite simply a wonderful, peaceful place to stay. A welcome change from busy, commercial campsites."

CORNWALL

When the sun shines, there's nowhere quite like Cornwall. Stunning beaches, coves, coastal walks and pretty fishing ports make it another family favourite.

HOTELS & B&Bs

Bedruthan Steps Hotel

Mawgan Porth, Cornwall, TR8 4BU
01637 860860
www.bedruthan.com
Open all year
Low season/peak season £75pp/£116pp double, discounted rates for children

Wonderfully welcoming to families, set above a beautiful beach. The hotel has indoor and outdoor swimming pools, a cyber café and a surf school and for adults a spa. Recent winner of Cornwall Hotel of the Year 2005.

Fowey Hall Hotel

Hanson Drive, Fowey, Cornwall, PL23 1ET
01726 833866
www.luxuryfamilyhotels.com
Open all year
From £195 double

Fowey Hall is set in five acres of gardens overlooking the charming Cornish port of Fowey and near to the Eden Project. It is family-friendly with 12 family suites and four pairs of interconnecting rooms. Children of all ages are very well catered for with a kids club, indoor swimming pool, trampoline, pool table, table football, Nintendo, plasma TV screen (showing evening movies). There are also plenty of outdoor games and BBQs in the summer. See photo of estuary above.

St Enodoc Hotel

Rock, Cornwall, PL27 6LA
01208 863394
www.enodoc-hotel.co.uk
Open Mid Feb-Mid Jan
Low season/peak season £155/£215 double pp BB,
£10 extra child (in same room)

P

St Enodocs is in a lovely location set against
Cornwall's rugged north coast overlooking
Rock. The views sweep across the Camel
Estuary towards Padstow. The hotel is bright
and modern with 15 double bedrooms and
five spacious family suites. Children of all ages
welcomed and they will enjoy the outdoor
swimming pool.

SELF-CATERING

Polruan Cottages

1 Fowey View, The Quay, Polruan, PL23 1PQ
01726 870 582
www.polruancottages.co.uk
Open all year
Cottages priced individually

There are over 50 holiday cottages to hire
from this excellent company. The website
gives full details for each cottage, including
tariffs and availability. This family-run business
selects individually-owned homes, most of
which overlook Fowey harbour or the sea.

The Olde House

Chapel Ample, Wadebridge, Cornwall, PL27 6EN
01208 813 219
www.theoldehouse.co.uk
Open all year
From £325 low season to £1,265 peak season,
per cottage

The Olde House comes highly recommended.
Each cottage is well equipped for families.
There is a farm trail as well as the beaches
of Daymer Bay and Polzeath nearby. Their
leisure centre has an adventure playground,
tennis courts, snooker table, play barn,
heated indoor swimming pool and jacuzzi.
Prices include all facilities.

YHAs

Golant YHA

Penguite House, Golant, Nr Fowey, PL23 1LA
0870 770 5832
www.yha.org.uk
Mar-Oct
Group bookings winter

Set in three acres of beautiful grounds with
a further 14 acres of woodland behind to
explore. It overlooks the lovely Fowey Estuary,
just four miles from the sea. Families will
enjoy the traffic-free ground. There is also a
games room and TV. The restaurant serves
breakfast and supper with table licence.
Washing machine, cots and self-catering
kitchen also available.

Want to hang ten?

Learn to surf, there are five
great places listed in Sports &
Outdoor Pursuits, see pg 31.

Treyarnon Bay YHA

Treyarnon Bay, Padstow, Cornwall, PL28 8JR
0870 770 6076
www.yha.org.uk
Open all year
£45 3-bed (£50 ensuite), £55 4-bed, £66 5-bed

P ☒ ⊞ ♿

A fabulous location set on the wild Cornish coastline. YHA Treyarnon is right on the beach in the bay of Treyarnon. It was formerly a 1930s summer residence and has been recently updated. The hostel's location makes it a popular family base, particularly for those interested in surfing. There is a board store and courses.

YHA Lizard

Lizard Point, TR12 7NT
0870 770 6120
www.yha.org.uk
Mar-Oct, flexible during winter mths
£46 3-bed, £49 4-bed, £60 5-bed, £70 6-bed

P ⌂ ⊞ 🚐 ♿

With stunning views of Lizard Point, this 5 Star YHA is family-friendly with three ensuite rooms, BBQ area and bike store. See photo on pg 210.

CAMPSITES

Lower Treave Caravan Park

Crows-An-Wra, Penzance, Cornwall, TR19 6HZ
01736 810 559
www.lowertreave.demon.co.uk
Apr-Nov open
Low season/peak season £4/£5pp, £2 child, caravan hire £215-£315 per week

P ⌂ 🛒

Lower Treave is a well-run campsite close to the beautiful beaches of Sennen and Porthcurno. The well-landscaped site covers 4½ acres and provides 80 spacious touring pitches on four terraced levels.

Trevedra Farm Caravan & Campsite

Sennen, Penzance, Cornwall, TR19 7BE
01736 871818 summer, 871835 winter
Easter or 1st Apr-31st Oct
£4 adult, £2 11-15yrs, £3 hook-up, £1 pitch only

P 🛒

Run by the same family for 65yrs. A working farm where you can watch cows being milked. Located close to the beautiful Sennen Cove and coastal footpath. There is a separate camping field with its own toilet/shower facilities. The shop has daily deliveries, bread, cakes, take-away breakfast, lunch and evening meals in peak season. There is a launderette & utility room. Booking essential in peak season.

Treyarnon Bay Campsite

Treyarnon Bay, Padstow, Cornwall, PL28 8JR
01841 520681
www.treyarnonbay.co.uk
Apr-Sep
£11 per unit peak, £7 per unit off-peak

P 🛒

Sea views from site, only 200yrds from a family beach and cliff walks. The site has two toilet blocks, a shower block and laundry. The hotel next door with bar and evening entertainment welcomes campers.

LONDON

Showing your children the sites of London can make a great weekend. The museums, interactive exhibitions, historical palaces, theatres and parks will keep you busy!

HOTELS

Express By Holiday Inn

295 North End Rd, West Kensington, W14 9NS
020 7384 5151
www.exhiearlscourt.co.uk
£80 family room (2+2)

There are 15 London hotels in this chain offering good value accommodation. This hotel is particularly close to public transport with easy access to central London. The rooms are clean but on the small size, all are ensuite and have tea and coffee making facilities. Self-serve continental breakfast. Parking available at a charge. Visit their website for low season offers.

YHAs

Hampstead Heath YHA

4 Wellgarth Rd, Golders Green, London, NW11
0870 770 5846
www.yha.org.uk
Open all year
£39 2-bed, £61 3-bed, £78 4-bed, £96.30 6-bed

This hostel is set in Hampstead Heath in North West London. It is busy but popular with families as it has a garden as well as a games room, TV and internet access.

St Pancras YHA

79-81 Euston Rd, London, NW1 2QE
0870 7706044
www.yha.org.uk
Open daily all year
From £44-£130 B&B

This is a modern hostel opposite St Pancras station. It offers comfortable, basic accommodation in family rooms close to central London transport links.

BRISTOL

If you don't always have the bed space for friends and family to stay, there is plenty of accommodation in Bristol to choose from.

HOTELS

Henbury Lodge

Station Rd, Henbury, BS10 7QQ
0117 950 2615
www.henburylodge.com
From £94 per room, £15 per child 2-14yrs

P &

A luxury Georgian country hotel in Bristol, Henbury lodge has very large family rooms. And for those of you planning large family celebrations, parties can also be catered for (the dining room seats 34).

Westbury Park Hotel

37 Westbury Rd, Bristol, BS9 3AU
0117 962 0465
www.westburypark-hotel.co.uk
Doubles from £60. Family rooms from £75

P

A detached Victorian house on the edge of Bristol's famous Durdham Downs. It is an AA four diamond rated hotel and also has the English Tourist Board Silver Award. There are two large rooms family rooms and also a twin interconnecting with a double bedroom.

SELF-CATERING

Bristol YHA

14 Narrow Quay, Bristol, BS1 4QA
0870 770 5726
www.yha.org.uk
Open all year
£40 2-bed, £66 ensuite 4-bed for B&B

This is a great base for visiting families or relatives as it is set down on the quayside with views over the waterways. The hostel has been sympathetically restored to create a relaxing place to stay, with games room, TV area, washing machines, self catering kitchen and the café has a table licence.

Days Serviced Apartments

30-38 St Thomas St, Redcliffe, Bristol, BS1 6JZ
0117 954 4800
www.premgroup.com
From £70 per unit per night

P &

These centrally-based, luxury, one or two bedroom serviced apartments are located a minute's walk from St Mary Redcliffe Church. Each apartment has a fully equipped kitchen with cooker, refrigerator, freezer, dishwasher, washing machine and microwave. Bed linen and towels are provided. There is secure car parking on request, an on-call manager and a shopping service is also available.

CAMPSITES

Brook Lodge Farm Camping & Caravan Park

Cowslip Green, Bristol, Somerset, BS40 5RB
01934 862 311
www.brooklodgefarm.com
Telephone for pricing and further information.

P

Brook Lodge Farm is a family-run country touring park, based in the private grounds of a small farm. It is ten miles from Bristol city centre, making it an ideal place to stay if you want to camp close to Bristol. Among its many charms, there is an abundance of wildlife, a stream and outdoor swimming pool.

HOLIDAYS FURTHER AFIELD

AIR TRAVEL

Bristol and the West Country are well served for travelling further afield, with Bristol International Airport (BIA), which has scheduled flights to many destinations.

Bristol International Airport

Bristol, BS48 3DY
0870 1212 747
www.bristolairport.co.uk

Being a relatively small airport, everything is within easy walking distance, making departures and arrivals fairly straight forward. There are shops and restaurants either side of customs.

Airportcarz

Bristol Int Airport, Lulsgate Bottom, BS48 3DY
01275 474888
www.airportcarz.com
Located on the way to Pick-up Car Park via covered walkway

Private hire taxis based at UK airports. They have people carriers suitable for larger families and minibuses for disabled travellers.

SEA TRAVEL

Travelling by ferry can be one of the least stressful ways to do long journeys. Many ferry companies have onboard activities to while away the journey including climbing areas, games rooms and cinemas. Booking a cabin on longer crossings can also have its advantages.

Brittany Ferries

08703 665 333, www.brittany-ferries.co.uk
Plymouth to Roscoff and Santander
Poole to Cherbourg

Condor Ferries Limited

0845 345 2000, www.condorferries.co.uk
Weymouth & Poole to Guernsey, Jersey & St Malo

Irish Ferries

08705 17 17 17, www.irishferries.com
Pembroke to Rosslare

Stena Line

08705 707 070, www.stenaline.co.uk
Fishguard to Rosslare

Swansea Cork Ferries

01792 456 116, www.swansea-cork.ie
Swansea and Cork

WORK & TRAVEL

Sophia Denham
Rachel Miller

CONTENTS

INTRODUCTION

The stereotype of the lazy teenager, lying in bed until midday is terribly unfair. Today's teenagers are busier than ever. If you're not at school, you're tackling mountains of coursework. Many of you have part-time jobs to try and earn a little cash, others might do voluntary work and most of you juggle hobbies and interests.

On top of that, you are expected to line up work experience and think about what you want to do with the rest of your lives!

Managing all the activities that take place outside school can be a big challenge. In this chapter, we guide you through the maze of jobs and voluntary work. We've got the low-down on organising work experience and there are masses of exciting ideas for travel and gap years.

WORK EXPERIENCE

Most schools expect their pupils to line up some work experience in the summer term of Year 10, others in Year 11. It can be hard to choose the right placement for you — a good place to start is to focus on your interests or favourite school subjects. If you already have a career plan, it is an excellent chance to see if that job is really for you! Or you could surprise yourself and choose something radically different.

Start planning well ahead, as you will be competing with hundreds of your fellow year 10s. Some placements are more popular than others: hospitals, TV and radio stations, football clubs and modelling agencies are in demand, so if they appeal, don't leave your application to the last minute.

Work experience placements usually last a week or two and they give you the chance to experience a real working environment. Sometimes, a group of companies or departments will get together to offer work experience to a group of pupils. This route can give you a broader experience and the chance to work as a team.

Whatever you do, work experience is a brilliant opportunity, helping to develop skills such as planning, time keeping, taking responsibility, confidence building and decision-making.

A good start to your search is the Health and Safety Approved Employer Database, as listed companies are already geared up for work experience placements. All placements must be health and safety approved for the purposes of work experience. Pupils on work experience are classed as employees for the period of the placement and are covered by the host company's insurance. Companies that are new to work experience can apply for Health and Safety Approval. This can take a few weeks, so it pays to start looking early.

Your parents can help with CVs and mock interview practice but organising the placement is down to you, it's all part of the experience. And it's not necessarily a good idea to go to work with your parents — you just won't get the same confidence boost if you're under their wings.

Connexions

www.connexionswest.org.uk
0117 987 3700

The Connexions West website has comprehensive guidelines and information on all aspects of work experience.

Placement ideas

Primary schools

Dental surgeries

Department stores

Kennels

Hotels

Fire Brigade

Banks

Radio stations

TV companies

Ministry of Defence

Universities or colleges

Nurseries

Law firms

Restaurants

Car manufacturers

[Based on the work experiences of the Bristol teenagers that completed our questionnaire]

PART-TIME WORK

Clothes, music, coffees, snacks, games, films, concerts, travel, mobile phones — these essential items don't come cheap. Getting a job is a great way to fund your spending habits and it gives you a real sense of independence.

Popular options are babysitting, paper rounds and also Saturday jobs in shops or restaurants. Other ideas include pet feeding and walking, car washing, gardening and plant watering.

If you are looking for a job, get friends and family to keep an eye out for you, word of mouth can be very helpful. Check the Bristol Evening Post, visit your local Connexions centre or you could put your own advert on a local noticeboard.

One tried and tested option is the fast food industry, if you don't mind flipping burgers.

Alternatively, the retail sector loves part-timers, especially in the run up to Christmas. Department stores pay well or you could try one of the big supermarkets which offer flexible hours.

Make sure you've got a good CV. Even if your experience is limited, it will help to make you stand out. If you get an interview, spend some time finding out about the company. They are bound to ask you why you want to work there. Make sure you've got an answer!

BABYSITTING

This is a great option, as babysitters are always in demand. You need to be at least 13 years old. Don't be fooled into thinking you're getting paid to watch TV! You do have to be responsible and take the job seriously.

You're in charge and it's your job to make sure the kids are happy and safe. Make sure you know the needs of the kids you're looking after — babysitting for a newborn is quite different to minding a 10 year old. Eating, bathing and homework are all activities that you may have to help with.

Babysitting facts

What age can you leave a child at home without a babysitter?

There is no law that states the minimum age that a child can be left alone. However, it is an offence to leave a child alone when doing so puts him or her at risk.

So how do you decide if you can safely leave a child alone?

The NSPCC advises, "You are the best judge of your child's level of maturity and responsibility".

Most children under 13 should not be left for more than a short period. No child under 16 should be left overnight.

For futher advice contact:

Children's Legal Centre
01206 872 466
www.childrenslegalcentre.com

NSPCC Public Enquiry Line
0207 825 2775
www.nspcc.org.uk

You need to be prepared for an emergency, however unlikely. Ask the parents for a mobile phone contact and details of where they are going to be. It sounds obvious, but you must also ensure that you know the telephone number of their home and the address, essential if you need to dial 999. As an extra precaution, it can be useful to have the number of a trusted neighbour in case you need someone on the spot.

Check whether the child is taking any medicine, if they have asthma or any allergies and what to do in case of a reaction. It's a good idea to learn basic first aid and it could give you an edge over other babysitters.

Negotiate rates for the job in advance and also check how you are getting home. If you don't have someone to pick you up, ask for a ride home from the parents that you are babysitting for. If you live nearby, ask them to walk you home.

JOBS & CAREERS

Connexions

www.connexionswest.org.uk
0117 987 3700

This is the main point of contact for young people aged 14-19 yrs old when it comes to finding work. If you want to see a personal advisor, go to your local office:

Bristol: 4 Colston Ave, Bristol BS1 4ST
0117 987 3700

Bath & NE Somerset: 28 Southgate St, Bath BA1 1TP
01225 461501

Filton: 28-30 Gloucester Rd North, Filton, South Glos BS7 0SJ
0117 969 8101

Kingswood: 21-23 High St, Kingswood, South Glos BS15 4AA
0117 961 2760

Weston-Super-Mare: 45 Boulevard, Weston-super-Mare BS23 1PG
01934 644443

Radio 1 One Life

www.bbc.co.uk/radio1/onelife/work

Everything you need to know about work, from CVs and interviews to your rights and skills development.

Monster

www.teenzone.monster.co.uk

Monster is a huge global recruitment service. Go to Teen Zone for advice and information.

The Site.org

www.thesite.org/workandstudy

Great information on everything from getting a job, working abroad and work experience to becoming an entrepreneur.

The lowdown on work for under 16s

What age do I have to be to work?
13yrs

I'm 13, what can I do? Local by-laws list the jobs that 13yr olds can do, contact the education department of your local council for more information

What about acting jobs? You can work in the theatre or television as a child but you need a performance license

How many hours can I work during term time? A maximum of 12 hours a week

What about hours on a Saturday? A maximum of five hours on Saturdays for 13-14yr olds, or eight hours for 15-16yr olds

What can't I do? You can't work in a factory; during school hours; before 7am or after 7pm

Do I need a work permit? Yes, you need an employment permit issued by the education department of the local council

Can I work in the school holidays? Yes but you must have a two week break from any work during the school holidays in each calendar year

What hours can I work in the school holidays? 13-14yr olds can work a maximum of 25hrs per week; 15-16yr olds can work a maximum of 35hrs per week

Do I need a permit for work experience? No

When can I work full-time? Children are of compulsory school age up to the last Friday in June in the academic year of their 16th birthday. After that you can apply for your National Insurance Number and work full time.

VOLUNTARY WORK

Giving up your time to help other people is not only about doing good. It's a great way to learn new skills, improve confidence, make friends and have fun. And you can feel pretty proud of yourself at the same time! Some schemes will give you an accreditation and the range of opportunities is amazing.

If you need some inspiration, the following organisations all rely on volunteers:
Care homes, disability clubs, hospitals, Mencap, National Trust, Red Cross, sports organisations, St Johns Ambulance, victim support, youth and community groups. The list starts with general points of enquiry and is then followed by specific groups requiring volunteers.

Do-it!
www.do-it.org.uk

Run by YouthNet UK, this website has hundreds of volunteering opportunities.

The Guardian newspaper

Check out The Guardian newspaper on a Wednesday. The Society section advertises volunteering opportunities.

Charity Shops

Most local charities and charity shops are grateful for volunteers.

Volunteer Reading Help
0207 729 4087
www.vrh.org.uk

Youth Information
www.youthinformation.com

Click on Employment and Training, then choose Volunteering.

Avon Wildlife Trust
32 Jacobs Well Rd, Bristol, BS8 1DR
0117 917 7270
www.avonwildlifetrust.org.uk

Opportunities for teenagers to volunteer, see website for details.

British Trust for Conservation Volunteers
01302 572244
www.btcv.org.uk
16+yrs
£30-60pw

BTCV Bristol
0117 929 1624
www.btcv.org/avon

A local group looking for volunteers to help them improve the environment by undertaking practical conservation work. Activities take place on Tuesdays, Wednesdays, Thursdays and Saturdays. U16s need to be accompanied by a parent or guardian, over 16s need parental consent.

Bristol Volunteers
www.bristolvolunteers.org.uk
0117 989 7733

Job shop of volunteering opportunities in Bristol.

Bristol Zoo Volunteers
Bristol Zoo Gardens, Clifton, Bristol, BS8 3HA
0117 974 7363

Volunteers over 18 can become involved in animal encounters, enclosure talks, activities with children, Zoo to You events and fund raising. You will need to commit a minimum of six hours per fortnight for a year.

Canal Camps
01923 711114
www.wrg.org.uk

The chance to restore derelict canals to their former glory. Holidays cost just £42 a week but are only for over 18s. Can provide the opportunity to qualify for a section of the Duke of Edinburgh's Gold Award.

Caring at Christmas

Little Bishop St, St Paul's, Bristol, BS2 9JF
0117 924 4444
www.caringatchristmas.org.uk
info@caringatchristmas.org.uk

If you are over 16 you can offer your services at Christmas. U18s work in the kitchen.

Cathedral Camps

01525 716237
www.cathedralcamps.org.uk
16-30yrs
£65pw

Connexions West

www.connexionswest.org.uk
0117 987 3700

Talk to a personal advisor for more ideas and help getting rewarding voluntary work in your area. You could even volunteer at Connexions, as it is committed to involving young people in the design, delivery, management and evaluation of its service. The kind of things you could get involved in are:

- Working with the marketing department to design leaflets

- Planning the re-decoration of the Connexions centres so young people feel welcome

- Coming to meetings where decisions are made and giving your views.

CSV

www.csv.org.uk

Community Service Volunteers (CSV) provides volunteering and training opportunities that tackle real need and enrich lives, including gap year volunteering.

Millennium Volunteers

www.millenniumvolunteers.gov.uk

An initiative for young people aged 16-24 in which you volunteer your time to help others, doing what you enjoy. The scheme encourages you to get involved in local issues you care about, from environmental issues or youth leadership, to music and dance. Over 100,000 Millennium Volunteers have already

received MV awards by doing 100 or 200 hours of voluntary work.

Local contacts:

Bath and North East Somerset
01225 318879
Bristol (Young Bristol)
0117 907 1010
North Somerset Volunteer Agency
01934 410192
South Gloucestershire
01454 317289.

National Trust Acorn Holidays

0870 429 2429
www.nationaltrust.org.uk/volunteers
16+yrs

Most National Trust working holidays are for over 18s, however there are about four holidays a year aimed at ages 16+.

St John Ambulance

The Harry Crook Centre, Raleigh Rd, Bedminster, BS1 3AP
0117 953 3880
www.sja.org.uk/avon/
info@avon.sja.org.uk

There are 23 different divisions of St John Ambulance in Bristol and Bath, so you'll have no trouble finding a local venue. Badgers (5-10yrs) and Cadets (10-18yrs) are taught basic first aid, learn about their community and have some fun and games. There are also opportunities to help out at events, supported by other St John Ambulance staff.

Volunteering Bristol

Royal Oak House, Royal Oak Avenue, BS1 4GB
0117 989 7733
www.bristolvolunteers.org.uk
Mon-Fri 10am-4pm
(Closed for lunch, 12pm-12.30pm)

There are hundreds of opportunities to offer your services at Volunteering Bristol, many for under 18s. However, it can be hard to find volunteering work over a school holiday as many organisations prefer a longer-term commitment and offer training. Check out the special booklet outlining the opportunities for regular weekend and evening voluntary work.

Volunteering England

www.volunteering.org.uk
0845 305 6979

The national volunteer development agency, which promotes volunteering as a powerful force for change, both for those who volunteer and for the wider community.

Young Bristol

32 Bond St, Broadmead, Bristol, BS1
0117 907 1010
www.youngbristol.com

This group, with its city centre drop-in, offers young people aged 16-24yrs the chance to volunteer through placements and youth-led projects. It also offers support, advice and the chance to do awards such as the Duke of Edinburgh. Great website, complete with message board, worth a browse.

MAKING YOUR VOICE HEARD

If you are passionate about the environment, politics or life in general, you may want to find a group that can give you a voice. The following organisations offer young people the chance to make a difference.

Young Bristol

32 Bond St, Broadmead, Bristol, BS1
0117 907 1010
www.youngbristol.com

Make your views known on this website. It runs polls on issues that concern young people and there are online debates on everything from current affairs to Big Brother.

Changemakers

www.changemakers.org.uk
020 7702 1511

Community-based activities designed to encourage active citizenship. If you're 16-25 yrs old, you can become a young advocate working with other young people in your community.

Friends of the Earth

10-12 Picton St, Montpelier, Bristol, BS6 5QA
0117 942 0129

A chance to campaign and make a difference to the environment in Bristol.

National Youth Agency

www.nya.org.uk/

The aim of the National Youth Agency is to enable young people to undergo personal and social development so that they can fulfil their potential within a just society.

Your Turn

www.commonpurpose.org.uk

Aimed at young people in Year 9, this programme is for schools that want their students to gain the knowledge and skills to operate as active citizens. If you're a young person who enjoys being a leader and wants to understand how your region works, so that you can make a difference, then Your Turn's for you.

GAP YEARS

By Sophia Denham, 21, who's been there, done that and bought the t-shirt!

Taking a gap year and travelling the world is becoming more popular each year, but planning your gap year can be daunting. Make sure you are realistic about every part of your trip, and plan well in advance, to ensure it's as successful as possible. Whether you want to live and work abroad, learn a language, travel independently, teach English, volunteer or do conservation work, there are loads of options to choose from and — trust me — choosing the right one for you is the hardest part.

If you're looking for a relaxing holiday, then volunteering is not for you — expect early mornings, hard, hands-on, dirty work and mostly being left to use your own initiative. It's not all bad though, and most people love every minute as well as the free time you get to explore the country.

There are masses of options, it's often easier to figure out what you want to do before looking, otherwise you'll be stuck for weeks thinking, "Shall I do orang-utan conservation in Borneo or work in an orphanage in Vietnam?" Match the project with your abilities, so if you're good with children, go for teaching; if you can play football, go for football coaching — it's much more rewarding if you want to do it and are already good at.

The most important thing is to check that the organisation is a genuine not-for-profit organisation, and that it will look after you and support you. Don't just do it for your CV. You need to be determined, hard-working, and enthusiastic about helping people in need, and most of all, be prepared for a culture shock. A good organisation will cover all the issues, from health problems to how to give your parents a call. You also get a degree of protection, in case anything serious happens to you, or there are any major disasters in the country.

There is a catch – some of the best and safest organisations to go with can be the priciest, and sometimes you have to pay for flights on top of these costs. The cost of volunteering varies (see pg 228). If you want to go far afield, such as Asia, Africa or South America, then the costs are higher. Alternatively, you can volunteer in Eastern Europe in places such as Romania or Bulgaria, for less. There are grants and scholarships available with most organisations if you have trouble raising the money, but from personal experience, a few months of hard slog in a supermarket will cover the cost!

If you're not one for "do-gooding" or just don't fancy paying to volunteer, just travelling and working is also an amazing experience — but make sure you check whether you need a working visa or not and then get one, it's not worth the hassle of being deported because you didn't bother with a visa.

Round-the world-tickets are the best value if you're going to a lot of countries. You can get these at good travel agents such as Student Flights or Flight Centre. Insurance is a necessity and Endsleigh do comprehensive cover. Avoid the cheap insurance websites, as you won't get the full cover you need.

Check out the gorvernment website, www.fco.gov.uk, where you can look up travel advice by country and get the most up-to-date information about any recent disasters and the status of local wars, as well as general safety advice about that country.

It's also worth doing a gap safety course. I did the Objective Gap Safety course (www. objectivegapsafety.com). It's a one-day training course, but gives you vital safety information on how to keep yourself out of trouble and what to do in certain situations. Several companies offer courses like these and they cost between £120 and £160, well worth the investment.

WORK YOUR WAY AROUND

Another way to see the world is to earn your dosh as you go, which has both upsides and downsides. The first obstacle is, obviously, finding a job, which can prove difficult in busy places at busy times, especially if it's full of backpackers desperate for some money. Hostels usually have boards with job ads, and

some hostels offer the opportunity for you to work to pay for your bed. Once you've got a job, depending where you are, there may be a limit on how long you can work for them (in Australia it's three months), due to working visa requirements. This needn't be a problem though, as it's usually enough time to save up to travel somewhere else.

The upsides of working and travelling are that you don't have to work for as long before you leave; you replenish your funds as you spend them; it's ideal for meeting people to travel with; and you can travel for longer. It also means you are more immersed into the culture and the local community.

So what did I do? After six months' full time work in the UK, I taught English in Sri Lanka (which actually, after Boxing Day, also turned into tsunami relief work) for three months, followed by three weeks in Australia, six weeks travelling around New Zealand, a glorious four weeks on the islands of Fiji and finally four weeks in the USA. All that work paid off and I had the time of my life. Now, all I want to do is see more of the world!

Work Visas

Australia
www.immi.gov.au

Go to the section in the website on Working Holiday Visas.

New Zealand
www.immigration.govt.nz

Go to the section in the website on Working Holiday Visas.

USA
www.usimmigrationsupport.org

Go to the section on H-2B Work Visas.

Europe

To work in Europe, check with the individual country embassies beforehand to see if any work visas or permits are required.

GAP YEAR CONTACTS

Aid Camps

www.aidcamps.org

Offers short-term voluntary work placements in India, Africa and Sri Lanka.

Au Pair in America

www.aupairamerica.co.uk

Massive database of families in the United States looking for au pairs.

Base Camp Group

www.basecampgroup.com

Learn to be a ski or snowboard instructor in Europe or North America and then teach others during your year off.

British International Twinning Association

0117 328 4450
www.bristol-city.gov.uk/twinning

Help and advice if you are looking to work in any one of the towns Bristol is twinned with. These include towns in the following countries: France, Germany, Portugal, Georgia, China, Mozambique and Nicaragua.

BUNAC

www.bunac.org.uk
020 7251 3472
BUNAC offer a range of work and volunteer-based opportunities abroad in countries including, Canada, Australia, New Zealand, Ghana, South Africa, Costa Rica, Cambodia and Peru.

Connexions

www.connexionswest.org.uk
0117 987 3700

Advice and information on taking a year off. Connexions also has a database, Exodus, which has information on career opportunities abroad.

Cross-Cultural Solutions

www.crossculturalsolutions.org

Work side-by-side with local people in countries such as: Brazil, China, Costa Rica, Ghana, Guatemala, India, Peru, Russia, Tanzania and Thailand. A well-established, not-for-profit organisation.

Camp America

www.campamerica.co.uk

American summer camps are part of the American way of life and there are over 12,000 throughout the whole of the USA. Camp counsellors pay their own travel costs but do receive some pocket money in return for their efforts.

Childcare International

www.childint.com

This specialist agency can help you find work as an au pair, mother's help or nanny in America, Canada, Australia or Europe.

GAP

www.gap.org.uk

A not-for-profit organisation, specialising in voluntary work placements for 17-25 year-olds, in 27 countries. Offers good preparation, paired placements and support overseas.

Gap Sports Abroad

www.gapsportsabroad.com

This programme enables you to combine adventurous travel with sports projects in developing communities. You could be coaching football in Coast Rica, organising rugby matches in South Africa, helping over-stretched staff in hospitals; or researching stories for African newspapers and TV stations.

Gap Year Directory

www.gapyeardirectory.co.uk

A good website to help you explore all the options and directing you to the many oraganisations that can help.

Greenforce

www.greenforce.org

Greenforce runs global conservation expeditions throughout the year, lasting one to six months: Marine projects in Borneo, the Bahamas and Fiji and terrestrial projects in Ecuador, Tanzania and Nepal/Tibet.

I-to-i

www.i-to-i.com

Offers a variety of volunteer experiences throughout the world, as well as TEFL (Teaching English as a Foreign Language) training. I-to-I has helped with tsunami relief in Sri Lanka, provides teachers in Ghana, has released turtle hatchlings into the pacific ocean in Costa Rica and has built homes for the people of Honduras.

Project Trust

www.projecttrust.org.uk

Its main philosophy is to provide young people with an opportunity to understand a community overseas by immersing themselves in it; living and working there for a year.

Raleigh International

www.raleighinternational.org
020 7371 8585

Its overseas programmes offer sustainable community and environmental projects as well as an adventure phase, lasting ten weeks in all. Destinations include Costa Rica, Borneo, Nicaragua, Ghana and Namibia.

Season Workers

www.seasonworkers.com

This website advertises gap year placements, courses, summer jobs and ski resort jobs.

Ski le Gap

www.skilegap.com

For gap-year students from Britain, Ski Le Gap provides young people with the ultimate skiing gap-year experience in Canada.

Teaching & Projects Abroad

www.teaching-abroad.com

Leading organiser of volunteer placements across five continents, offering a diverse range of teaching, care, conservation, medical, journalism and work experience projects.

Travellers Worldwide

www.travellersworldwide.com

Live and work abroad helping children, adults, animals and entire communities in less advantaged countries. Placements can last from two weeks to a year.

UKSA (The United Kingdom Sailing Academy)

www.uksa.org

UKSA is a charity that offers gap year sailing and watersports courses for all abilities in Australia and the UK.

Vacation Work Publications

www.vacationwork.co.uk

A specialist publisher with a range of guides, including the Live and Work In and the Survival Kit series, covering many countries.

It also publishes Summer Jobs USA, The Au Pair & Nanny's Guide to Working Overseas, the International Directory of Voluntary Work, Working in Ski Resorts and Taking a Gap Year.

VSO (Voluntary Services Overseas)

020 8780 7200
www.vso.org.uk

VSO Undergraduate Scheme
Youth volunteering for ages 18-25yrs.

VentureCo

www.ventureco-worldwide.com

Offers the chance to volunteer and lead expeditions in South America and Africa.

World Challenge

www.world-challenge.co.uk
020 8728 7200

World Challenge offers leadership training and expeditions for young people from 16-18yrs. It also offers special Travelsafe Training. Topics include: documentation, budgeting, managing culture shock, taking risks, first aid and more.

Worldwide Volunteering UK

www.wwv.org.uk
01935 825588

A database with nearly 1000 volunteer organisations and 300,000 placements.

Volunteering price guide

Based on long-haul destinations, not including flights.

1 Month	£800-£1,600
2 Months	£1,200-£1,900
3 Months	£1,500-£2,500
Extra month	£350-£700

TRAVEL AGENTS

STA Travel

www.statravel.co.uk
43 Queens Rd, Bristol, BS8 1QQ
0117 929 4399
National: 0870 1600 599

Staffed by experienced travellers, STA can help with all aspects of gap year planning including travel, accommodation and insurance.

Flight Centre

www.flightcentre.co.uk
37 Queens Rd, Bristol BS8 1QE
0117 929 8560
Branches also at: Whiteladies Rd, The Galleries and the High St. See website for details.

Flight Centre is one of the world's largest independent travel retailers. It is aimed at the cost-conscious traveller and specialises in cheap flights and holiday packages. See also Student Flights.

Student Flight

www.studentflight.co.uk

Part of the Flight Centre group, see details above. Student Flights caters to the youth travel market, offering airfare deals to students, backpackers and independent travellers. It also offers budget accommodation, bus rail and ferry passes, student discount cards and discounted travel insurance.

Endsleigh Insurance

www.endsleigh.co.uk
0800 028 3571

The only insurance company recommended by the National Union of Students (NUS), Endsleigh offers special gap year insurance packages.

SCHOOLS & STUDYING

Rachel Miller

Emma Woodworth

CONTENTS

INTRODUCTION

This chapter has information that both parents and students will find useful during (and just prior to) the years of secondary education.

Applying for schools is stressful — every child's needs are different and finding the right path for them is one of the most important decisions a parent can make. We explain admissions and appeals, from starting secondary school up to sixth form.

In order to make school life go as smoothly as possible, we have compiled a comprehensive list of the best websites to help with coursework and revision. We've got information on the extensive resources available at Bristol's libraries and we've also got the lowdown on getting online.

It's not all about schoolwork either. If you fancy doing an evening course or learning first aid, we can point you in the right direction.

STATE EDUCATION

Local Education Authorities (LEAs) are part of local councils and they are accountable for early-years education, schools, adult education and youth services. LEAs are also responsible for promoting high standards of education and work to improve standards and tackle failure. They provide support for special educational needs, access and school transport, pupil welfare and educating excluded pupils.

Schools in Bristol and its surrounding area fall under four different LEAs.

Education & Life Long Learning
PO Box 57, The Council House, College Green, Bristol, BS99 7EB
0117 903 7900, www.bristol-lea.org.uk

South Gloucestershire Council Education Service
Bowling Hill, Chipping Sodbury, South Gloucestershire, BS37 6JX
01454 868009, www.southglos.gov.uk

North Somerset Council Education Department
PO Box 51, Town Hall, Weston-s-Mare, BS23 1ZZ
01934 888888, www.n-somerset.gov.uk

Bath and North East Somerset Council Education Department
PO Box 25, Riverside, Temple St, Keynsham, Bristol, BS31 1DN
01225 477000, www.bathnes.gov.uk

TYPES OF LEA SCHOOLS

All LEA-run schools are self-managing and do not charge fees. They work in partnership with other schools and LEAs, and receive LEA funding. Each has its own characteristics.

Community schools

Community schools are very similar to former county schools. The LEA employs the school's staff, owns the school's land and buildings and is the admissions authority.

Voluntary-aided schools

These schools are run by the Church of England or Roman Catholic Church in partnership with the LEA. The governing body determines admissions. For further details, contact individual schools.

Voluntary-controlled schools

Management of these schools is shared between the LEA and the relevant religion. The LEA is responsible for admissions and allocating school places.

City Technology Colleges

City Technology Colleges (CTCs) are independent, non fee-paying schools for pupils, 11-18yrs. Their purpose is to offer pupils of all abilities the opportunity to study successfully towards the world of work. All CTCs offer a wide range of vocational post-16 qualifications alongside A-Levels.

Academies

Academies are publicly-funded, independent, secondary schools that are designed to provide a first class free education for local pupils.

Special schools

LEAs provide these schools for certain children with special educational needs (SEN). The great majority, however, are educated in ordinary schools.

CHOOSING SCHOOLS

Children transfer to secondary school in the September after their eleventh birthday.

The most important thing you can do before choosing a school for your child is to do your research. A list of secondary schools can be found in the Yellow Pages or obtained from the LEA admissions department. Allow plenty of time to look around schools before application forms have to be submitted.

Visit the school

One of the best ways to assess a school is by visiting it in person. This way, you gain first-hand knowledge of where your child will be spending their day. You can learn a great deal from touring the school and observing the children, the teachers and the way they work together. Things to consider:

- The location of the school. Is there nearby public transport or a school bus?
- Observe the children's work and check the school's resources. Is it a happy school where everyone is serious about learning?
- Find out how the school involves parents.
- Was the school welcoming? Would it suit your child?

Most secondary schools hold open days and evenings, where you can meet the staff and view children's work. You could also make an appointment to visit the school and meet with a senior member of staff. Schools usually have Parent Teacher Associations (PTAs) or Friends Associations which may be able to give you extra information.

LEA booklets

Your Local Education Authority (LEA) produces a booklet, which lists all the schools in your area and has information:

- About the schools and their admission arrangements (including admission form)
- How many pupils they admit and how popular they are

This can be obtained from any school in the LEA or from the LEA admissions department. They are also available in public libraries.

The school prospectus

Each year, every school publishes a brochure called a prospectus. It usually tells you more about a particular school than the LEA booklet can and contains further information about the admissions process.

The performance tables

Every year, the Department for Education and Skills (DfES) publishes performance tables for primary and secondary schools. Though they cannot give a complete picture, they serve as a guide to how well a school is doing.

www.dfes.gov.uk/performancetables

Ofsted reports

It is helpful to read the Office for Standards in Education (Ofsted) reports, produced by the government's school inspectors. A report is available for every school in the country.

www.ofsted.gov.uk/reports

ADMISSION & APPEAL PROCEDURES

You have the right to say which school you would prefer your child to attend, regardless of the school's location (even if it does not fall into the LEA in which you live). But your right to express a preference does not guarantee you a place at the school if it is oversubscribed.

Time your application

LEA booklets are usually available during the summer the year before the child is due to start school. The application form, which must be returned by the given deadline, (usually in the autumn term) will be included in the booklet. Late applications will be processed last and you may not get your preferred choice of school. Arrangements vary in each area so contact your local LEA for advice.

Find out who handles admissions

Admissions are handled either by the local authority, or by the school itself. If you have not applied, **do not** assume your child will get a place at the school you want. Remember also, that you need to apply for each of your children as they reach secondary school age. Having one child at a school does not automatically mean a place for siblings.

When completing the application form, it is important to state your second and third preferred school in case your first choice is unsuccessful.

If there are sufficient places available, your child will be offered a place at your preferred school. However in schools which are oversubscribed, the LEA uses specific criteria when allocating places. These are usually:

- Siblings already attending the school
- Medical, psychological or special educational reason
- Geographical location to home.

Appeals procedure

If you are not allocated a place at your preferred school, you will be offered an alternative school. You have the right to accept the alternative place or formally appeal to an independent panel for a place at your preferred school. The letter you receive from the admission authority should also provide information about your right to appeal and how to go about it.

SERVICES PROVIDED BY LEA

Free transport

Free transport is provided if pupils:

- Attend the nearest appropriate school as determined by the city council and
- The distance between home and school is 3 miles or more for pupils 8-16yrs

Free school meals

These are available if you are entitled to Income Support, Income Based Job-seeker's Allowance, support under Part VI of the Immigration and Asylum Act 1999 or Child Tax Credit with an income below £13,910.

Grants

The LEA may be able to help with costs for families who are in financial difficulty. Contact your LEA for further details.

Welfare

Child welfare in schools is primarily the concern of the staff and head teacher of the school. A welfare officer also supports schools and parents in ensuring full-time school attendance, promoting good home/school liaison, supporting excluded pupils, and dealing with special educational needs, bullying and welfare benefits.

Educational psychology

Schools are allocated an educational psychologist. They may get involved if there are any concerns with a child's learning, general development, behaviour and special educational needs.

School nurse

Each school has a named nurse who works in partnership with parents, teachers and children offering help and support with any emotional/behavioural or physical concerns parents may have.

ASSESSMENT AT SCHOOL

National testing

Pupil progress is assessed through Standard Attainment Tests (SATs) in English, Maths and Science. These occur at the end of Key Stages 1 (Yr 2), 2 (Yr 6) and 3 (Yr 9).

Key Stage 4 qualifications

There are a range of options for pupils in years 10 and 11. These include:

- Entry level certificates. These are designed for students who are unlikely to achieve a GCSE grade
- General Certificates of Secondary Education (GCSE) based on coursework and exams
- GCSE short courses (with two making up a full GCSE)
- General National Vocational Qualifications (GNVQ)
- National Vocational Qualifications (NVQ)
- Vocational Qualifications (VQs) earned through practical work-based placements.

Individual schools do not necessarily offer all of these options, so when choosing a school, make sure it suits your preferences.

POST 16 CHOICES

A student can leave full-time education at the end of the academic year they turn 16. If they wish to pursue a college education it is important to note that some courses fill up by the previous November, although most applications and decisions will be made after Christmas in Year 11.

School sixth form centres

Many secondary schools have a sixth form centre attached. Courses offered depend on the needs of their students.

Sixth form colleges

These are similar to schools and a student can transfer to one at the completion of their Stage 4 programme.

Colleges of further education

These offer a wider range of courses than sixth form colleges and provide education and training for students of all ages.

Modern apprenticeships

This is a work-based learning programme supporting young people through nationally recognised qualifications.

Post 16 courses

- Entry level certificates, GCSEs, GNVQs, NVQs. See Key Stage 4 above.
- The A level qualification is a level up from GCSE and a combination of these is required for university entrance. It consists of two parts, the AS and the A2. The Advanced Subsidiary (AS) is a stand alone qualification. It is valued as half an A level qualification. The A2 is the second half of a full A level qualificaton.
- Vocational AS & A levels (or AVCEs) are designed to develop the skills needed for a wide range of jobs such as engineering, hospitality & catering, leisure & tourism.

- Key Skills are the essential skills you need to do well in education and training, to succeed at work and to get on in life.
- BTEC Nationals and City & Guilds qualifications are nationally-recognised occupational qualifications offered in a number of subjects.
- Modern Apprenticeships are work-based learning programmes supporting young people through nationally-recognised NVQ and Key Skills qualifications.

Examination boards

www.ocr.org.uk
www.aqa.org.uk
www.edexcel.or.uk

There are a number of examination boards in the UK. These all have websites from which programmes of study, syllabuses and past papers can be accessed. Information regarding courses studied can be obtained from individual schools. The three main awarding bodies are OCR, AQA and Edexcel. See their websites above.

Costs

There are no tuition fees for students under 19, although there may be some course costs:

- Textbooks, stationery and materials
- Travel costs to and from college/work experience placements
- Educational visits and residential courses.

Help with costs

Some students aged 16 and over may be eligible for financial help through the learner support fund. There are two types of fund:

School learner support funds

These are administered by the LEA for 6th form students in school. Pupils in financial need can apply to their LEA.

College learner support funds

Administered directly by further education colleges. Contact the college Student Support Officer for details.

The support funds are means tested and are intended to help with the cost of equipment, books, travel and field trips.

Educational Maintenance Allowance

www.dfes.gov.uk/ema

Part of the government's commitment to help young people fulfil their educational potential. Payments are means tested.

Care to Learn

www.dfes.gov.uk/caretolearn
0845 600 2809

This is a childcare funding scheme to support young parents in education and training. All parents aged 16-18yrs who study could be eligible to claim for childcare and associated transport costs up to £5,000 per child p.a.

USEFUL WEBSITES

City and Guilds

www.city-and-guilds.co.uk

City & Guilds is the leading provider of vocational qualifications in the UK.

Connexions (West of England)

www.connexionswest.org.uk

Aims to give young people the best start in life by helping them make the transition to adulthood and working life. Connexions can advise on work, training and further education opportunities as well as drug abuse, sexual health and relationships, housing and money matters. There is a vacancy database of jobs with training for 16-19yrs.

Department for Education and Skills

www.dfes.gov.uk/keyskills

DfES: The Parent Centre

www.parentcentre.gov.uk

Information about schools and the curriculum, as well as a facility to search for local schools.

Educate the Children

www.educate.org.uk

Guidelines on the education system and information about local schools.

Popular Questions

www.dfes.gov.uk/popularquestions

information on careers, education and skills.

StudentZone

www.studentzone.org.uk

Provides information on issues such as careers, news, travel, legal and finance matters, sport and much more.

SPECIAL EDUCATIONAL NEEDS

Children with special educational needs (SEN) have learning difficulties, or disabilities that make it harder for them to learn than most children of the same age. These children may need extra help.

Special needs could include problems with: thinking and understanding, physical or sensory skills, behaviour and emotions or speech and language.

Help for children with SEN will usually be in the child's mainstream school, sometimes with help from outside specialists.

If you are worried your child may be having difficulties

If you think your child may have a special educational need, you should talk to your child's tutor, the SENCO (the special educational needs co-ordinator), the head teacher or head of year.

The Independent Panel for Special Education Advice (IPSEA) offers free advice on LEAs' legal duties to assess and provide for children with SEN. See their website www.ipsea.org.uk

EDUCATIONAL SUPPORT

Advisory Centre for Education
Unit 1C, 22 Highbury Grove, London, N5 2EA
www.ace-ed.org.uk
0808 800 5793, 2pm-5pm

Telephone advice on a range of issues relating to state education in England and Wales.

Support for ADD/ADHD
45 Vincent Close, Broadstairs, Kent, CT10 2ND
www.adders.org
01843 851145, 24 hr

Promoting awareness of Attention Deficit/ Hyperactivity Disorder

AFASIC
2nd Floor, 50-52 Great Sutton St, London, EC1V 0DJ
www.afasic.org.uk
020 7490 9410, Mon-Fri 9am-5pm
Helpline 0845 3555577 Mon-Thu 11am-2pm

Association for All Speech Impaired Children.

Belgrave School
10 Upper Belgrave Rd, BS8 2XH
0117 974 3133
www.dyslexiacentre.co.uk
Full-time school (24 pupils, 7-12 yrs) with dyslexia and related difficulties.

Bristol Dyslexia Centre
10 Upper Belgrave Rd, BS8 2XH
0117 973 9405
www.dyslexiacentre.co.uk
Private tuition for children with learning difficulties.

British Dyslexia Association
98 London Rd, Reading, Berkshire RG1 5AU
www.bda-dyslexia.org.uk
0118 966 2677
Mon-Fri 10am-12.45pm & 2pm-5pm

The Dyslexia Institute
14 Whiteladies Rd, Bristol, BS8 1PD
0117 923 9166
www.dyslexia-inst.org.uk
Advice, assessments and tuition. Additional teaching centre at Staple Hill.

Dyspraxia Foundation
8 West Alley, Hitchin, Herts, SG5 1EG
www.dyspraxiafoundation.org.uk
01462 454986

Parents for Inclusion
Unit 2, 70 South Lambeth Rd, London SW8 1RL
0800 6523145 helpline
www.parentsforinclusion.org

Helps disabled children in mainstream school.

The National Association for Gifted Children — NAGC
Suite 14, Challenge House, Sherwood Drive, Bletchley, MK3 6DP
www.nagcbritain.org.uk
0845 450 0221

Supportive Parents, Parent Partnership Service
3rd Floor Royal Oak House, Royal Oak Ave, BS1 4GB
www.supportiveparents.org.uk
0117 989 7725 Helpline, Mon/Wed/Fri 10am-2pm
Term time support for parents of children with any level of special educational need.

SICK CHILDREN
www.dfes.gov.uk/sickchildren

The LEA and schools must ensure that children who cannot attend school because of medical needs have access to as much education as their medical condition allows.

HOME SCHOOLING

While school is not compulsory, parents do have a responsibility to ensure their child has an effective education, which can be at home.

Education Otherwise
PO Box 7420, London, N9 9SG
Tel: 0870 730 0074
www.educationotherwise.org.uk

A self-help group offering support and information on home education.

Home Education Advisory Service
www.heas.org.uk

Provides advice and support for families who wish to educate their children at home.

PRIVATE TUITION

There are many independent tutors or agencies providing extra educational support for your child. Tuition can be on a one-to-one basis or in small groups. Independent tutors can be found via the internet, in the Yellow Pages, Primary Times (available in schools & libraries), in newspapers and via schools. Check any tutor you find for your child has passed a police check.

Kumon
www.kumon.co.uk
0800 854 714

This style of educational support is becoming increasingly popular. Devised 40 years ago by Toru Kumon, a Japanese school teacher. It is based on repeated exercises in maths and English. It is about making sure the foundations of learning are solid before moving on to the next level. Parental involvement is essential! There are centres across the West. See advertisement in the Colour Reference Section, pg 183.

INDEPENDENT EDUCATION

Private schools are independent of local or central government control. Most of them have their own board of governors and a bursar who is responsible for financial and other aspects of school management. The head is responsible to the governors but has the freedom to appoint staff, admit pupils and take day-to-day decisions. Independents include day and boarding schools and can be single-sex or co-educational.

Choosing a school

Most schools advertise in the Yellow Pages, local papers and educational publications. Having obtained a prospectus, arrange a visit. It's worth going to open days, but also try to visit on a normal working day.

Curriculum

Independent schools are not required to follow the National Curriculum and therefore set their own. Some schools place emphasis on the arts or sciences, others on sport.

Admission and selection

Many junior schools and even some senior schools admit pupils on a first-come-first-served basis. Senior schools usually set some form of entrance test. Standards of these vary.

How much?

Basic fees vary widely depending on the age of the child, location and facilities. Approximate fee range per term in 2006:

Pre-Prep (age 2-7)	£1200-£2770
Junior/Prep (age 7-13)	£1325-£3270
Senior (age 11/13-18)	£2200-£4060

Many schools include lunches in basic fees. Uniforms, trips and other incidental costs will add to the bill. You may have to pay for books, entries for public examinations, stationery and medical supplies.

Scholarships and bursaries

Scholarships are awarded to students who have shown academic or sporting excellence. They rarely cover the whole fee.

Many schools also have bursaries to help you pay the fees. These are often means-tested. Some schools offer grants to children of clergy, teachers and armed forces personnel. Some give concessions for siblings.

Bristol Independent Schools

www.bristolindependentschools.co.uk
Bristol's independent schools have made it easy to investigate the range of independent education offered. There are links to 11 schools' websites.

The Independent Schools Council information service (ISCis)

www.isc.co.uk
020 7766 7071

The Independent Schools Guide

www.gabbitas.net
A complete directory of the UK's independent schools and special schools.

STUDYING & REVISION

Studying dominates much of your time when you're a teenager. Thanks to the internet, there are masses of places to go if you get stuck with your homework. The following websites all come highly recommended. Do not, however, be tempted to cut and paste huge chunks off the internet — your teacher can tell you know!

Ask for kids

www.askforkids.com

This search engine allows your kids to surf the net in confidence. The site also offers study resources, with everything from dictionaries to clip art.

BBC jam

www.bbc.co.uk/jam

The BBC's new broadband learning service for 5 to 16 year olds is a mix of curriculum-based activities, video games, audio and animation. It is being developed over two years and will be fully up and running by September 2008. In the meantime, there's already lots of information for secondary school pupils on subjects such as business studies, French, geography and design and technology.

Bitesize

www.bbc.co.uk/schools/gcsebitesize

The BBC's dedicated revision resource, offering advice, chat, games and quizzes.

GCSE.com

www.gcse.com

This site offers revision help in the following subjects: French, maths, English, physics and ICT.

Homework Elephant

www.homeworkelephant.co.uk

It claims to have over 5000 carefully selected resources to assist with your homework problems. You can search by subject and there is a list of interactive sites for revision. There is also a team of experts to answer any questions you want to post on the site.

Revision tips

Do's & don'ts.

Do draw up a revision timetable but don't spend a whole day designing it!

Do get a copy of the syllabus, as you don't want to spend hours revising stuff you won't be asked about.

Do revise with a friend but don't waste too much time chatting.

Do use different techniques to revise: diagrams, mind maps, lists and memory joggers.

Don't leave the TV on, you can't watch and revise.

Do have a go at past exam papers and questions in revision books.

Don't keep working for hours at a time, take regular breaks.

Homework High

www.homeworkhigh.com

This is Channel 4's learning and revision website. You can email questions, get advice and there is lots of help with homework for pupils studying for GCSEs.

Onion St

www.bbc.co.uk/schools/communities/onionst

Onion St is a BBC initiative that aims to be a supportive community for 11-16 year olds. You can get advice on schoolwork and it's a safe environment to share ideas and develop friendships with other people of the same age. Read and watch interviews with experts, get advice on revision technique and take a break in the music and art rooms.

S-cool

www.s-cool.co.uk

Great revision website which provides high-quality GCSE and A-level revision material for free.

Spelling it Right
www.spelling.hemscott.net

If spelling is a challenge, then this website can help.

Top Marks
www.topmarks.co.uk

A free web site designed to provide easy access to the best educational websites. The resources are geared towards UK curriculum requirements and all sites featured on the website are carefully reviewed by teachers.

LIBRARIES

Bristol libraries offer an amazing range of resources and services for young people. Central Library, in particular, has excellent provision, whether you want to study, go online or borrow a computer game. However, all the local libraries have resources for young people. As well as books, DVDs, CDs and games, there is internet access and some libraries run homework clubs. To find out more about what your local library has to offer see the contact details on the Bristol City Council website:
www.bristol-city.gov.uk/libraries

Bristol Central Library

College Green, Bristol BS1 5TL
0117 903 7215
To book time on a PC, call in
or phone 0117 903 7216/7234

The Central Library has a range of services for young people. It offers a large selection of non-fiction and reference books for homework and study as well as fiction. There is a very popular collection of XBox and PS2 console games for loan, a graphic novels collection, CDs and films for loan and a range of teen-oriented magazines. Dedicated PCs are available for young people, they are free to access, have filtered internet access and offer a range of specially selected websites. The library runs regular events for teenagers, such as pizza and console game-playing evenings.

Librarians are always happy to help with specific enquiries and young people aged 12-17yrs have their own special ticket that has extra benefits over the children's ticket, CDs and films (with appropriate ratings) can be borrowed, reservation request are free and to top that there are no fines. Joining is easy and free — all that is required is some proof of ID.

The Online Reference Library

You don't necessarily have to go to a library to access its resources. The 24-hour online reference library allows library members to access high quality websites from home or from any library computer during normal opening hours. All you need is a valid library card number. To access these sites, go to www.bristol-city.gov.uk/libraries, select 24-hour online reference library and click on the appropriate link.

Britannica Online

Includes the complete encyclopedia, as well as Merriam-Webster's Collegiate Dictionary and Thesaurus, Britannica Student Encyclopedia and the Britannica Book of the Year.

Oxford Dictionary of National Biography

50,000 biographies of people who shaped the history of the British Isles and beyond, from the earliest times to the year 2001.

Times Digital Archive

A complete facsimile copy of the Times newspaper, from 1785-1985. All the text is fully indexed and searchable — advertisements, captions for photographs and illustrations, personal notices, sports results, even wartime casualty lists.

Photographs in this section were taken by Nlarge young photographers who took part in The Libraries Through the Lens project. They produced a portfolio of images to promote libraries to children and young people across England.

Bristol Records Office

"B" Bond Warehouse, Smeaton Rd BS1 6XN
0117 922 4224

Next to the Create Centre, Bristol Records Office is a real treasure trove of fascinating records documenting the history of Bristol.

LOCAL LIBRARIES

www.bristol-city.gov.uk

Bristol City libraries allow you to borrow and return books from different libraries. Library opening hours are subject to change, so do check Bristol City Council's website or contact the appropriate young people's librarian:

Bristol's Children/Young People's Librarian

Janet Randall 0117 903 8565

South Gloucestershire Children/Young People's Librarian

Wendy Nicholls 01454 868451

GETTING ONLINE

Whether you have got your own computer or not, Bristol offers lots of ways to get online.

INTERNET CAFES

Bristol Life

27-29 Baldwin St, Bristol, BS1 1LT
0117 945 9926

£2/hr or £1/hr for members. Membership is £3 for three months. 50p to check email for 10 mins.

Café Eden

24 High St, Portishead, Bristol, BS20 6EN
01275 847673

U16s 70p per half hour; over 16s £1.20 per half hour.

Internet & Chat Rooms

Soph, our resident teenager, gives you the lowdown.

You should be aware of the dangers associated with the internet. Online chat rooms are especially risky because you don't know who you're talking to. However, some services are much safer than others.

MSN Messenger and Yahoo Messenger, for instance, allow you to talk to your friends and have total control over who can talk to you. Alternatively, online "blog" sites are also good, where you can keep a diary and post photos online. Only your friends can view it, so it's secure. Examples of these are www.bebo.com or www.myspace.com.

Skype www.skype.com is a programme that allows you to call your friends from computer to computer, for free, as long as they have Skype too. You will need a microphone and headphones. It's a great way to keep in touch (and your parents won't hassle you about phone bills anymore!).

Easton Internet Café

137 Lawrence Hill, Bristol, BS5 0BT
0117 955 8996

50p per half hour; half hour free if you spend £5.

Surf N Play

14 High St, Westbury-on-Trym, Bristol, BS9 3DU
0117 950 8833
wwwsurfnplay.co.uk

£3/hr or 5p a minute; can buy time in bulk. Membership schemes available for gaming or internet only.

The Lan Rooms

6 Cotham Hill, Bristol, BS6 6LF
0117 973 3886

£2.50/hr; £1 for 24mins, £10 a year (gives five hours of free gaming).

WIRELESS HOTSPOTS

Got a laptop? Now you can access the internet or send emails when you are out and about in lots of areas of Bristol.

City centre

Bristol City Council has installed a number of wi-fi transmitters, known as StNet. This means you can access the internet or send emails from a laptop anywhere in the centre of Bristol, within a two square mile area. The wi-fi hotspot zone extends from the top of Park St down to St Augustine's Parade and includes the Watershed. The University area is also a hotspot.

Bristol Wireless Community Co-operative

www.bristolwireless.net

A large wireless network giving free internet access covering Easton, Lawrence Hill, St Paul's, St Werburgh's, Windmill Hill and Knowle. There are plans to extend the hotspot to Bedminster and Southville.

LIBRARIES

Most libraries offer free PC use and internet access. See above.

MULTIMEDIA KIOSKS

Special touch-screen kiosks are dotted about the city centre and they provide internet access and the opportunity to email, as well as tourist information, news and links to the Bristol City Council website.

EVENING CLASSES

Bristol School of Art, Media & Design (UWE)

Bower Ashton campus, Kennel Lodge Rd, BS3 2JT
0117 328 4716
www.uwe.ac.uk

UWE offers drawing and animation workshops for children and young people aged up to 17yrs. These run on Saturday mornings as well as during the Easter and ummer holidays.

Bristol School of Art (Filton College)

Filton Ave, Filton, Bristol, BS34 7AT
0117 931 2121
www.filton.ac.uk

There are a whole range of part-time as well as full-time courses and they are free if you are between 16 and 18 years of age on the 31st August in the year in which you start the course.

City of Bristol College

College Green Centre, St George Rd, BS1 5UA
0117 312 5000
www.cityofbristol.ac.uk

College centres across Bristol, including: Ashley Down, Parkway, College Green, Downend, Lawrence Weston, Hartcliffe, Folly Lane, Bedminster, Queen Charlotte St, Parkway, Soundwell, St Paul's and Easton.

City of Bristol College offers full and part-time courses including GCSE and A-Levels. Its Community Learning provision includes a vast array of part-time and evening courses in everything from arts and crafts to languages and dance. Courses are free if you are between 16 and 18 years of age on the 31st August in the year in which you start the course.

Filton College

Filton Ave, Filton, BS34 7AT
0117 931 2121
www.filton.ac.uk

Filton College offers both part-time and full-time courses. School leavers have a wide choice of courses open to them including art and design, IT, engineering, construction, media and photography and travel and tourism. There are also specialist academies for sport and performing arts. Part-time evening courses are open to all. Under 16s may have to get permission from school to say that the course won't interfere with their schoolwork and they may also have to be accompanied by an adult.

University of Bristol

8-10 Berkeley Square, BS8 1HH
0117 928 9000
www.bris.ac.uk

The University offers a range of evening classes open to the public, including drama, see Interests and Clubs pg 43.

FIRST AID & LIFESAVING

Learing basic first aid or life saving skills is extremely worthwhile.

Junior Lifesaving
Winterbourne Swimming Pool
0800 953 0059
Friday evenings
£25 for ten week course

Children aged 8-14yrs can become a Rookie Lifesaver. The programme has four components: water safety, rescue, self rescue and emergency response.

National Pool Lifeguard Qualification
01454 319373

This 37-hour training programme is available to competent swimmers aged 16yrs+. The course is available at several pools in Bristol, call for further details.

St John Ambulance
The Harry Crook Centre, Raleigh Rd, Bedminster, BS1 3AP
0117 953 3880
www.sja.org.uk/avon/
info@avon.sja.org.uk

There are 23 different divisions of St John Ambulance in Bristol and Bath, so you'll have no trouble finding a local venue. Cadets (10-18yrs) are taught basic first aid. There are also opportunities to help out at events, supported by other St John Ambulance staff.

POST 18 COURSES & CAREERS

Whether you are planning to continue into higher education or start your career now, your school or Connexions West will be able to help. There is a huge amount of advice out there, this list of website should get you started.

Brilliant Careers (Channel 4)
www.channel4.com/microsites/B/brilliantcareers
A great web site that has everything from personality tests to career matching.

Careers Gateway
www.careers-gateway.co.uk
A-Z of jobs with links to other UK websites including professional bodies, trade associations, and education and training providers.

Career Portal
www.trotman.co.uk
This award-winning online careers service is part of the National Grid for Learning. It can help you find the right university, organise a gap year or plan your career. It also publishes lots of relevant books including Choosing your A-Levels and Post 16 Options.

CID (Careers Information Database)
Available at school or at Connexions, this database can help you find the right career path to suit your skills and interests.

Go4it
www.connexionswest.org.uk/go4it
This is a Connexions database that highlights all the learning and training opportunities available to over 16s.

Kudos
This career-matching programme is available through Connexions or at your school and is aimed at 13-20 year-olds. You take a 30-minute questionnaire and Kudos provides you with a personal report suggesting which career path might be right for you. It has details of over 1,700 careers including salary and labour market information,

UCAS
www.ucas.com
The central organisation that processes applications for all full-time undergraduate courses at UK universities and colleges. It has information on all courses, deadlines, how to apply, fees, bursaries and grants.

University Options
www.universityoptions.co.uk
This website can help you to choose the right course, the best university or college, and it gives advice on how to apply.

HEALTHCARE

Elspeth Pontin

Lindsey Potter

CONTENTS

INTRODUCTION

Most families are registered with a GP however if you have just moved to the area a list of local surgeries can be found in the Yellow pages, from NHS Direct, Avonweb or your local Primary Care Trust, see below.

In this chapter we give a list of contact points such as your nearest A&E, walk-in centres and NHS Direct.

Bristol has a history of offering a wide range of complementary care. Over the years, readers of our sister publication, The Titch Hikers' Guide to Bristol for Families, have recommended practices which offer services to both growing kids and their parents. There is a brief overview of the therapies offered followed by a directory of clinics.

If you are looking for specific help to a health problem, check out our Advice and Support chapter.

GENERAL HEALTHCARE

HEALTHCARE SERVICES

Avonweb
www.avon.nhs.uk

Online site providing information about local NHS services, such as GPs, dentists, hospitals and opticians.

NHS Direct
0845 46 47
www.nhsdirect.nhs.uk

A confidential advice line, staffed by nurses, offering healthcare advice 24 hours a day. They will assess your needs and either give advice or refer you to your out of hours GP or hospital. They also give information about local NHS services, such as GPs and dentists.

HOSPITALS & WALK-INS

A&Es

The following hospitals all have accident and emergency departments.

Bristol Eye Hospital
Lower Maudlin St, BS1 2LY
0117 923 0060

For emergencies related to eyes!

Frenchay Hospital
Frenchay Park Rd, Bristol
0117 970 1212 (ext 3887)

Royal United Hospital, Minor Injuries
Combe Park, Bath, BS1 3NG
01225 428331

For emergencies but not immediate life threatening illnesses or injuries.

Southmead Hospital
Westbury-on-Trym, Southmead Rd, BS10 5NB
0117 950 5050

Minor injuries unit open daily from 9am-9pm.

The Bristol Royal Hospital for Children
Upper Maudlin St, Bristol, BS1
0117 927 6998

The Bristol Royal Infirmary
Marlborough St, Bristol
0117 923 0000

Walk-in centres

NHS walk-in centres provide treatment for minor injuries and illnesses seven days a week. You don't need an appointment and will be seen by an experienced NHS nurse.

Bristol (City Gate) NHS Walk-in Centre
33 Broad St, BS1 2EZ
0117 906 9600
www.nhs.uk
Daily 8am-8pm

South Bristol NHS Walk-in Centre
5 Knowle West Health Park, Downton Rd, Knowle West, BS4 1WH
0117 903 0003
www.nhs.uk
Daily 9am-9pm

Nurses here also offer blood tests and ear syringing services.

MENTAL HEALTH

Avon and Wiltshire Mental Health Partnership NHS Trust

Bath NHS House, Newbridge Hill, Bath, BA1 3QE
01225 731732
www.awp.nhs.uk

Information regarding mental health needs for both service users and carers.

LATE NIGHT PHARMACIES

In all chemist shops (or pharmacies) there is a pharmacist on duty who is able to give advice on the treatment of many health problems. There will always be a pharmacy in your area open outside normal shop hours, see our listing in Shopping and Services, pg 164.

ADVICE & COMPLAINTS

Complaints

If you are not happy with the care that you have received from any aspect of the NHS, you have every right to complain. For information about how to make a complaint, see www.nhs.uk or contact your local PCT:

Bath and North East Somerset PCT

St Martin's Hospital, Midford Rd, Bath, BA2 5RP
01225 831800
www.banes-pct.nhs.uk

Bristol North PCT

King Square House, King Square, Bristol, BS2 8EE
0117 976 6600
www.bristolnorthpct.nhs.uk

Bristol South and West PCT

King Square House, King Square, Bristol, BS2 8EE
0117 976 6600
www.bristolswpct.nhs.uk

North Somerset PCT

Waverley House, Old Church Rd, Clevedon, BS21
01275 546 770
www.northsomerset.nhs.uk

South Gloucestershire PCT

1 Monarch Court, Emerald Park, Emerson's Green, BS16 7FH
0117 330 2468
www.sglos-pct.nhs.uk

ACCIDENTS

Accidents are the most common cause of death in children.

Child Accident Prevention Trust

18-20 Farringdon Lane, London, EC1R 3HA
020 7608 3828
www.capt.org.uk

This is a national charity committed to reducing the number of children and young people killed, disabled and seriously injured as a result of accidents.

St. John's Ambulance

The Harry Crook Centre, Raleigh Rd, Bedminster, Bristol, BS3 1AP
0117 953 3880
www.avon.sja.org.uk
courses@avon.sja.org.uk

St John Ambulance run adult and paediatric first aid courses, for groups of six to 12 people. They can be run in your own home, place of work or other suitable venue.

COMPLEMENTARY HEALTHCARE

This section puts several branches of western medicine under the same umbrella as those medicines which were traditionally thought of as alternative. They are now termed complementary. Some of these services can be received within the NHS but many are private; some offer reduced rates.

Below, we give an overview of the different types of complementary medicine, followed by an A-Z directory of local practitioners.

Institute of Complementary Medicine

PO Box 194, London, SE16 7QZ
0207 237 5165
www.icmedicine.co.uk

The Institute is a charity providing information on all complementary medicines.

Acupuncture

Used in traditional Chinese medicine for 4,000 years. It involves the painless insertion of fine needles into specific points on the body. It is sometimes available on the NHS.

British Acupuncture Council

63 Jeddo Rd, London, W12 9HQ
0208 735 0400
www.acupuncture.org.uk

Free information and lists of local practitioners. Look for letters such as MBAcC, after a practitioner's name.

Aromatherapy

Aromatherapy is the holistic application of essential oils, often involving massage. Aromatherapy can be used on small children and can be beneficial during pregnancy, labour and postnatally.

The International Federation of Aromatherapists

61-63 Churchfield Rd, London, W3 6AY
0208 992 9605
www.ifaroma.org

Provides lists of local practitioners. Look out for MIFA after a practitioner's name.

The Register of Qualified Aromatherapists

PO Box 3431, Danbury, Chelmsford, Essex
01245 227 957

Professional association of aromatherapy practitioners who have undergone training of the highest standards. Write with SAE or phone to find an aromatherapist in your area.

Chiropractors

Chiropractors diagnose and treat conditions rising from the mechanical dysfunction of the joints and their effects on the nervous system. Chiropractors use their hands to adjust the joints of your spine and extremities where signs of restriction in movement are found.

The British Chiropractic Association

Blagrave House, 17 Blagrave St, Reading, RG1 1QB
0118 950 5950
www.chiropractic-uk.co.uk

Make sure your pracitioner is registered with the General Chiropractic Council (GCC).

Counselling

The British Association of Counselling and Psychotherapy

BACP House, 35-37 Albert St, Rugby, CV21 2SG
0870 4435252
www.bacp.co.uk

Lists of local therapists are available online or by sending an SAE. Look for BACP, UKCP, UKRC, BCP after a counsellor's name.

Cranial Osteopaths

Craniosacral therapy is based around the gentle and natural motion of fluids which surround the brain (inside the cranium) and spine (which ends at the sacrum), but which influence the whole body. Treatment can be useful in children with such problems as glue ear and hyperactivity. Adult treatments for back pain, stress or emotional problems, headaches and migraines.

Also see Osteopaths below.

The Craniosacral Therapy Association of the UK
Monomark House, 27 Old Gloucester St, London, WC1N 3XX
07000 784735
www.craniosacral.co.uk

Practitioner listing and information on craniosacral therapy.

Homeopathy

Homeopathic medicines are derived from a variety of plants, animal materials and minerals. It is believed that natural substances, prepared in a special way and used in often dilute form can restore health.

The British Homeopathic Association
Hahnemann House, 29 Park St West, Luton, LU1 3BE
0870 444 3950
www.trusthomeopathy.org

Details of medically-qualified homeopaths.

Bristol Hoemopathic Hospital
Cotham Hill, Cotham, BS6 6JU
0117 973 1231
www.ubht.nhs.uk/homeopath

Established over 80 years ago. Offering outpatients services here and in Bath. For an NHS referral see their website.

Osteopathy

Osteopathy treats faults which occur in the musculo-skeletal system due to stress, injury and sometimes disease.

General Osteopathic Council
Osteopathy House, 176 Tower Bridge Rd, London, SE1 3LU
0207 357 6655
www.osteopathy.org.uk

List of registered osteopaths and fact sheets. Under the Osteopaths Act 1993, all qualified Osteopaths have to be listed with the General Osteopathic Council.

Reflexology

Working on reflex points on the feet to treat imbalances in the whole body. It is drug free and can be used to treat many conditions.

Association of Reflexologists
27 Old Gloucester St, London, WC1 3XX
0870 5673320
www.aor.org.uk

Lists of registered reflexologists.

British Reflexology Association
Monks Orchard, Whitbourne, Worcester, WR6 5RB
01886 821 207
www.britreflex.co.uk

Lists registered reflexologists.

Shiatsu

Practitioners use fingers, palms, elbows, knees and feet to apply pressure to the energy lines, to stimulate the body's energy flow. It can help in a wide range of conditions — from specific injuries to more general symptoms of poor health and stress.

The Shiatsu Society UK
Eastlands Court, St Peters Rd, Rugby, CV21 3QP
0845 130 4560
www.shiatsu.org

The governing body for all Shiatsu practioners. Look for the letters MRSS after the name. Provides practitioner listings.

A-Z DIRECTORY OF COMPLEMENTARY PRACTICES

AcuMedic Chinese Medical Centre
Manvers Chambers, Manvers St, Bath, BA1 1PE
01225 483 393
www.acumedic.com

Treatments for dermatology, gynaecology, pain and musculoskeletal disorders.

Bristol Centre for Craniosacral Therapy
26 Cairns Rd, Bristol, BS6 7TY
0117 942 8647
www.bristolcraniosacral.co.uk

Treating children with problems from glue ear to hyperactivity. Adult treatments include stress, migraines and back pain.

Bristol Natural Health Service
407 Gloucester Rd, Horfield, BS7 8TJ
0117 944 4448

Offers a wide range of therapies and aims to help your select the most appropriate therapy for your needs.

Bristol School of Shiatsu
4 Brecknock Rd, Knowle, BS4 2DD
0117 977 2809
www.shiatsubristol.co.uk
shiatsubss@blueyonder.co.uk

Contact for details of local practitioners.

Children's Homeopathic Clinic
St Werburghs City Farm, Watercress Rd,
St Werburghs, BS2 9YJ
0117 914 1694
www.bristol-natural-health-service.co.uk

Low cost homeopathic treatment for 0-18 yrs.

Children's Nutrition Clinic
01225 789513, 07734 839496
optnutclinic@aol.com

Natural treatments for children's health
problems including asthma, eczema, learning
problems, digestive complaints, lack of energy
and recurrent colds/infections. Clinics in Bath
and Bristol.

Clinic of Natural Medicine
126 Whiteladies Rd, Clifton, BS8 2RP
0117 946 6035

Wide range of therapies, free initial 15 minute
consultation to select a suitable treatment.

Clover House Children's Complementary Therapy Centre
447 Bath Rd, Saltford, Bristol, BS31 3AZ
01225 344047
www.cloverhouse.org

An appointment includes seeing three
therapists covering aromatherapy, nutrition &
imagery to help with fears surrounding illness.

Kingswood Natural Health Centre
355-359 Two Mile Hill Rd, Kingswood, BS15 1AF
0117 914 5590
www.kingswoodnaturalhealth.co.uk

Provides a range of complementary and
holistic therapies.

Natural Health Clinic
39 Cotham Hill, Cotham, BS6 6JY
0117 974 1199
www.thenaturalhealthclinic.com

Wide selection of practitioners including
homeopathy and cranial osteopathy.
Concessions offered.

Oriental Medicine Practice
35 North View, Westbury Park, BS6 7PY
0117 907 8890
www.orientalmedicine.co.uk

Offers acupuncture, shiatsu, Chinese herbs,
nutritional consultation and allergy testing.

Sneyd Park Osteopaths
4 Rockleaze Rd, Sneyd Park, Bristol, BS9 1NF
0117 968 5107
www.bristolosteopaths.com

Treats a range of complaints. Specialising in
mechanical, visceral and cranial approaches.

The Centre for Whole Health
12 Victoria Place, Bedminster, BS3 3BP
0117 923 1138

Offers acupuncture, Chinese herbal medicine,
counselling, homeopathy, massage and
osteopathy.

The Chandos Clinic
21 Chandos Rd, Redland, BS6 6PG
0117 974 5084
www.chandosclinic.co.uk

Offers all the main complementary therapies.

The Clifton Practice
8-10 Whiteladies Rd, Clifton, BS8 1PD
0117 946 6070
www.thecliftonpractice.co.uk

Offers all the main complementary therapies.

The Fishponds Practice
834 Fishponds Rd, Fishponds, Bristol, BS16 3XA
0117 949 1290

Offers a range of therapies.

Vital Health Clinic
8 North View, Westbury Park, BS6 7QB
0117 973 0878

Chiropractors and osteopaths treating a range
of muscular skeletal problems.

Pictures of health

Photographs in this chapter have been
kindly supplied by the Sea Cadet Corp.
They are a voluntary nautical youth
organisation for boys and girls aged
12-18yrs. See their entry on pg 47.

www.sea-cadet.org

ADVICE
& SUPPORT

Nicola O'Brien

Lindsey Potter

CONTENTS

INTRODUCTION

Life does not always run smoothly. At times of trouble it can sometimes be difficult to know where to turn. Whatever your concerns, there is help out there. There is an incredible network of charities and support agencies in the UK, offering a huge range of services, both regionally and nationally. In this chapter, we have created a directory which lists organisations and charities that can either help you or advise you on where to find help. It's by no means exhaustive, but we cover most bases and it should point you in the right direction.

Contact details frequently change and new support services are starting up all the time. Please let us know any updates via our website, www.freedomguide.co.uk.

FOR YOUNG PEOPLE

This section lists organisations that offer services that are particularly accessible to young people. However there are many other support groups listed under Families so cross reference where necessary.

Bereavement, Relationships pg 255

Sexual Abuse pg 256

GENERAL ADVICE

ChildLine

www.childline.org.uk
Children's correspondence address:
Childline, Freepost, NATN1111, London, E1 6BR
Admin 020 7650 3200
Helpline 0800 1111

UK's free helpline for children and young people. It provides a confidential telephone counselling service for any child with any problem, 24/7. It comforts, advises, protects. Now part of the NSPCC.

The Line
0800 884444
Mon-Fri 3.30pm-9.30pm, Sat-Sun 2pm-8pm
Textphone 0800 400222
Mon-Fri 9.30am-9.30pm, Sat-Sun 9.30am-8pm

For children living away from home.

Childtime

The Old Treasury, 30A College Green, BS1 5TB
www.childtime.org.uk
0117 929 1533
Helps children who are experiencing emotional or psychological difficulties, in partnership with parents and relevant professionals. Subsidised fees on sliding scale.

Connexions West of England

www.connexionswest.org.uk

Offering an information service to 13-19yr olds on a vast range of issues: studying, health, relationships, bullying, jobs and drugs to name a few. It has five centres across the region in Bath, Bristol, Filton, Kingswood and Weston-super-Mare.

**Connexions West of England,
Bath & North East Somerset**
28 Southgate St, Bath, BA1 1TP
01225 461501

Connexions West of England, Bristol
4 Colston Ave, Bristol, BS1 4ST
0117 987 3700

The Site

www.thesite.org.uk

Owned and run by charity YouthNet UK. The website aims to be the first place all young adults turn to when they need support and guidance through life. The website provides fact sheets and articles on all the key issues facing young people including: sex and relationships; drinking and drugs; work and study; housing, legal and finances; and health and wellbeing.

Off the Record

2 Horfield Rd, St Michael's Hill, Bristol, BS2 8EA
www.otrbristol.org.uk
Helpline 0808 808 9120
Mon-Wed 9.30am-8pm
Drop-in Mon-Wed 11.30am-5pm

Free, confidential information, advice and informal support for all ages. Free, counselling via appointments for those aged 11-25yrs.

Samaritans

www.samaritans.org
08457 909090

ALCOHOL, DRUGS & ADDICTION

Alcohol and you

www.alcoholandyou.org

A website created by At-Bristol to inspire 11-16 year olds to think sensibly about alcohol with all the facts and a quiz to test your knowledge.

Advice and Counselling on Alcohol and Drugs (ACAD)

15/16 Lower Park Row, Bristol, BS1 5BN
www.acad.org.uk
0117 929 3028
Group drop-in Mon-Thu 9am-5pm, Fri 9am-4pm

Free advice and counselling by appointment (or drop-ins) for people directly or indirectly affected by alcohol-related problems.

Al-Anon Family Group

www.al-anonuk.org.uk
Helpline 0207 403 0888
Daily 10am-10pm

Confidential understanding and support for family and friends of problem drinkers. Details of local support groups.

Alateen, a service for young people (12-20yrs) who have been affected by someone else's drinking.

Bristol Drugs Project

11 Brunswick Square, Bristol, BS2 8PE
0117 987 1500
www.bdp.org.uk
Drop-in &/or needle exchange:
Mon-Sat 9.30am-12.30pm

Free and confidential advice and counselling for anyone concerned about drug use.

Gamcare

0845 6000 133
www.gamcare.org.uk

Informative website with pages dedicated to youth gambling issues. The helpline offers advice and support to those affected by gambling problems.

BULLYING & CHILD PROTECTION

Bullying Online

www.bullying.co.uk

Charity that offers advice and support on all aspects of bullying, including mobile phone bullying.

Kidscape

www.kidscape.org.uk
Helpline 08451 205 204

A UK charity established specifically to prevent bullying and child sexual abuse. Kidscape staff equip vulnerable children under the age of 16, with practical, non-threatening knowledge and skills to keep themselves safe and reduce the likelihood of future harm.

NSPCC (National Society for the Prevention of Cruelty to Children)

www.nspcc.org.uk
Helpline 0808 800 5000 24hr
Child Protection Helpline 0808 800 5000 24hr
Textphone 0800 056 0566 24 hr

NSPCC Asian Child Protection Helpline
0800 096 7719
Mon-Fri 11am-7pm

HEALTH

Brook Young People's Services

1 Unity St, College Green, Bristol, BS1 5HH
www.brook.org.uk
0117 929 0090
Helpline 0800 018 5023
Mon-Fri 9am-5pm
Walk-in Mon-Tue 1-3pm, 4-6pm
Appt only Wed & Fri 12am-2pm,
Walk-in Wed/Thu 4-6pm, Sat 10-12pm

Expert counselling and advice on sexual health for under 25s. Provides all methods of contraception and emergency contraception; screening and testing. Connexions advice, and ACCSEX — a project aimed at young disabled people. Extremely informative website.

Eating Disorder Association

www.edauk.com
0845 6347650 youth line for 18yrs or under
0845 6341414 adult helpline

The website is very informative giving information and help on all aspects of eating disorders including Anorexia Nervosa, Bulimia Nervosa, Binge Eating Disorder and related eating disorders.

Family Planning Association

www.fpa.org.uk
0845 310 1334
Mon-Fri 9am-6pm

Support and advice on sexual health plus information on local drop-in clinics.

Frank

www.talktofrank.com
0800 77 66 00

Visit this site or phone the helpline (24hrs) for free confidential advice and information on drug issues, whatever your age.

Walk-in centres

www.nhs.uk

NHS walk-in centres provide treatment for minor injuries and illnesses seven days a week. You don't need an appointment and will be seen by an experienced NHS nurse.

Bristol (City Gate) NHS Walk-in Centre

33 Broad St, BS1 2EZ
0117 906 9600
Daily 8am-8pm

South Bristol NHS Walk-in Centre

5 Knowle West Health Park, Downton Rd, Knowle West, BS4 1WH
0117 903 0003
Daily 9am-9pm

Nurses here also offer blood tests and ear syringing services.

Sexwise

0800 28 29 30
7am-12midnight

A free confidential advice line on sex, relationships and contraception for young people aged 18yrs or under.

YOUNG PARENTS

The Young Mothers Group and Information Project

c/o The Mill Youth Centre, Lower Ashley Rd, BS5 0YJ
0117 935 5639

Offers advice, support and out-reach visits to mothers under 25yrs. The Information Project is peer-led: trained volunteers talk in schools, colleges & youth clubs about the realities of young parenthood.

Young Mothers' Group Trust

Unit 31/32, Easton Business Centre, Felix Rd, BS5 0HE
0117 941 5838

Provides housing and advice for single homeless mothers (16-24yrs) or those facing homelessness.

FOR FAMILIES

GENERAL SUPPORT

Bristol City Council

Social Services and Health Department, Amelia Court PO Box 30, Bristol, BS99 7NB
0117 922 2000
Mon-Fri 8.30am-5pm (until 4.30pm on Fri)
Emergency out of hours: 01454 615 165

Services include: social workers, family support workers, special needs provision, respite care, adoption and fostering, child protection, services and support for disabled children and their families.

Bristol City Council Child Protection

Citywide services are provided for:
Adoption 0117 954 8545
Disabled Children's Service 0117 903 8250
www.bristol-city.gov.uk

The telephone directory provides a list of all local Child Protection offices, to contact the nearest to the child's home.

Children's Information Service

The Proving House, Sevier St, Bristol, BS2 9LB
0845 129 7217
www.cisbristol.co.uk
Mon/Fri 8am-4pm, Tue-Thu 8am-8pm

Provides free, impartial and confidential information/guidance on a full range of children's services and resources in Bristol.

Parentline Plus

www.parentlineplus.org.uk
Freephone 0808 800 2222
Textphone 0800 783 66783

Call centres run by parents, offering a confidential, anonymous listening ear and practical help. The lines are often busy so keep trying!

ADOPTION & FOSTERING

Bristol Family Placement Team (Recruitment)

Social Services, Avonvale Rd, Redfield, BS5 9RH
www.bristol-city.gov.uk/fostering
0117 954 8545

This team offers information, training and support to anyone interested in fostering children or young people. They welcome applicants from all sections of the community. See their advertisement in the Colour Reference Section, pg 182.

Our Place

139 Fishponds Rd, Eastville, Bristol, BS5 6PR
0117 951 2433

Offering foster and adoptive families the opportunity to mix with others and share experiences. Fun activities, seminars and workshops run by professionals, no charges.

South West Adoption Network (SWAN)

Leinster House, Leinster Ave, Knowle, BS4 1NL
www.swan-adoption.org.uk
Helpline 0845 601 2459
Tue-Thu 10am-2pm, Tue 7pm-9pm

A post-adoption centre offering advice, counselling, support groups and workshops.

BEREAVEMENT

Cruse Bereavement Care

9A St James Barton, Bristol, BS1 3LT
www.crusebereavementcare.org.uk
National Helpline
0870 167 1677
0117 926 4045
Mon-Fri 10am-2pm

Provides free 1:1 or family counselling.

The Compassionate Friends

53 North St, Bristol, BS3 1EN
www.tcf.org.uk
Helpline 0845 1232304 24hr
Admin 08451 203786
10am-4pm & 6.30pm-10.30pm

Self-help befriending organisation offering support to families after the death of a child.

Winstons Wish

www.winstonswish.org.uk
01242 515157
Helpline 0845 2030405
Mon-Fri 9am-5pm

Helping bereaved children and their families rebuild their lives. Also assists schools and carers with the needs of bereaved children.

RELATIONSHIPS

The Bridge Foundation

12 Sydenham Rd, Bristol, BS6 5SH
0117 942 4510
www.bridgefoundation.org.uk

A consultation and therapy service for couples, young children and families. Fees are charged but are discretionary for some.

Bristol Gay & Lesbian Switchboard

8 Somerville Rd, Bishopston, Bristol, BS7 9AA
www.bristolblag.org. uk
0117 942 0842
Daily 8pm-10pm

Provides information and support to gay, lesbian, transgender and tranvestite people.

Freedom Youth
0117 377 3677

Supporting young people with gay and lesbian issues.

Bristol Family Mediation

Alexander House, Telephone Ave, Bristol, BS1 4BS
www.bristolfamilymediation.org.uk
0117 929 2002
Mon-Fri 9am-5pm

Help pre or post-separating/divorcing couples make mutual decisions or resolve issues. A not-for-profit organisation. Outreach offices in Bath and Weston-super-Mare, see website.

It's not your fault

www.itsnotyourfault.org.uk

A website for children, young people and their parents who are undergoing a family break-up.

IN CRISIS

Avon Sexual Abuse Centre

PO Box 665, BS99 1XY
www.napac.org.uk
National Helpline 0800 0853 330
0117 935 1707
Mon/Wed/Thu 9.30am-4pm

A free and confidential counselling service available to adults, children and their families.

MEDICAL CONDITIONS & SPECIAL NEEDS

GENERAL SUPPORT GROUPS

Break

www.break-charity.org
01263 822161

Provides special care services for children, adults and families with special needs, including subsidised holidays and respite care.

Bristol Family Link Scheme

Family Placements, Avonvale Rd, Redfield, BS5 9RH
www.sharedcarenetwork.org.uk
0117 954 8502

Family-based short breaks for disabled children and young people.

Disabled Living Centre, West of England

The Vassall Centre, Gill Ave, Fishponds, BS16 2QQ
www.dlcbristol.org
0117 965 3651 (also Minicom)
For appts: Mon-Fri 10am-4pm (some Sats)

Consultation by appointment providing professional, impartial information and advice on products and equipment to aid independent living. Also has a Multimedia Resource Area, coffee shop and garden.

Hop Skip & Jump

Grimsbury Rd, Kingswood, Bristol, BS15 9SE
www.hopskipandjump.org.uk
0117 967 7282
Mon-Fri 9am-5.30pm, Sat 10am-4pm
Donations welcome

Charity-run play centre for children, 0-16yrs, with special needs, where parents can relax while children are looked after by qualified care workers, siblings welcome.

The Yellow Book

www.southglos.gov.uk
01454 866 345

A definitive guide book giving information and services relevant to caring for children with special needs in South Gloucestershire. Download guide from website.

Time 2 Share

Unit 55, Easton Business Centre, Felix Rd, BS5 OHE
www.time2share.org.uk
0117 941 5868
Mon-Fri 9.30am-2.00pm

Support for families who care for children with learning difficulties. Provides sitters and caters for individual needs. Families are matched on a one to one basis with a volunteer; support and training is available.

West of England Centre for Disabled Living

Leinster Ave, Knowle, Bristol, BS4 1AR
www.wecil.co.uk
Helpline & Minicom 0117 903 8900
Admin 0117 983 2828

Phone service provided by disabled people, offering free, confidential advice covering all aspects of disability.

A-Z MEDICAL DIRECTORY

ALLERGIES

Allergy UK

www.allergyuk.org
Helpline 01322 619 898
Mon-Fri 9am-5pm
Membership £20

Aims to increase understanding and awareness and assist in allergy management. Information, advice and support.

ASTHMA

Asthma UK

www.asthma.org.uk
Advice Line 020 7786 4900
Helpline 08457 010203
Mon-Fri 9am-5pm

Helpline staffed by asthma nurses. Publishes fact sheets and lists of support groups.

AUTISM

Autism (National Autistic Society)

www.nas.org.uk
Helpline 0845 070 4004
Mon-Fri 10am-4pm
Local contact 0117 939 0141

The local group meets regularly and there are family social events throughout the year.

BLOOD DISORDERS

OSCAR (Sickle Cell and Thalassaemia Centre, Bristol)

256 Stapleton Rd, Easton, Bristol, BS5 0NP
www.sicklecellsociety.org
0117 951 2200

Providing information, support and counselling.

BRAIN INJURIES

Cerebra

www.cerebra.org.uk
Helpline 0800 328 1159

Information, contact and support network for families and carers of brain-injured children.

CEREBRAL PALSY

Scope Bristol (Cerebral Palsy)

www.scopebristol.co.uk
0117 950 5099
Mon-Thu 9am-3pm, Fri 9am-12pm

Information, grants scheme, Connexions Young People's Information Point (YPIP), Lifestyles Project, physio and equipment.

CYSTIC FIBROSIS

Cystic Fibrosis Trust

www.cftrust.org.uk
Helpline 0845 859 1000

Information, advice and support for those affected by CF and their families and carers.

COELIAC DISEASE

Coeliac UK

www.coeliac.co.uk
Helpline 0870 444 8804

Supporting coeliac research and helping sufferers manage their health and diet.

DEAFNESS

Avon Deaf Child Society & Bristol Centre for Deaf People

www.ndcs.org.uk
Helpline 0808 800 8880 (voice & textphone)
Textphone 0117 924 9868
Minicom 0117 944 1344

Support for deaf children and their families. Sign language and lip-reading taught to hearing-impaired parents and children.

Family Centre (Deaf Children)

www.fcdc.org.uk
Minicom 01454 315405
01454 315404

Support, information, educational and social activities for hearing families with deaf children across the Avon area.

DIABETES

Diabetes UK

www.diabetes.org.uk
0207 424 1000
Mon-Fri 9am-5pm

Specially trained staff offering advice to those with diabetes.

Local Contact
Diabetes UK South West 01823 324 007

DOWNS SYNDROME

Downs Syndrome Association

www.downs-syndrome.org.uk
0845 230 0372

South West Development Officer
01275 858230

BADSS (local parent support group)
www.dsa-bristol.org.uk
0117 986 7992

Information library, parents support network, outings and events.

EPILEPSY

Epilepsy (British Epilepsy Association)

www.epilepsy.org.uk
Helpline 0808 800 5050
Mon-Thu 9am-4.30pm, Fri 9am-4pm

Information support groups and a newsletter.

HIV

Aled Richards Centre

8-10 West St, Old Market, BS2 0BH
0117 955 1000
www.tht.org.uk

The Terrence Higgins Trust has a wide range of publications and information on HIV, AIDS and sexual health.

HYPERACTIVE CHILDREN

Hyperactive Children's Support Group

www.hacsg.org.uk
01243 539966
Mon-Fri 10am-1pm

Including allergic/ADD children. Advice and support with a dietary and nutrition approach for parents, carers and professionals.

MENINGITIS

The Meningitis Trust

Fern House, Bath Rd, Stroud, GL5 3TJ
01453 768 000
www.meningitis-trust.org
Helpline 0845 6000 800 24 hr

Financial, emotional and practical support to sufferers and their families. Information and local contacts available on admin line.

MENTAL ILLNESS

MENCAP Avon North

Kingswood House, South Rd, Kingswood, BS15 8JF
www.avonnorthmencap.org.uk
0117 961 4372

Support, advice and information for people with learning disabilities and their families.

Young Minds

0800 018 2138
www.youngminds.org.uk

Information for parents who may be concerned about the mental health of their child.

Scoliosis Association (UK)

Helpline 020 8964 1164
www.sauk.org.uk

Information and support and how to detect it early in children.

SKIN DISORDERS

Eczema (National Eczema Society)

www.eczema.org
Helpline 0870 241 3604
Mon-Fri 8am-8pm

Help and support for those people affected by eczema. Provides list of local support groups.

Psoriasis Association

www.psoriasis-association.org.uk
Helpline 0845 676 0076
Mon-Thu 9.15am-4.45pm, Fri 9.15am-4.15pm

Offers support and advice to children and adults suffering from psoriasis.

VISUAL IMPAIRMENT

Look West

c/o RNIB Bristol, Stillhouse Lane, Bristol, BS3 4EB
01225 421 717
www.look-uk.org.uk

Parent self-help group of visually impaired children and their families. Has its own holiday caravan equipped to meet the needs of a visually impaired child. Children's groups include The Explorers and Discoverers.

RNIB Bristol

10 Stillhouse Lane, Bedminster, Bristol, BS3 4EB
www.rnib.org.uk
Helpline 0845 766 9999
Voice/minicom 0117 953 7750
Mon-Fri 10am-4pm

Support and facilities for those with any level of visual impairment, including combined sight and hearing loss.

SERIOUS ILLNESS

ACT (Association for Children with Life Threatening or Terminal Conditions and their Families)

Orchard House, Orchard Lane, Bristol, BS1 5DT
www.act.org.uk
Helpline 0117 922 1556
Mon-Fri 8.30am-5pm

Information on support services available for families. Online discussion group.

CLIC Sargent (Cancer and Leukaemia in Childhood)

Abbeywood, Bristol, BS34 7JU
www.clicsargent.org.uk
0117 311 2600
Mon-Fri 8.30am-5pm
Helpline 0845 301 0031
Mon-Fri 9am-5pm

CLIC and Sargent Cancer Care merged in 2005. Provides specialist clinical care, family support, family accommodation close to paediatric oncology centres, holidays, financial help and advice, research.

The Jessie May Trust

35 Old School House, Kingswood Foundation Estate, Britannia Rd, Kingswood, Bristol, BS15 8DB
www.jessiemaytrust.org.uk
Admin 0117 961 6840
Care Team 0117 958 2172

Providing a palliative care service for children and young people who are not expected to live beyond the age of 19. Respite, support, advice, terminal nursing care and bereavement support.

The Rainbow Centre

27 Lilymead Ave, Bristol, BS4 2BY
www.rainbowcentre.org.uk
0117 985 3343

Aims to provide the highest quality support and help to children with life-threatening illness, and their families. Also bereavement support, art and play therapy, and complementary therapies.

ACKNOWLEDGEMENTS

We have had tremendous support from people all over Bristol and the West. Their enthusiasm for this publication has been extremely encouraging. Please let us know your views and ideas. We are also grateful for pictures for future publications. It is your book and we need your voice.

www.freedomguides.co.uk

PO Box 296, Bristol, BS99 7LR

Special thanks from the editors to the following:

Researchers

Diana Beavon, Sophia Denham, Paula Brown, Lu Hersey, Nicola O'Brien, Cathy Panter, Elspeth Pontin, Alex Reed, Lucy Saunders, Alison Simmonds, Jo Smart, Jane Wisbey and Emma Woodworth.

Contributors

Sarah Davies, Sophia Denham, Bertie Ellis, Fiona & Rory MccGwire, Alan Miller, Cathy Panter, Angela Potter, Keith Potter, Tim Potter and Pete Smart.

Database & website

Mark Furnevall, www.sunspace.ltd.uk

Cover Design

karen painter design, www.karenpainterdesigns.co.uk, karenpainter@blueyonder.co.uk

Photography

See inside flyer for cover credits. Those not credited on pg 262 were taken by Marina Allan, Julia Swan and Tim Potter. Thanks also to Henry Lowrey, Will Burton, Emily Thompson and Anna Barham who attended photo shoots in cold and very wet weather.

Other young people photographed include: Zoe Alexander, Bertie Allan, Charles Allan, Ellen Earp, Jack Escrit, Jess Hand, Laurence Hand, Chloë Harrison, Molly Harrison, Hugo, Livy Hunt, Phoebe Lau, Catherine Perry, Tom Pie, Lucy Row, Emma Shovlin, Sophie, Harriet Surman, Lily Swan, Peter Swan, Rose Swan, Helen Walker and Lucy Weaver.

Questionnaires

Thanks very much to all the teenagers who completed our questionnaires, providing great inspiration and inside information:

Liz Brown, Hannah Simpson, Rachel Smith, Naomi Pullen, Ian Irwin, Alice Sharp, Molly Surridge, Rachel Clark, Alexander Hale, Hannah Lexton, Eddie Fieldhouse, James Hilton, Thomas Heller, Nathalie Flower, Emma Sage, Katie Lockett, Clair Thomas, Rachel Evans, Caitlin Telfer, Jake Ainsley, Clare Anglin, Christina Evans, Roanna Faith Price, Stephen Powell, Isaac Percival, Charley Norman, Charlotte Frost, Jackie Balley, Jo, Kamal Gregory, Farzana H, Ian H, Gwen, Christopher Phillips, Catherine Ewins, Chloë Janssen-Lester, Jackie Bally and James Nichol.

Further thanks to Claire Horsburgh at St Brendan's Sixth Form College and Alison Bedford at St Mary Redcliffe.

Acknowledgements

PHOTOGRAPHS

Sports & Outdoor Pursuits

Pg 5 Nick Escrit, Pg 9 www.qehbristol.co.uk, Pg 13 www.qehbristol.co.uk, Pg 15 www.qehbristol.co.uk, Pg 18 Kath Sidaway, Pg 20 www.seacadets.org, Pg 22 Acorn Adventure, Pg 23 www.howies.co.uk, Pg 24 Paul Korkus, Photomedia, Castle Combe Kart Track, Pg 26 Kath Sidaway, Pg 27 & 29 Nick Escrit, Pg 30 www.howies.co.uk, Pg 32 www.bristolbikefest.com

Interest & Clubs

Pg 33 Bristol Old Vic, Pg 34 www.nationaltrust.org.uk, Pg 35 Circus Maniacs, Pg 36 Nick Hand & Quartier Vert, Pg 36 www.danceblast.co.uk, Pg 41 & 43 Bristol Old Vic, Pg 44 37th Kingswood Drum & Bugle Corps, Pg 47 www.seacadets.co.uk, Pg 49 Helen Walker

Out & About in Bristol

Pg 51 Nick Hand, Pg 56 Bristol City Museum & Art Gallery, Pg 59 Bristol Old Vic, Pgs 60-61 Nick Hand, Pg 64 Bristol Rugby www.bristolrugby.co.uk, Pg 68 Kath Sidaway, Pg 70 Nick Hand

Eating Out

Pg 71 Nick Hand, Pg 73 www.shakenstephens.co.uk, Pg 74 Nick Hand, Pg 76-77 www.watershed.co.uk, Pg 81 Nick Hand, Pg 83 www.janeausten.co.uk, Pg 85 Nick Hand

Out & About in the West Country

Pg 91 Kath Sidaway, Pg 95 www.thermaebathspa.com, Pg 97 www.romanbaths.co.uk, Pg 98 www.museumofcostume.co.uk, Pg 103 www.megamaze.co.uk, Pg 104 Nick Escrit, Pg 106 Kath Sidaway, Pg 107 www.bayisland.co.uk, Pg 110 www.sudeleycastle.co.uk, Pg 112-113 www.nationaltrust.org.uk, Pg 119 www.fleetairarm.com, Pg 121 Used courtesy of Amgueddfa Cymru — National Museum Wales, Pg 122 Steve Dempster www.countrywalkers.co.uk, Pg 125 & 126 Kath Sidaway, Pg 130 www.howies.co.uk

Shopping & Services

Pg 133 Nick Hand, Pgs 140 & 145 Helen Walker, Pg 146 Joanna Thirlwall, Pgs 148-149 Nick Hand, Pg 151 www.travellingman.com, Pg 153 Helen Walker, Pg 157 Bruce the dog, Pg 159 Helen Walker, Pg 160 Sophia Denham, Pg 164 www.howies.co.uk

Transport

Pg 169-172 www.firstgroup.com, Pg 173 www.sustrans.org.uk, Pg 174 Nlarge, The Libraries Through the Lens Project

Colour section

Pg 185 www.ashtoncourtfestival.com, Pg 187 www.ashtoncourtfestival.com, Pg 187 www.qehbristol.co.uk, Pg 189 www.ashtoncourtfestival.com, Pg 191 www.qehbristol.co.uk

Holidays and Weekends Away

Pg 198 Acorn Adventure, Pg 201 www.yha.org.uk, Pg 205 Nick Escrit, Pg 206 & 210 www.yha.org.uk, Pg 212 Kath Sidaway, Pg 216 Acorn Adventure

Work & Travel

Pgs 217 (NZ) & 235 (Fiji) Sophia Denham, Pg 218 www.shakenstevens.co.uk, Pgs 221 & 223 Bristol Zoo Volunteers

Schools & Studying

Pg 229 www.qehbristol.co.uk, Pg 230 Helen Walker, Pg 232 www.empiremuseum.co.uk, Pg 235 www.bristolzoo.org.uk, Pg 237 & 239 www.qehbristol.co.uk, Pg 240 & 242 Nlarge, The Libraries Through the Lens Project

Healthcare

Pgs 245-247 www.sea-cadet.org

Advice & Support

Pg 252 Nick Hand

INDEX

Index

Index

Index

Index

QUICK INDEX